Second Workshop on Neural Machine Translation 2018

Held at ACL 2018

Melbourne, Australia
20 July 2018

ISBN: 978-1-5108-6714-7

ACL 2018

Neural Machine Translation and Generation

Proceedings of the Second Workshop

July 20, 2018
Melbourne, Australia

amazon  Google

Introduction

iii

Machine Translation and Generation focusing on Neural Machine Translation (NMT) technology. This workshop aims to cultivate research on the leading edge in neural machine translation and other aspects of machine translation, generation, and multilinguality that utilize neural models. In this year's workshop we are extremely pleased to be able to host four invited talks from leading lights in the field, namely: Jacob Devlin Rico Sennrich, Jason Weston, and Yulia Tsvetkov. In addition this year's workshop will feature a session devoted to a new shared task on efficient machine translation. We received a total of 25 submissions, and accepted 16 for inclusion in the workshop, an acceptance rate of 64%. Due to the large number of invited talks, and to encourage discussion, only the two papers selected for best paper awards will be presented orally, and the remainder will be presented in a single poster session. We would like to thank all authors for their submissions, and the program committee members for their valuable efforts in reviewing the papers for the workshop. We would also like to thank Amazon, Apple and Google for their generous sponsorship.

Organizers:

Alexandra Birch, (Edinburgh)
Andrew Finch, (Apple)
Thang Luong, (Google)
Graham Neubig, (CMU)
Yusuke Oda, (Google)

Program Committee:

Roee Aharoni, (Bar Ilan University)
Joost Bastings, (University of Amsterdam)
Yonatan Belinkov, (Qatar Computing Research Institute)
Marine Carpuat, (University of Maryland)
Boxing Chen, (National Research Council, Canada)
Eunah Cho, (Amazon)
Michael Denkowski, (Amazon)
Kevin Duh, (JHU)
Cong Duy Vu Hoang, (University of Melbourne)
Markus Freitag, (Google)
Isao Goto, (NHK)
Jiatao Gu, (The University of Hong Kong)
Barry Haddow, (Edinburgh)
Sebastien Jean, (Montreal)
Yuta Kikuchi, (Preferred Networks)
Philipp Koehn, (Johns Hopkins University)
Yannis Konstas, (Heriot-Watt University)
Shumpei Kubosawa, (NEC)
Mirella Lapata, (University of Edinburgh)
Shujie Liu, (Microsoft)
Lemao Liu, (Tencent AI Lab)
Haitao Mi, (Ant Financial US)
Hideya Mino, (NHK)
Makoto Morishita, (Nara Institute of Science and Technology)
Preslav Nakov, (QCRI)
Hieu Pham, (Google)
Alexander Rush, (Harvard)
Abigail See, (Stanford)
Rico Sennrich, (Edinburgh)
Raphael Shu, (The University of Tokyo)
Akihiro Tamura, (Ehime University)
Rui Wang, (NICT)
Xiaolin Wang, (NICT)
Taro Watanabe, (Google)
Xingxing Zhang, (University of Edinburgh)

Invited Speakers:

Jacob Devlin, (Google)
Rico Sennrich, (Edinburgh)
Yulia Tsvetkov, (CMU)
Jason Weston, (Facebook)

Table of Contents

Workshop Program

July 20, 2018

09:00–09:10   *Welcome and Opening Remarks*

             Findings of the Second Workshop on Neural Machine Translation and Generation
Alexandra Birch, Andrew Finch, Minh-Thang Luong, Graham Neubig and Yusuke Oda

09:10–10:00   *Keynote 1*
Jacob Devlin

10:00–10:30   *Shared Task Overview*

10:30–11:00   *Coffee Break*

11:00–11:30   *Marian: Fast Neural Machine Translation in C++*

11:30–12:20   *Keynote 2*
Rico Sennrich

12:20–13:20   *Lunch Break*

13:20–13:50   **Best Paper Session**

13:50–14:40   *Keynote 3*
Jason Weston

14:40–15:30   *Keynote 4*
Yulia Tsvetkov

15:30–16:00   *Coffee Break*

16:00–17:30   Poster Session

NICT Self-Training Approach to Neural Machine Translation at NMT-2018
Kenji Imamura and Eiichiro Sumita

Fast Neural Machine Translation Implementation
Hieu Hoang, Tomasz Dwojak, Rihards Krislauks, Daniel Torregrosa and Kenneth Heafield

OpenNMT System Description for WNMT 2018: 800 words/sec on a single-core CPU
Jean Senellart, Dakun Zhang, Bo WANG, Guillaume KLEIN, Jean-Pierre Ramatchandirin, Josep Crego and Alexander Rush

Marian: Cost-effective High-Quality Neural Machine Translation in C++
Marcin Junczys-Dowmunt, Kenneth Heafield, Hieu Hoang, Roman Grundkiewicz and Anthony Aue

On Individual Neurons in Neural Machine Translation
D. Anthony Bau, Yonatan Belinkov, Hassan Sajjad, Nadir Durrani, Fahim Dalvi and James Glass

Parameter Sharing Strategies in Neural Machine Translation
Sébastien Jean, Stanislas Lauly and Kyunghyun Cho

Modeling Latent Sentence Structure in Neural Machine Translation
Joost Bastings, Wilker Aziz, Ivan Titov and Khalil Simaan

Extreme Adaptation for Personalized Neural Machine Translation
Paul Michel and Graham Neubig

Exploiting Semantics in Neural Machine Translation with Graph Convolutional Networks
Diego Marcheggiani, Joost Bastings and Ivan Titov

17:30–17:40   ***Closing Remarks***

Findings of the Second Workshop on
Neural Machine Translation and Generation

Alexandra Birch♠, Andrew Finch♡, Minh-Thang Luong♣, Graham Neubig◇, Yusuke Oda°
♠University of Edinburgh, ♡Apple, ♣Google Brain, ◇Carnegie Mellon University °Google Translate

Abstract

This document describes the findings of the Second Workshop on Neural Machine Translation and Generation, held in concert with the annual conference of the Association for Computational Linguistics (ACL 2018). First, we summarize the research trends of papers presented in the proceedings, and note that there is particular interest in linguistic structure, domain adaptation, data augmentation, handling inadequate resources, and analysis of models. Second, we describe the results of the workshop's shared task on efficient neural machine translation (NMT), where participants were tasked with creating NMT systems that are both accurate and efficient.

1 Introduction

Neural sequence to sequence models (Kalchbrenner and Blunsom, 2013; Sutskever et al., 2014; Bahdanau et al., 2015) are now a workhorse behind a wide variety of different natural language processing tasks such as machine translation, generation, summarization and simplification. The 2nd Workshop on Neural Machine Translation and Generation (WNMT 2018) provided a forum for research in applications of neural models to machine translation and other language generation tasks (including summarization (Rush et al., 2015), NLG from structured data (Wen et al., 2015), dialog response generation (Vinyals and Le, 2015), among others). Overall, the workshop was held with two goals:

First, it aimed to synthesize the current state of knowledge in neural machine translation and generation: This year we will continue to encourage submissions that not only advance the state of the art through algorithmic advances, but also analyze and understand the current state of the art, pointing to future research directions. Towards this goal, we received a number of high-quality research contributions on the topics of linguistic structure, domain adaptation, data augmentation, handling inadequate resources, and analysis of models, which are summarized in Section 2.

Second, it aimed to expand the research horizons in NMT: Based on panel discussions from the first workshop, we organized a shared task. Specifically, the shared task was on "Efficient NMT". The aim of this task was to focus on not only accuracy, but also memory and computational efficiency, which are paramount concerns in practical deployment settings. The workshop provided a set of baselines for the task, and elicited contributions to help push forward the Pareto frontier of both efficiency and accuracy. The results of the shared task are summarized in Section 3

2 Summary of Research Contributions

We published a call for long papers, extended abstracts for preliminary work, and cross-submissions of papers submitted to other venues. The goal was to encourage discussion and interaction with researchers from related areas. We received a total of 25 submissions, out of which 16 submissions were accepted. The acceptance rate was 64%. Three extended abstracts, two cross-submissions and eleven long papers were accepted after a process of double blind reviewing.

Most of the papers looked at the application of machine translation, but there is one paper on abstractive summarization (Fan et al., 2018) and one paper on automatic post-editing of translations (Unanue et al., 2018).

The workshop proceedings cover a wide range of phenomena relevant to sequence to sequence

Proceedings of the 2nd Workshop on Neural Machine Translation and Generation, pages 1–10
Melbourne, Australia, July 20, 2018. ©2018 Association for Computational Linguistics

model research, with the contributions being concentrated on the following topics:

Linguistic structure: How can we incorporate linguistic structure in neural MT or generation models? Contributions examined the effect of considering semantic role structure (Marcheggiani et al., 2018), latent structure (Bastings et al., 2018), and structured self-attention (Bisk and Tran, 2018).

Domain adaptation: Some contributions examined regularization methods for adaptation (Khayrallah et al., 2018) and "extreme adaptation" to individual speakers (Michel and Neubig, 2018)

Data augmentation: A number of the contributed papers examined ways to augment data for more efficient training. These include methods for considering multiple back translations (Imamura et al., 2018), iterative back translation (Hoang et al., 2018b), bidirectional multilingual training (Niu et al., 2018), and document level adaptation (Kothur et al., 2018)

Inadequate resources: Several contributions involved settings in which resources were insufficient, such as investigating the impact of noise (Khayrallah and Koehn, 2018), missing data in multi-source settings (Nishimura et al., 2018) and one-shot learning (Pham et al., 2018).

Model analysis: There were also many methods that analyzed modeling and design decisions, including investigations of individual neuron contributions (Bau et al., 2018), parameter sharing (Jean et al., 2018), controlling output characteristics (Fan et al., 2018), and shared attention (Unanue et al., 2018)

3 Shared Task

Many shared tasks, such as the ones run by the Conference on Machine Translation (Bojar et al., 2017), aim to improve the state of the art for MT with respect to accuracy: finding the most accurate MT system regardless of computational cost. However, in production settings, the efficiency of the implementation is also extremely important. The shared task for WNMT (inspired by the "small NMT" task at the Workshop on Asian Translation (Nakazawa et al., 2017)) was focused on creating systems for NMT that are not only accurate, but also efficient. Efficiency can include a number of concepts, including memory efficiency and computational efficiency. This task concerns itself with both, and we cover the detail of the evaluation below.

3.1 Evaluation Measures

The first step to the evaluation was deciding *what* we want to measure. In the case of the shared task, we used metrics to measure several different aspects connected to how good the system is. These were measured for systems that were run on CPU, and also systems that were run on GPU.

Accuracy Measures: As a measure of translation accuracy, we used BLEU (Papineni et al., 2002) and NIST (Doddington, 2002) scores.

Computational Efficiency Measures: We measured the amount of time it takes to translate the entirety of the test set on CPU or GPU. Time for loading models was measured by having the model translate an empty file, then subtracting this from the total time to translate the test set file.

Memory Efficiency Measures: We measured: (1) the size on disk of the model, (2) the number of parameters in the model, and (3) the peak consumption of the host memory and GPU memory.

These metrics were measured by having participants submit a container for the virtualization environment Docker[1], then measuring from outside the container the usage of computation time and memory. All evaluations were performed on dedicated instances on Amazon Web Services[2], specifically of type m5.large for CPU evaluation, and p3.2xlarge (with a NVIDIA Tesla V100 GPU).

3.2 Data

The data used was from the WMT 2014 English-German task (Bojar et al., 2014), using the preprocessed corpus provided by the Stanford NLP Group[3]. Use of other data was prohibited.

---

[1]https://www.docker.com/
[2]https://aws.amazon.com/
[3]https://nlp.stanford.edu/projects/nmt/

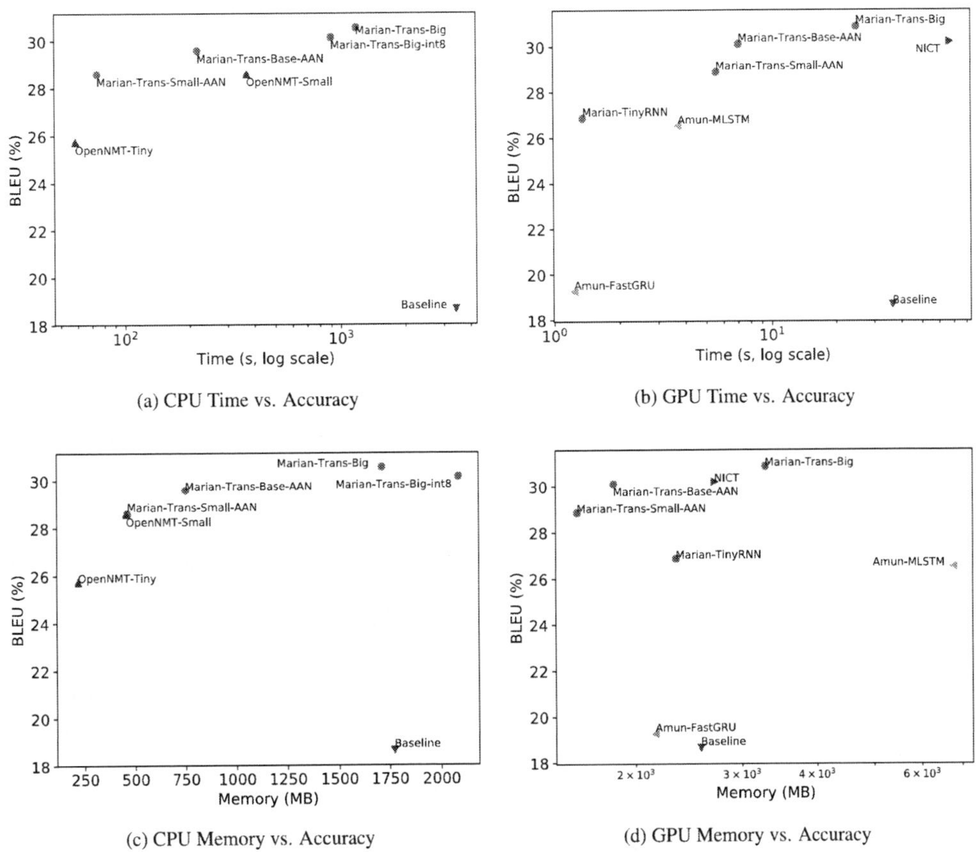

(a) CPU Time vs. Accuracy

(b) GPU Time vs. Accuracy

(c) CPU Memory vs. Accuracy

(d) GPU Memory vs. Accuracy

Figure 1: Time and memory vs. accuracy measured by BLEU, calculated on both CPU and GPU

3.3 Baseline Systems

Two baseline systems were prepared:

Echo: Just send the input back to the output.

Base: A baseline system using attentional LSTM-based encoder-decoders with attention (Bahdanau et al., 2015).

3.4 Submitted Systems

Four teams, Team Amun, Team Marian, Team OpenNMT, and Team NICT submitted to the shared task, and we will summarize each below. Before stepping in to the details of each system, we first note general trends that all or many systems attempted. The first general trend was a fast C++ decoder, with Teams Amun, Marian, and NICT using the Amun or Marian decoders included in the Marian toolkit,[4] and team OpenNMT

using the C++-decoder decoder for OpenNMT.[5] The second trend was the use of data augmentation techniques allowing the systems to train on data other than the true references. Teams Amun, Marian, and OpenNMT all performed model distillation (Kim and Rush, 2016), where a larger teacher model is used to train a smaller student model, while team NICT used back translation, training the model on sampled translations from the target to the source (Imamura et al., 2018). Finally, a common optimization was the use of lower-precision arithmetic, where Teams Amun, Marian, and OpenNMT all used some variety of 16/8-bit or integer calculation, along with the corresponding optimized CPU or GPU operations. These three improvements seem to be best practices for efficient NMT implementation.

---

[4] https://marian-nmt.github.io

[5] http://opennmt.net

3.4.1 Team Amun

Team Amun's contribution (Hoang et al., 2018a) was based on the "Amun" decoder and consisted of a number of optimizations to improve translation speed on GPU. The first major unique contribution was a strategy of batching together computations from multiple hypotheses within beam search to exploit parallelism of hardware. Another contribution was a methodology to create a fused GPU kernel for the softmax calculation, that calculates all of the operations within the softmax (e.g. max, exponentiation, and sum) in a single kernel. In the end they submitted two systems, **Amun-FastGRU** and **Amun-MLSTM**, which use GRU (Cho et al., 2014) and multiplicative LSTM (Krause et al., 2016) units respectively.

3.4.2 Team Marian

Team Marian's system (Junczys-Dowmunt et al., 2018) used the Marian C++ decoder, and concentrated on new optimizations for the CPU. The team distilled a large self-attentional model into two types of "student" models: a smaller self-attentional model using average attention networks (Zhang et al., 2018), a new higher-speed version of the original Transformer model (Vaswani et al., 2017), and a standard RNN-based decoder. They also introduced an auto-tuning approach that chooses which of multiple matrix multiplication implementations is most efficient in the current context, then uses this implementation going forward. This resulted in the **Marian-TinyRNN** system using an RNN-based model, and the **Marian-Trans-Small-AAN**, **Marian-Trans-Base-AAN**, **Marian-Trans-Big**, **Marian-Trans-Big-int8** systems, which use different varieties and sizes of self-attentional models.

3.4.3 Team OpenNMT

Team OpenNMT (Senellart et al., 2018) built a system based on the OpenNMT toolkit. The model was based on a large self-attentional teacher model distilled into a smaller, fast RNN-based model. The system also used a version of vocabulary selection (Shi and Knight, 2017), and a method to increase the size of the encoder but decrease the size of the decoder to improve the efficiency of beam search. They submitted two systems, **OpenNMT-Small** and **OpenNMT-Tiny**, which were two variously-sized implementations of this model.

3.4.4 Team NICT

Team NICT's contribution (Imamura and Sumita, 2018) to the shared task was centered around using self-training as a way to improve NMT accuracy without changing the architecture. Specifically, they used a method of randomly sampling pseudo-source sentences from a back-translation model (Imamura et al., 2018) and used this to augment the data set to increase coverage. They tested two basic architectures for the actual translation model, a recurrent neural network-based model trained using OpenNMT, and a self-attentional model trained using Marian, finally submitting the self-attentional model using Marian as their sole contribution to the shared task **NICT**.

3.5 Shared Task Results

A brief summary of the results of the shared task (for newstest2015) can be found in Figure 1, while full results tables for all of the systems can be found in Appendix A. From this figure we can glean a number of observations.

First, encouragingly all the submitted systems handily beat the baseline system in speed and accuracy.

Secondly, observing the speed/accuracy curves, we can see that Team Marian's submissions tended to carve out the Pareto frontier, indicating that the large number of optimizations that went into creating the system paid off in aggregate. Interestingly, on GPU, RNN-based systems carved out the faster but less accurate part of the Pareto curve, while on CPU self-attentional models were largely found to be more effective. None of the submissions consisted of a Transformer-style model so small that it under-performed the RNN models, but a further examination of where the curves cross (if they do) would be an interesting examination for future shared tasks.

Next, considering memory usage, we can see again that the submissions from the Marian team tend to be the most efficient. One exception is the extremely small memory system OpenNMT-Tiny, which achieves significantly lower translation accuracies, but fits in a mere 220MB of memory on the CPU.

In this first iteration of the task, we attempted to establish best practices and strong baselines upon which to build efficient test-time methods for NMT. One characteristic of the first iteration of the task was that the basic model architectures used relatively standard, with the valuable contributions lying in solid engineering work and best practices in neural network optimization such as low-precision calculation and model distillation. With these contributions, we now believe we have very strong baselines upon which future iterations of the task can build, examining novel architectures or methods for further optimizing the training speed. We also will examine other considerations, such as efficient adaptation to new training data, or latency from receiving a sentence to translating it.

4 Conclusion

This paper summarized the results of the Second Workshop on Neural Machine Translation and Generation, where we saw a number of research advances, particularly in the area of efficiency in neural MT through submissions to the shared task. The workshop series will continue next year, and continue to push forward the state of the art on these topics for faster, more accurate, more flexible, and more widely applicable neural MT and generation systems.

Acknowledgments

We would like to warmly thank Amazon for its support of the shared task, both through its donation of computation time, and through its provision of a baseline system for participants to build upon. We also thank Google and Apple for their monetary support of the workshop.

References

Dzmitry Bahdanau, Kyunghyun Cho, and Yoshua Bengio. 2015. Neural machine translation by jointly learning to align and translate. In *Proc. ICLR*.

Joost Bastings, Wilker Aziz, Ivan Titov, and Khalil Simaan. 2018. Modeling latent sentence structure in neural machine translation. In *Proc. WNMT*.

D. Anthony Bau, Yonatan Belinkov, Hassan Sajjad, Nadir Durrani, Fahim Dalvi, and James Glass. 2018. On individual neurons in neural machine translation. In *Proc. WNMT*.

Yonatan Bisk and Ke Tran. 2018. Inducing grammars with and for neural machine translation. In *Proc. WNMT*.

Ondřej Bojar, Rajen Chatterjee, Christian Federmann, Yvette Graham, Barry Haddow, Shujian Huang, Matthias Huck, Philipp Koehn, Qun Liu, Varvara Logacheva, et al. 2017. Findings of the 2017 conference on machine translation (wmt17). In *Proc. WMT*, pages 169–214.

Ondrej Bojar et al. 2014. Findings of the 2014 workshop on statistical machine translation. In *Proc. WMT*, pages 12–58.

Kyunghyun Cho, Bart van Merrienboer, Caglar Gulcehre, Dzmitry Bahdanau, Fethi Bougares, Holger Schwenk, and Yoshua Bengio. 2014. Learning phrase representations using RNN encoder–decoder for statistical machine translation. In *Proc. EMNLP*, pages 1724–1734.

George Doddington. 2002. Automatic evaluation of machine translation quality using n-gram co-occurrence statistics. In *Proc. HLT*, pages 138–145.

Angela Fan, David Grangier, and Michael Auli. 2018. Controllable abstractive summarization. In *Proc. WNMT*.

Hieu Hoang, Tomasz Dwojak, Rihards Krislauks, Daniel Torregrosa, and Kenneth Heafield. 2018a. Fast neural machine translation implementation. In *Proc. WNMT*.

Vu Cong Duy Hoang, Philipp Koehn, Gholamreza Haffari, and Trevor Cohn. 2018b. Iterative back-translation for neural machine translation. In *Proc. WNMT*.

Kenji Imamura, Atsushi Fujita, and Eiichiro Sumita. 2018. Enhancement of encoder and attention using target monolingual corpora in neural machine translation. In *Proc. WNMT*.

Kenji Imamura and Eiichiro Sumita. 2018. Nict self-training approach to neural machine translation at nmt-2018. In *Proc. WNMT*.

Sèbastien Jean, Stanislas Lauly, and Kyunghyun Cho. 2018. Parameter sharing strategies in neural machine translation. In *Proc. WNMT*.

Marcin Junczys-Dowmunt, Kenneth Heafield, Hieu Hoang, Roman Grundkiewicz, and Anthony Aue. 2018. Marian: Cost-effective high-quality neural machine translation in c++. In *Proc. WNMT*.

Nal Kalchbrenner and Phil Blunsom. 2013. Recurrent continuous translation models. In *Proc. EMNLP*, pages 1700–1709.

Huda Khayrallah and Philipp Koehn. 2018. On the impact of various types of noise on neural machine translation. In *Proc. WNMT*.

Huda Khayrallah, Brian Thompson, Kevin Duh, and Philipp Koehn. 2018. Regularized training objective for continued training for domain adaption in neural machine translation. In *Proc. WNMT*.

Yoon Kim and Alexander M. Rush. 2016. Sequence-level knowledge distillation. In *Proc. EMNLP*, pages 1317–1327.

Sachith Sri Ram Kothur, Rebecca Knowles, and Philipp Koehn. 2018. Document-level adaptation for neural machine translation. In *Proc. WNMT*.

Ben Krause, Liang Lu, Iain Murray, and Steve Renals. 2016. Multiplicative lstm for sequence modelling. *arXiv preprint arXiv:1609.07959*.

Diego Marcheggiani, Joost Bastings, and Ivan Titov. 2018. Exploiting semantics in neural machine translation with graph convolutional networks. In *Proc. WNMT*.

Paul Michel and Graham Neubig. 2018. Extreme adaptation for personalized neural machine translation. In *Proc. WNMT*.

Toshiaki Nakazawa, Shohei Higashiyama, Chenchen Ding, Hideya Mino, Isao Goto, Hideto Kazawa, Yusuke Oda, Graham Neubig, and Sadao Kurohashi. 2017. Overview of the 4th workshop on asian translation. In *Proc. WAT*, pages 1–54, Taipei, Taiwan. Asian Federation of Natural Language Processing.

Yuta Nishimura, Katsuhito Sudoh, Graham Neubig, and Satoshi Nakamura. 2018. Multi-source neural machine translation with missing data. In *Proc. WNMT*.

Xing Niu, Michael Denkowski, and Marine Carpuat. 2018. Bi-directional neural machine translation with synthetic parallel data. In *Proc. WNMT*.

Kishore Papineni, Salim Roukos, Todd Ward, and Wei-Jing Zhu. 2002. BLEU: a method for automatic evaluation of machine translation. In *Proc. ACL*, pages 311–318.

Ngoc-Quan Pham, Jan Niehues, and Alexander Waibel. 2018. Towards one-shot learning for rare-word translation with external experts. In *Proc. WNMT*.

Alexander M. Rush, Sumit Chopra, and Jason Weston. 2015. A neural attention model for abstractive sentence summarization. In *Proc. EMNLP*, pages 379–389.

Jean Senellart, Dakun Zhang, Bo Wang, Guillaume Klein, Jean-Pierre Ramatchandirin, Josep Crego, and Alexander Rush. 2018. OpenNMT system description for WNMT 2018: 800 words/sec on a single-core CPU. In *Proc. WNMT*.

Xing Shi and Kevin Knight. 2017. Speeding up neural machine translation decoding by shrinking run-time vocabulary. In *Proc. ACL*, pages 574–579.

Ilya Sutskever, Oriol Vinyals, and Quoc VV Le. 2014. Sequence to sequence learning with neural networks. In *Proc. NIPS*, pages 3104–3112.

Inigo Jauregi Unanue, Ehsan Zare Borzeshi, and Massimo Piccardi. 2018. A shared attention mechanism for interpretation of neural automatic post-editing systems. In *Proc. WNMT*.

Ashish Vaswani, Noam Shazeer, Niki Parmar, Jakob Uszkoreit, Llion Jones, Aidan N. Gomez, Lukasz Kaiser, and Illia Polosukhin. 2017. Attention is all you need. In *Proc. NIPS*.

Oriol Vinyals and Quoc Le. 2015. A neural conversational model. *arXiv preprint arXiv:1506.05869*.

Tsung-Hsien Wen, Milica Gasic, Nikola Mrkšić, Pei-Hao Su, David Vandyke, and Steve Young. 2015. Semantically conditioned lstm-based natural language generation for spoken dialogue systems. In *Proc. EMNLP*, pages 1711–1721.

Biao Zhang, Deyi Xiong, and Jinsong Su. 2018. Accelerating neural transformer via an average attention network. In *Proc. ACL*.

A Full Shared Task Results

For completeness, in this section we add tables of the full shared task results. These include the full size of the image file for the translation system (Table 1), the comparison between compute time and evaluation scores on CPU (Table 2) and GPU (Table 3), and the comparison between memory and evaluation scores on CPU (Table 4) and GPU (Table 5).

Table 1: Image file sizes of submitted systems.

Team	System	Size [MiB]
edin-amun	fastgru	4823.43
	mlstm.1280	5220.72
Marian	cpu-transformer-base-aan	493.20
	cpu-transformer-big	1085.93
	cpu-transformer-big-int8	1085.92
	cpu-transformer-small-aan	367.92
	gpu-amun-tinyrnn	399.08
	gpu-transformer-base-aan	686.59
	gpu-transformer-big	1279.32
	gpu-transformer-small-aan	564.32
NICT	marian-st	2987.57
OpenNMT	cpu1	339.02
	cpu2	203.89
Organizer	echo	110.42
	nmt-1cpu	1668.25
	nmt-1gpu	3729.40

Table 2: Time consumption and MT evaluation metrics (CPU systems).

Dataset	Team	System	Time Consumption [s]			BLEU %	NIST
			CPU	Real	Diff		
Empty	Marian	cpu-transformer-base-aan	6.48	6.55	—	—	—
		cpu-transformer-big	7.01	9.02	—	—	—
		cpu-transformer-big-int8	7.31	7.51	—	—	—
		cpu-transformer-small-aan	6.32	6.33	—	—	—
	OpenNMT	cpu1	0.64	0.65	—	—	—
		cpu2	0.56	0.56	—	—	—
	Organizer	echo	0.05	0.06	—	—	—
		nmt-1cpu	1.50	1.50	—	—	—
newstest2014	Marian	cpu-transformer-base-aan	281.72	281.80	275.25	27.44	7.362
		cpu-transformer-big	1539.34	1541.00	1531.98	28.12	7.436
		cpu-transformer-big-int8	1173.32	1173.41	1165.90	27.50	7.355
		cpu-transformer-small-aan	100.36	100.42	94.08	25.99	7.169
	OpenNMT	cpu1	471.41	471.43	470.78	25.77	7.140
		cpu2	77.41	77.42	76.86	23.11	6.760
	Organizer	echo	0.05	0.06	0.00	2.79	1.479
		nmt-1cpu	4436.08	4436.27	4434.77	16.79	5.545
newstest2015	Marian	cpu-transformer-base-aan	223.86	223.96	217.41	29.59	7.452
		cpu-transformer-big	1189.04	1190.97	1181.95	30.56	7.577
		cpu-transformer-big-int8	907.95	908.43	900.92	30.15	7.514
		cpu-transformer-small-aan	80.21	80.25	73.92	28.61	7.312
	OpenNMT	cpu1	368.93	368.95	368.30	28.60	7.346
		cpu2	59.02	59.02	58.46	25.75	6.947
	Organizer	echo	0.05	0.06	0.00	3.24	1.599
		nmt-1cpu	3401.99	3402.14	3400.64	18.66	5.758

Table 3: Time consumption and MT evaluation metrics (GPU systems).

Dataset	Team	System	Time Consumption [s]			BLEU %	NIST
			CPU	Real	Diff		
Empty	edin-amun	fastgru	4.18	4.24	—	—	—
		mlstm.1280	4.44	4.50	—	—	—
	Marian	gpu-amun-tinyrnn	4.27	4.33	—	—	—
		gpu-transformer-base-aan	5.62	5.68	—	—	—
		gpu-transformer-big	6.00	6.05	—	—	—
		gpu-transformer-small-aan	5.48	5.54	—	—	—
	NICT	marian-st	5.78	5.84	—	—	—
	Organizer	nmt-1gpu	3.73	3.80	—	—	—
newstest2014	edin-amun	fastgru	5.68	5.74	1.50	17.74	5.783
		mlstm.1280	8.64	8.70	4.20	23.85	6.833
	Marian	gpu-amun-tinyrnn	5.90	5.96	1.63	24.06	6.879
		gpu-transformer-base-aan	14.58	14.64	8.95	27.80	7.415
		gpu-transformer-big	36.74	36.80	30.74	28.34	7.486
		gpu-transformer-small-aan	12.46	12.52	6.97	26.34	7.219
	NICT	marian-st	82.07	82.14	76.30	27.59	7.375
	Organizer	nmt-1gpu	51.24	82.14	47.50	16.79	5.545
newstest2015	edin-amun	fastgru	5.41	5.47	1.23	19.26	5.905
		mlstm.1280	8.15	8.22	3.71	26.51	7.015
	Marian	gpu-amun-tinyrnn	5.62	5.68	1.35	26.86	7.065
		gpu-transformer-base-aan	12.67	12.73	7.04	30.10	7.526
		gpu-transformer-big	30.81	30.90	24.84	30.87	7.630
		gpu-transformer-small-aan	11.04	11.10	5.56	28.87	7.379
	NICT	marian-st	72.84	72.90	67.06	30.19	7.541
	Organizer	nmt-1gpu	39.95	40.01	36.21	18.66	5.758

Table 4: Peak memory consumption (CPU systems).

Dataset	Team	System	Memory [MiB]		
			Host	GPU	Both
Empty	Marian	cpu-transformer-base-aan	531.39	—	531.39
		cpu-transformer-big	1768.56	—	1768.56
		cpu-transformer-big-int8	1193.13	—	1193.13
		cpu-transformer-small-aan	367.22	—	367.22
	OpenNMT	cpu1	403.86	—	403.86
		cpu2	194.61	—	194.61
	Organizer	echo	1.15	—	1.15
		nmt-1cpu	1699.71	—	1699.71
newstest2014	Marian	cpu-transformer-base-aan	761.07	—	531.39
		cpu-transformer-big	1681.81	—	1768.56
		cpu-transformer-big-int8	2084.66	—	1193.13
		cpu-transformer-small-aan	476.21	—	367.22
	OpenNMT	cpu1	458.08	—	403.86
		cpu2	219.79	—	194.61
	Organizer	echo	1.20	—	1.15
		nmt-1cpu	1770.69	—	1699.71
newstest2015	Marian	cpu-transformer-base-aan	749.29	—	531.39
		cpu-transformer-big	1712.08	—	1768.56
		cpu-transformer-big-int8	2086.02	—	1193.13
		cpu-transformer-small-aan	461.27	—	367.22
	OpenNMT	cpu1	455.21	—	403.86
		cpu2	217.64	—	194.61
	Organizer	echo	1.11	—	1.15
		nmt-1cpu	1771.35	—	1699.71

Table 5: Peak memory consumption (GPU systems).

Dataset	Team	System	Memory [MiB]		
			Host	GPU	Both
Empty	edin-amun	fastgru	442.55	668	1110.55
		mlstm.1280	664.88	540	1204.88
	Marian	gpu-amun-tinyrnn	346.80	522	868.80
		gpu-transformer-base-aan	487.18	484	971.18
		gpu-transformer-big	1085.29	484	1569.29
		gpu-transformer-small-aan	366.26	484	850.26
	NICT	marian-st	510.43	484	994.43
	Organizer	nmt-1gpu	378.81	640	1018.81
newstest2014	edin-amun	fastgru	456.29	1232	1688.29
		mlstm.1280	686.29	5144	5830.29
	Marian	gpu-amun-tinyrnn	346.93	1526	1872.93
		gpu-transformer-base-aan	492.91	1350	1842.91
		gpu-transformer-big	1081.69	2070	3151.69
		gpu-transformer-small-aan	366.55	1228	1594.55
	NICT	marian-st	922.53	1780	2702.53
	Organizer	nmt-1gpu	377.18	2178	2555.18
newstest2015	edin-amun	fastgru	473.72	1680	2153.72
		mlstm.1280	684.84	6090	6774.84
	Marian	gpu-amun-tinyrnn	350.19	1982	2332.19
		gpu-transformer-base-aan	489.62	1350	1839.62
		gpu-transformer-big	1082.52	2198	3280.52
		gpu-transformer-small-aan	372.56	1228	1600.56
	NICT	marian-st	929.70	1778	2707.70
	Organizer	nmt-1gpu	383.02	2178	2561.02

A Shared Attention Mechanism for Interpretation of Neural Automatic Post-Editing Systems

Inigo Jauregi Unanue[1,2], Ehsan Zare Borzeshi[2], Massimo Piccardi[1]
[1] University of Technology Sydney, Sydney, Australia
[2] Capital Markets Cooperative Research Centre, Sydney, Australia

{ijauregi,ezborzeshi}@cmcrc.com, massimo.piccardi@uts.edu.au

Abstract

Automatic post-editing (APE) systems aim to correct the systematic errors made by machine translators. In this paper, we propose a neural APE system that encodes the source (src) and machine translated (mt) sentences with two separate encoders, but leverages a shared attention mechanism to better understand how the two inputs contribute to the generation of the post-edited (pe) sentences. Our empirical observations have showed that when the mt is incorrect, the attention shifts weight toward tokens in the src sentence to properly edit the incorrect translation. The model has been trained and evaluated on the official data from the WMT16 and WMT17 APE IT domain English-German shared tasks. Additionally, we have used the extra 500K artificial data provided by the shared task. Our system has been able to reproduce the accuracies of systems trained with the same data, while at the same time providing better interpretability.

1 Introduction

In current professional practice, translators tend to follow a two-step approach: first, they run a machine translator (MT) to obtain a first-cut translation; then, they manually correct the MT output to produce a result of adequate quality. The latter step is commonly known as *post-editing* (PE). Stemming from this two-step approach and the recent success of deep networks in MT (Sutskever et al., 2014; Bahdanau et al., 2014; Luong et al., 2015), the MT research community has devoted increasing attention to the task of automatic post-editing (APE) (Bojar et al., 2017).

The rationale of an APE system is to be able to automatically correct the systematic errors made by the MT and thus dispense with or reduce the work of the human post-editors. The data for training and evaluating these systems usually consist of triplets (src, mt, pe), where src is the sentence in the source language, mt is the output of the MT, and pe is the human post-edited sentence. Note that the pe is obtained by correcting the mt, and therefore these two sentences are closely related. An APE system is "monolingual" if it only uses the mt to predict the post-edits, or "contextual" if it uses both the src and the mt as inputs (Béchara et al., 2011).

Despite their remarkable progress in recent years, neural APE systems are still elusive when it comes to interpretability. In deep learning, highly interpretable models can help researchers to overcome outstanding issues such as learning from fewer annotations, learning with human-computer interactions and debugging network representations (Zhang and Zhu, 2018). More specifically in APE, a system that provides insights on its decisions can help the human post-editor to understand the system's errors and consequently provide better corrections. As our main contribution, in this paper we propose a contextual APE system based on the seq2seq model with attention which allows for inspecting the role of the src and the mt in the editing. We modify the basic model with two separate encoders for the src and the mt, but with a single attention mechanism shared by the hidden vectors of both encoders. At each decoding step, the shared attention has to decide whether to place more weight on the tokens from the src or the mt. In our experiments, we clearly observe that when the mt translation contains mistakes (word order, incorrect words), the model learns to shift the attention toward tokens in the source language, aiming to get extra "context" or information that will help to correctly edit the translation. Instead, if

Proceedings of the 2nd Workshop on Neural Machine Translation and Generation, pages 11–17
Melbourne, Australia, July 20, 2018. ©2018 Association for Computational Linguistics

the *mt* sentence is correct, the model simply learns to pass it on word by word. In Section 4.4, we have plotted the attention weight matrices of several predictions to visualize this finding.

The model has been trained and evaluated with the official datasets from the WMT16 and WMT17 Information Technology (IT) domain APE English-German (en-de) shared tasks (Bojar et al., 2016, 2017). We have also used the 500K artificial data provided in the shared task for extra training. For some of the predictions in the test set, we have analysed the plots of attention weight matrices to shed light on whether the model relies more on the *src* or the *mt* at each time step. Moreover, our model has achieved higher accuracy than previous systems that used the same training setting (official datasets + 500K extra artificial data).

2 Related work

In an early work, (Simard et al., 2007) combined a rule-based MT (RBMT) with a statistical MT (SMT) for monolingual post-editing. The reported results outperformed both systems in standalone translation mode. In 2011, (Béchara et al., 2011) proposed the first model based on contextual post-editing, showing improvements over monolingual approaches.

More recently, neural APE systems have attracted much attention. (Junczys-Dowmunt and Grundkiewicz, 2016) (the winner of the WMT16 shared task) integrated various neural machine translation (NMT) components in a log-linear model. Moreover, they suggested creating artificial triplets from out-of-domain data to enlarge the training data, which led to a drastic improvement in PE accuracy. Assuming that post-editing is reversible, (Pal et al., 2017) have proposed an attention mechanism over bidirectional models, *mt*→ *pe* and *pe* → *mt*. Several other researchers have proposed using multi-input seq2seq models for contextual APE (Bérard et al., 2017; Libovický et al., 2016; Varis and Bojar, 2017; Pal et al., 2017; Libovický and Helcl, 2017; Chatterjee et al., 2017). All these systems employ separate encoders for the two inputs, *src* and *mt*.

2.1 Attention mechanisms for APE

A key aspect of neural APE systems is the attention mechanism. A conventional attention mechanism for NMT first learns the alignment scores (e^{ij}) with an alignment model (Bahdanau et al.,

2014; Luong et al., 2015) given the j-th hidden vector of the encoder ($\mathbf{h}^j$) and the decoder's hidden state ($\mathbf{s}_{i-1}$) at time $i - 1$ (Equation 1). Then, Equation 2 computes the normalized attention weights, with T_x the length of the input sentence. Finally, the context vector is computed as the sum of the encoder's hidden vectors weighed by the attention weights (Equation 3). The decoder uses the computed context vector to predict the output.

$$e^{ij} = aligment\_model(\mathbf{h}^j, \mathbf{s}^{i-1}) \qquad (1)$$

$$\alpha^{ij} = \frac{exp(e^{ij})}{\sum_{m=1}^{T_x} exp(e^{im})} \qquad (2)$$

$$\mathbf{c}^i = \sum_{j=1}^{T_x} \alpha^{i,j} \mathbf{h}^j \qquad (3)$$

In the APE literature, two recent papers have extended the attention mechanism to contextual APE. (Chatterjee et al., 2017) (the winner of the WMT17 shared task) have proposed a two-encoder system with a separate attention for each encoder. The two attention networks create a context vector for each input, $\mathbf{c}_{src}$ and $\mathbf{c}_{mt}$, and concatenate them using additional, learnable parameters, $\mathbf{W}_{ct}$ and $\mathbf{b}_{ct}$, into a merged context vector, $\mathbf{c}_{merge}$ (Equation 4).

$$\mathbf{c}^i_{merge} = [\mathbf{c}^i_{src}; \mathbf{c}^i_{mt}] * \mathbf{W}_{ct} + \mathbf{b}_{ct} \qquad (4)$$

(Libovický and Helcl, 2017) have proposed, among others, an attention strategy named the *flat attention*. In this approach, all the attention weights corresponding to the tokens in the two inputs are computed with a joint soft-max:

$$\alpha^{ij}_{(k)} = \frac{exp(e^{ij}_{(k)})}{\sum_{n=1}^{2} \sum_{m=1}^{T_x^{(n)}} exp(e^{im}_{(n)})} \qquad (5)$$

where $e^{ij}_{(k)}$ is the attention energy of the j-th step of the k-th encoder at the i-th decoding step and $T_x^{(k)}$ is the length of the input sequence of the k-th encoder. Note that because the attention weights are computed jointly over the different encoders, this approach allows observing whether the system assigns more weight to the tokens of the *src* or the *mt* at each decoding step. Once the attention weigths are computed, a single context vector ($\mathbf{c}$) is created as:

$$\mathbf{c}^i = \sum_{k=1}^{N} \sum_{j=1}^{T_x^{(k)}} \alpha_{(k)}^{i,j} \mathbf{U}_{c(k)} \mathbf{h}_{(k)}^j \qquad (6)$$

where $\mathbf{h}_{(k)}^j$ is the j-th hidden vector from the k-th encoder, $T_x^{(k)}$ is the number of hidden vectors from the k-th encoder, and $\mathbf{U}_{c(k)}$ is the projection matrix for the k-th encoder that projects its hidden vectors to a common-dimensional space. This parameter is also learnable and can further re-weigh the two inputs.

3   The proposed model

The main focus of our paper is on the interpretability of the predictions made by neural APE systems. To this aim, we have assembled a contextual neural model that leverages two encoders and a shared attention mechanism, similarly to the *flat attention* of (Libovický and Helcl, 2017). To describe it, let us assume that $\mathbf{X}_{src} = \{\mathbf{x}_{src}^1, ..., \mathbf{x}_{src}^N\}$ is the *src* sentence and $\mathbf{X}_{mt} = \{\mathbf{x}_{mt}^1, ..., \mathbf{x}_{mt}^M\}$ is the *mt* sentence, where N and M are their respective numbers of tokens. The two encoders encode the two inputs separately:

$$\begin{aligned} \mathbf{h}_{src}^j &= enc_{src}(\mathbf{x}_{src}^j, \mathbf{h}_{src}^{j-1}) \quad j = 1, ..., N \\ \mathbf{h}_{mt}^j &= enc_{mt}(\mathbf{x}_{mt}^j, \mathbf{h}_{mt}^{j-1}) \quad j = 1, ..., M \end{aligned} \qquad (7)$$

All the hidden vectors outputs by the two encoders are then concatenated as if they were coming from a single encoder:

$$\mathbf{h}_{join} = \{\mathbf{h}_{src}^1, ..., \mathbf{h}_{src}^N, \mathbf{h}_{mt}^1, ..., \mathbf{h}_{mt}^M\} \qquad (8)$$

Then, the attention weights and the context vector at each decoding step are computed from the hidden vectors of $\mathbf{h}_{join}$ (Equations 9-11):

$$e^{ij} = aligment\_model(\mathbf{h}_{join}^j, \mathbf{s}^{i-1}) \qquad (9)$$

$$\alpha^{ij} = \frac{exp(e^{ij})}{\sum_{m=1}^{N+M} exp(e^{im})} \qquad (10)$$

$$\mathbf{c}^i = \sum_{j=1}^{N+M} \alpha^{i,j} \mathbf{h}_{join}^j \qquad (11)$$

where i is the time step on the decoder side, j is the index of the hidden encoded vector. Given that the $\alpha^{i,j}$ weights form a normalized probability distribution over j, this model is "forced" to spread the weight between the *src* and *mt* inputs. Note that our model differs from that proposed by (Libovický and Helcl, 2017) only in that we do not employ the learnable projection matrices, $U_{c(k)}$. This is done to avoid re-weighing the contribution of the two inputs in the context vectors and, ultimately, in the predictions. More details of the proposed model and its hyper-parameters are provided in Section 4.3.

4   Experiments

4.1   Datasets

For training and evaluation we have used the WMT17 APE[1] IT domain English-German dataset. This dataset consists of 11,000 triplets for training, 1,000 for validation and 2,000 for testing. The hyper-parameters have been selected using only the validation set and used unchanged on the test set. We have also trained the model with the 12,000 sentences from the previous year (WMT16), for a total of 23,000 training triplets.

4.2   Artificial data

Since the training set provided by the shared task is too small to effectively train neural networks, (Junczys-Dowmunt and Grundkiewicz, 2016) have proposed a method for creating extra, "artificial" training data using round-trip translations. First, a language model of the target language (German here) is learned using a monolingual dataset. Then, only the sentences from the monolingual dataset that have low perplexity are round-trip translated using two off-the-shelf translators (German-English and English-German). The low-perplexity sentences from the monolingual dataset are treated as the *pe*, the German-English translations as the *src*, and the English-German back-translations as the *mt*. Finally, the (*src*, *mt*, *pe*) triplets are filtered to only retain sentences with comparable TER statistics to those of the manually-annotated training data. These artificial data have proved very useful for improving the accuracy of several neural APE systems, and they have therefore been included in the WMT17 APE shared task. In this paper, we have limited ourselves to using 500K artificial triplets as done in (Varis and Bojar, 2017; Bérard

---

[1] http://www.statmt.org/wmt17/ape-task.html

# encoders	2
encoder type	B-LSTM
encoder layers	2
encoder hidden dim	500
# decoders	1
decoder type	LSTM
decoder layers	2
decoder hidden dim	500
word vector dim	300
attention type	*general*
dropout	0.3
beam size	5

Table 1: The model and its hyper-parameters.

et al., 2017). To balance artificial and manually-annotated data during training, we have resampled the official 23K triplets 10 times.

4.3 Training and hyper-parameters

Hereafter we provide more information about the model's implementation, its hyper-parameters, the pre-processing and the training to facilitate the reproducibility of our results. We have made our code publicly available[2].

To implement the encoder/decoder with separate encoders for the two inputs (*src*, *mt*) and a single attention mechanism, we have modified the open-source OpenNMT code (Klein et al., 2017).

Table 1 lists all hyper-parameters which have all been chosen using only training and validation data. The two encoders have been implemented using a Bidirectional Long Short-Term Memory (B-LSTM) (Hochreiter and Schmidhuber, 1997) while the decoder uses a unidirectional LSTM. Both the encoders and the decoder use two hidden layers. For the attention network, we have used the OpenNMT's *general* option (Luong et al., 2015).

As for the pre-processing, the datasets come already tokenized. Given that German is a morphologically rich language, we have learned the subword units using the BPE algorithm (Sennrich et al., 2015) only over the official training sets from the WMT16 and WMT17 IT-domain APE shared task (23,000 sentences). The number of *merge* operations has been set to 30,000 under the intuition that one or two word splits per sentence could suffice. Three separate vocabularies have been used for the (*src*, *mt* and *pe*) sentences. Each vocabulary contains a maximum of 50,000 most-

---

[2]https://github.com/ijauregiCMCRC/Shared_Attention_for_APE

Model	TER	BLEU
MT (Bojar et al., 2017)	24.48	62.49
SPE (Bojar et al., 2017)	24.69	62.97
(Varis and Bojar, 2017)	24.03	64.28
(Bérard et al., 2017)	22.81	65.91
train 11K	41.58	43.05
train 23K	30.23	57.14
train 23K + 500K	**22.60**	**66.21**

Table 2: Results on the WMT17 IT domain English-German APE test set.

frequent subword units; the remaining tokens are treated as unknown (<*unk*>).

As mentioned in Section 4.2, we have trained our model with 500K extra triplets as in (Bérard et al., 2017). We have oversampled the 23K official triplets 10 times, added the extra 500K, and trained the model for 20 epochs. We have used Stochastic Gradien Descent (SGD) with a learning rate of 1 and a learning rate decay of 0.5. The learning rate decays if there are no improvements on the validation set.

In all cases, we have selected the models and hyper-parameters that have obtained the best results on the validation set (1,000 sentences), and reported the results blindly over the test set (2,000 sentences). The performance has been evaluated in two ways: first, as common for this task, we have reported the accuracy in terms of Translation Error Rate (TER) (Snover et al., 2006) and BLEU score (Papineni et al., 2002). Second, we present an empirical analysis of the attention weight matrices for some notable cases.

4.4 Results

Table 2 compares the accuracy of our model on the test data with two baselines and two state-of-the-art comparable systems. The MT baseline simply consists of the accuracy of the *mt* sentences with respect to the *pe* ground truth. The other baseline is given by a statistical PE (SPE) system (Simard et al., 2007) chosen by the WMT17 organizers. Table 2 shows that when our model is trained with only the 11K WMT17 official training sentences, it cannot even approach the baselines. Even when the 12K WMT16 sentences are added, its accuracy is still well below that of the baselines. However, when the 500K artificial data are added, it reports a major improvement and it outperforms them both significantly. In addition, we have compared our model with two recent systems that have used our

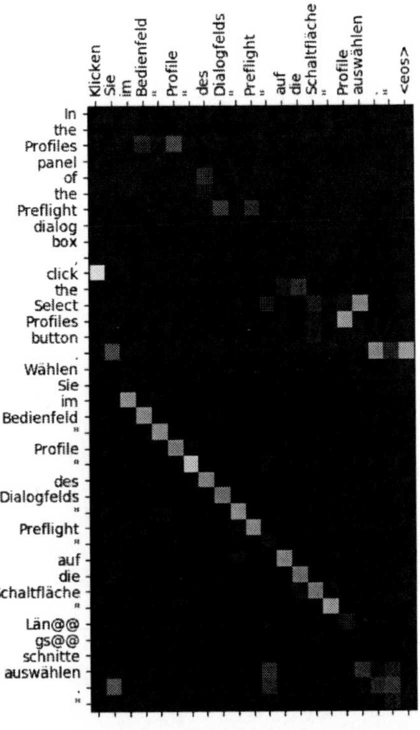

Figure 1: An example of perfect correction of an *mt* sentence.

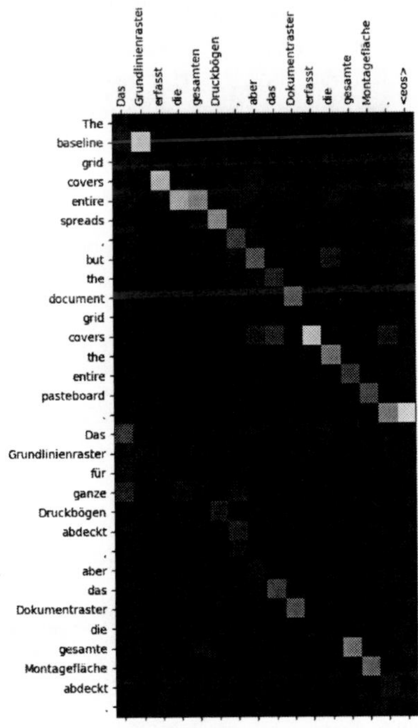

Figure 2: Partial improvement of an *mt* sentence.

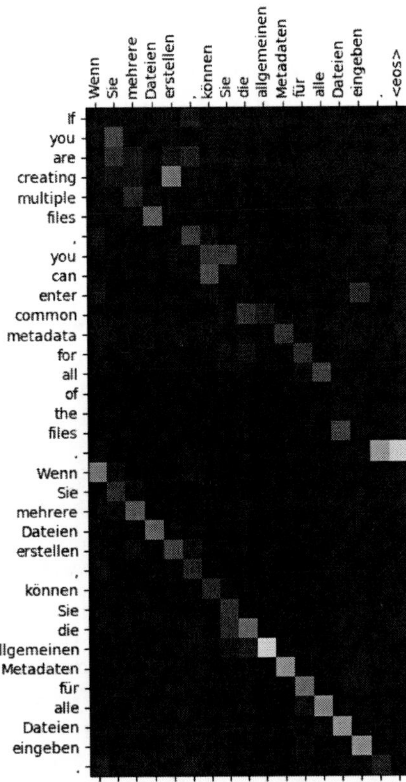

Figure 3: Passing on a correct *mt* sentence.

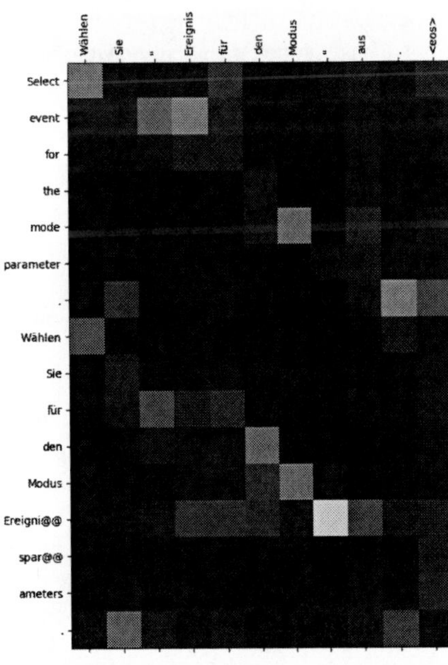

Figure 4: A completely incorrect prediction.

same training settings (500K artificial triplets + 23K manual triplets oversampled 10 times), reporting a slightly higher accuracy than both (1.43 TER and 1.93 BLEU p.p. over (Varis and Bojar, 2017) and 0.21 TER and 0.30 BLEU p.p. over (Bérard et al., 2017)). Since their models explicitly predicts edit operations rather than post-edited sentences, we speculate that these two tasks are of comparable intrinsic complexity.

In addition to experimenting with the proposed model (Equation 11), we have also tried to add the projection matrices of the flat attention of (Libovický and Helcl, 2017) (Equation 6). However, the model with these extra parameters showed evident over-fitting, with a lower perplexity on the training set, but unfortunately also a lower BLEU score of 53.59 on the test set. On the other hand, (Chatterjee et al., 2017) and other participants of the WMT 17 APE shared task [3] were able to achieve higher accuracies by using 4 million artificial training triplets. Unfortunately, using such a large dataset sent the computation out of memory on a system with 32 GB of RAM. Nonetheless, our main goal is not to establish the highest possible accuracy, but rather contribute to the interpretability of APE predictions while reproducing approximately the same accuracy of current systems trained in a comparable way.

For the analysis of the interpretability of the system, we have plotted the attention weight matrices for a selection of cases from the test set. These plots aim to show how the shared attention mechanism shifts the attention weights between the tokens of the *src* and *mt* inputs at each decoding step. In the matrices, the rows are the concatenation of the *src* and *mt* sentences, while the columns are the predicted *pe* sentence. To avoid cluttering, the ground-truth *pe* sentences are not shown in the plots, but they are commented upon in the discussion. Figure 1 shows an example where the *mt* sentence is almost correct. In this example, the attention focuses on passing on the correct part. However, the start (*Wählen*) and end (*Längsschnitte*) of the *mt* sentence are wrong: for these tokens, the model learns to place more weight on the English sentence (*click* and *Select Profiles*). The predicted *pe* is eventually identical to the ground truth.

Conversely, Figure 2 shows an example where the *mt* sentence is rather incorrect. In this case, the model learns to focus almost completely on

---

[3] http://www.statmt.org/wmt17/ape-task.html

Sentence	Focus
src	23%
mt	45%
Both	31%

Table 3: Percentage of the decoding steps with marked attention weight on either input (*src*, *mt*) or both.

the English sentence, and the prediction is very aligned with it. The predicted *pe* is not identical to the ground truth, but it is significantly more accurate than the *mt*. Figure 3 shows a case of a perfect *mt* translation where the model simply learns to pass the sentence on word by word. Eventually, Figure 4 shows an example of a largely incorrect *mt* where the model has not been able to properly edit the translation. In this case, the attention matrix is scattered and defocused.

In addition to the visualizations of the attention weights, we have computed an attention statistic over the test set to quantify the proportions of the two inputs. At each decoding time step, we have added up the attention weights corresponding to the *src* input ($\alpha^i_{src} = \sum_{j=1}^{N} \alpha^{ij}$) and those corresponding to the *mt* ($\alpha^i_{mt} = \sum_{j=N+1}^{N+M} \alpha^{ij}$). Note that, obviously, $\alpha^i_{src} + \alpha^i_{mt} = 1$. Then, we have set an arbitrary threshold, $t = 0.6$, and counted step i to the *src* input if $\alpha^i_{src} > t$. If instead $\alpha^i_{src} < 1 - t$, we counted the step to the *mt* input. Eventually, if $1 - t \leq \alpha^i_{src} \leq t$, we counted the step to both inputs. Table 3 shows this statistic. Overall, we have recorded 23% decoding steps for the *src*, 45% for the *mt* and 31% for both. It is to be expected that the majority of the decoding steps would focus on the *mt* input if it is of sufficient quality. However, the percentage of focus on the *src* input is significant, confirming its usefulness.

5 Conclusion

In this paper, we have presented a neural APE system based on two separate encoders that share a single, joined attention mechanism. The shared attention has proved a key feature for inspecting how the selection shifts on either input, (*src* and *mt*), at each decoding step and, in turn, understanding which inputs drive the predictions. In addition to its easy interpretability, our model has reported a competitive accuracy compared to recent, similar systems (i.e., systems trained with the official WMT16 and WMT17 data and 500K extra training triplets). As future work, we plan to continue to explore the interpretability of contemporary neural APE architectures.

6 Acknowledgements

We would like to acknowledge the financial support received from the Capital Markets Cooperative Research Centre (CMCRC), an applied research initiative of the Australian Government.

References

Dzmitry Bahdanau, Kyunghyun Cho, and Yoshua Bengio. 2014. Neural machine translation by jointly learning to align and translate. *arXiv preprint arXiv:1409.0473* .

Hanna Béchara, Yanjun Ma, and Josef van Genabith. 2011. Statistical post-editing for a statistical mt system. In *MT Summit*. volume 13, pages 308–315.

Olivier Bérard, Alexandre Pietquin, and Laurent Besacier. 2017. Lig-cristal system for the wmt17 automatic post-editing task. In *Proceedings of the Second Conference on Machine Translation*. pages 623–629.

Ondřej Bojar, Rajen Chatterjee, Christian Federmann, Yvette Graham, Barry Haddow, Shujian Huang, Matthias Huck, Philipp Koehn, Qun Liu, Varvara Logacheva, Christof Monz, Matteo Negri, Matt Post, Raphael Rubino, Lucia Specia, and Marco Turchi. 2017. Findings of the 2017 conference on machine translation (wmt17). In *Proceedings of the Second Conference on Machine Translation*. pages 169–214.

Ondřej Bojar, Rajen Chatterjee, Christian Federmann, Yvette Graham, Barry Haddow, Matthias Huck, Antonio Jimeno Yepes, Philipp Koehn, Varvara Logacheva, Christof Monz, Matteo Negri, Aurélie Névéol, Mariana Neves, Martin Popel, Matt Post, Raphael Rubino, Carolina Scarton, Lucia Specia, Marco Turchi, Karin Verspoor, and Marcos Zampieri. 2016. Findings of the 2016 conference on machine translation. In *Proceedings of the First Conference on Machine Translation: Volume 2, Shared Task Papers*. volume 2, pages 131–198.

Rajen Chatterjee, M Amin Farajian, Matteo Negri, Marco Turchi, Ankit Srivastava, and Santanu Pal. 2017. Multi-source neural automatic post-editing: Fbks participation in the wmt 2017 ape shared task. In *Proceedings of the Second Conference on Machine Translation*. pages 630–638.

Sepp Hochreiter and Jürgen Schmidhuber. 1997. Long short-term memory. *Neural computation* 9(8):1735–1780.

Marcin Junczys-Dowmunt and Roman Grundkiewicz. 2016. Log-linear combinations of monolingual and bilingual neural machine translation models for automatic post-editing. In *Proceedings of the First Conference on Machine Translation*. pages 751–558.

Guillaume Klein, Yoon Kim, Yuntian Deng, Jean Senellart, and Alexander M Rush. 2017. Opennmt: Open-source toolkit for neural machine translation. *arXiv preprint arXiv:1701.02810* .

Jindřich Libovický and Jindřich Helcl. 2017. Attention strategies for multi-source sequence-to-sequence learning. *arXiv preprint arXiv:1704.06567* .

Jindřich Libovický, Jindřich Helcl, Marek Tlustý, Pavel Pecina, and Ondřej Bojar. 2016. Cuni system for wmt16 automatic post-editing and multimodal translation tasks. In *Proceedings of the First Conference on Machine Translation*.

Minh-Thang Luong, Hieu Pham, and Christopher D Manning. 2015. Effective approaches to attention-based neural machine translation. *arXiv preprint arXiv:1508.04025* .

Santanu Pal, Sudip Kumar Naskar, Mihaela Vela, Qun Liu, and Josef van Genabith. 2017. Neural automatic post-editing using prior alignment and reranking. In *Proceedings of the 15th Conference of the European Chapter of the Association for Computational Linguistics: Volume 2, Short Papers*. volume 2, pages 349–355.

Kishore Papineni, Salim Roukos, Todd Ward, and Wei-Jing Zhu. 2002. Bleu: a method for automatic evaluation of machine translation. In *Proceedings of the 40th annual meeting on association for computational linguistics*. Association for Computational Linguistics, pages 311–318.

Rico Sennrich, Barry Haddow, and Alexandra Birch. 2015. Neural machine translation of rare words with subword units. *arXiv preprint arXiv:1508.07909* .

Michel Simard, Cyril Goutte, and Pierre Isabelle. 2007. Statistical phrase-based post-editing. In *NAACL HLT*. pages 505–515.

Matthew Snover, Bonnie Dorr, Richard Schwartz, Linnea Micciulla, and John Makhoul. 2006. A study of translation edit rate with targeted human annotation. In *Proceedings of association for machine translation in the Americas*. volume 200.

Ilya Sutskever, Oriol Vinyals, and Quoc V Le. 2014. Sequence to sequence learning with neural networks. In *Advances in neural information processing systems*. pages 3104–3112.

Dusan Varis and Ondřej Bojar. 2017. Cuni system for wmt17 automatic post-editing task. In *Proceedings of the Second Conference on Machine Translation*. pages 661–666.

Quan-shi Zhang and Song-Chun Zhu. 2018. Visual interpretability for deep learning: a survey. *Frontiers of Information Technology & Electronic Engineering* 19(1):27–39.

Iterative Back-Translation for Neural Machine Translation

Cong Duy Vu Hoang
Computing and Information Systems
University of Melbourne, Australia
vhoang2@student.unimelb.edu.au

Philipp Koehn
Computer Science Department
Johns Hopkins University, USA
phi@jhu.edu

Gholamreza Haffari
Faculty of Information Technology
Monash University, Australia
gholamreza.haffari@monash.edu

Trevor Cohn
Computing and Information Systems
University of Melbourne, Australia
tcohn@unimelb.edu.au

Abstract

We present iterative back-translation, a method for generating increasingly better synthetic parallel data from monolingual data to train neural machine translation systems. Our proposed method is very simple yet effective and highly applicable in practice. We demonstrate improvements in neural machine translation quality in both high and low resourced scenarios, including the best reported BLEU scores for the WMT 2017 German↔English tasks.

1 Introduction

The exploitation of monolingual training data for neural machine translation is an open challenge. One successful method is back-translation (Sennrich et al., 2016b), whereby an NMT system is trained in the reverse translation direction (target-to-source), and is then used to translate target-side monolingual data back into the source language (in the *backward* direction, hence the name back-translation). The resulting sentence pairs constitute a synthetic parallel corpus that can be added to the existing training data to learn a source-to-target model. Figure 1 illustrates this idea.

In this paper, we show that the quality of back-translation matters and propose *iterative back-translation*, where back-translated data is used to build better translation systems in forward and backward directions, which in turn is used to re-back-translate monolingual data. This process can be "iterated" several times. This is a form of co-training (Blum and Mitchell, 1998) where the two models over both translation directions can be used to train one another. We show that iterative back-translation leads to improved results over simple back-translation, under both high and

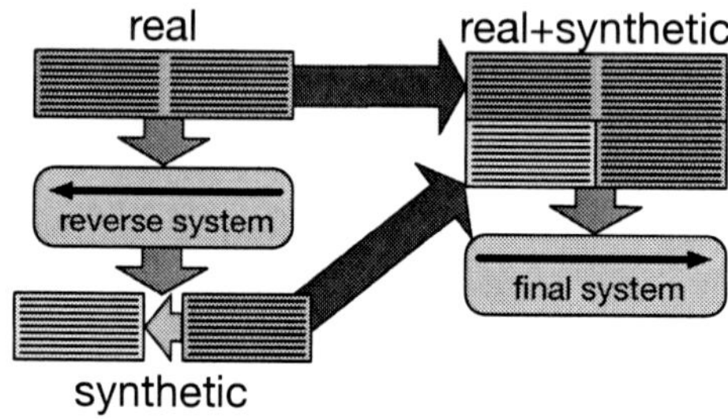

Figure 1: Creating a synthetic parallel corpus through back-translation. First, a system in the reverse direction is trained and then used to translate monolingual data from the target side backward into the source side, to be used in the final system.

low resource conditions, improving over the state of the art.

2 Related Work

The idea of back-translation dates back at least to statistical machine translation, where it has been used for semi-supervised learning (Bojar and Tamchyna, 2011), or self-training (Goutte et al., 2009, ch.12, p.237). In modern NMT research, Sennrich et al. (2017) reported significant gains on the WMT and IWSLT shared tasks. They showed that even simply duplicating the monolingual target data into the source was sufficient to realise some benefits. Currey et al. (2017) reported similar findings for low resource conditions, showing that even poor translations can be beneficial. Gwinnup et al. (2017) mention in their system description iteratively applying back-translation, but did not report successful experiments.

A more refined idea of back-translation is the *dual learning* approach of He et al. (2016) which integrates training on parallel data and training on monolingual data via round-tripping. We have to admit that we extensively experimented with

Proceedings of the 2nd Workshop on Neural Machine Translation and Generation, pages 18–24
Melbourne, Australia, July 20, 2018. ©2018 Association for Computational Linguistics

	English-German	English-French$_{100K}$	English-French$_{1M}$	English-Farsi
parallel en	141 280 704	2 651 040	26 464 159	2 233 688
parallel l$_2$	134 638 256	2 962 318	29 622 370	2 473 608
mono en	322 529 936	2 154 175 053	2 154 175 053	2 154 175 053
mono l$_2$	301 736 163	766 646 932	766 646 932	65 585 281

Table 1: Parallel and monolingual corpora used, including English-German, English-French and English-Farsi. Numbers denote the number of words, and l$_2$ is the second language in each pair. The de-en data is from WMT 2017 (parallel) and a subset of News 2016 (monolingual).

an implementation of this approach, but did not achieve any gains.

An alternative way to make use of monolingual data is the integration of a separately trained language model into the neural machine translation architecture (Gülçehre et al., 2015), but this has not yet to be proven to be as successful as back-translation.

Lample et al. (2018) explore the use of back-translated data generated by neural and statistical machine translation systems, aided by denoising with a language model trained on the target side.

3 Impact of Back-Translation Quality

Our work is inspired by the intuition that a better back-translation system will lead to a better synthetic corpus, hence producing a better final system. To empirically validate this hypothesis and measure the correlation between back-translation system quality and final system quality, we use a set of machine translation systems of differing quality (trained in the reverse "back-translation" direction), and check how this effects the final system quality.

We carried out experiments on the high-resource WMT German↔English news translation tasks (Bojar et al., 2017). For these tasks, large parallel corpora are available from related domains.[1] In addition, in-domain monolingual news corpora are provided as well, in much larger quantities. We sub-sampled the 2016 news corpus (see Table 1) for about twice as large as corpus as the parallel training corpus.

Following Sennrich et al. (2016b), a synthetic parallel corpus is created from the in-domain news monolingual data, in equal amounts to the existing real parallel corpus. The systems used to translate the monolingual data are canonical atten-

German–English	Back	Final
no back-translation	-	29.6
10k iterations	10.6	29.6 (+0.0)
100k iterations	21.0	31.1 (+1.5)
convergence	23.7	32.5 (+2.9)

English–German	Back	Final
no back-translation	-	23.7
10k iterations	14.5	23.7 (+0.0)
100k iterations	26.2	25.2 (+1.5)
convergence	29.1	25.9 (+2.2)

Table 2: WMT News Translation Task English↔German, reporting cased BLEU on newstest2017, evaluating the impact of the quality of the back-translation system on the final system. Note that the back-translation systems run in the opposite direction and are not comparable to the numbers in the same row.

tional neural machine translation systems (Bahdanau et al., 2015). Our setup is very similar to Edinburgh's submission to the WMT 2016 evaluation campaign (Sennrich et al., 2016a),[2] but uses the fast Marian toolkit (Junczys-Dowmunt et al., 2018) for training. We trained 3 different back-translation systems, namely:

10k iterations Training a neural translation model on the parallel corpus, but stopping after 0.15 epochs;

100k iterations As above, but stopping after 1½ epochs; and

convergence As above, but training until convergence (10 epochs, 3 GPU days).

Given these three different systems, we create three synthetic parallel corpora of different quality and train systems on each. Table 2 shows the quality of the final systems. For both direc-

---

[1]EU Parliament Proceedings, official EU announcements, news commentaries, and web crawled data.

[2]With true-casing and 50,000 BPE operations (Sennrich et al., 2016c) as pre-processing steps.

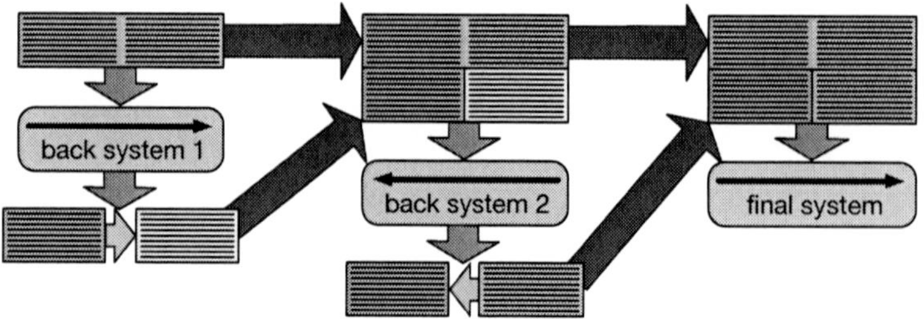

Figure 2: Re-Back-Translation: Taking the idea of back-translation one step further. After training a system with back-translated data (back system 2 above), it is used to create a synthetic parallel corpus for the final system.

tions, the quality of the back-translation systems differs vastly. The **10k iteration** systems perform poorly, and their synthetic parallel corpus provides no benefit over a baseline that does not use any back-translated data.

The longer trained systems have much better translation quality, and their synthetic parallel corpora prove to be beneficial. The back-translation system trained for 100k iteration already provides tangible benefits (+1.5 BLEU for both directions), while the converged system yields even bigger improvements (+2.9 for German–English, and +2.2 for English–German). These results indicate that the quality of the back-translation system is a significant factor for the success of the approach.

4   Iterative Back-Translation

We now take the idea of back-translation one step further. If we can build a better system with the back-translated data, then we can continue repeating this process: Use this better system to back-translate the data, and use this data in order to build an even better system. See Figure 2 for an illustration of this *re-back-translation* process (repeated back-translation). See Algorithm 1 for the details of this *iterated* back-translation process. The final system benefits from monolingual data in both the source and target languages.

We do not have to stop at one iteration of repeated back-translation. We can iterate training the two back-translation systems multiple times. We refer this process to *iterative back-translation*.

In our experiments, we validate our approach under both high-resource and low-resource conditions. Under high-resource conditions, we improve the state of the art with re-back-translation. Under low-resource conditions, we demonstrate

---

Algorithm 1 Iterative Back-Translation

Input: parallel data D^p, monolingual source, D^s, and target D^t text
1: Let $T_{\leftarrow} = D^p$
2: **repeat**
3:      Train target-to-source model $\Theta_{\leftarrow}$ on $T_{\leftarrow}$
4:      Use $\Theta_{\leftarrow}$ to create $S = \{(\hat{s}, t)\}$, for $t \in D^t$
5:      Let $T_{\rightarrow} = D^p \cup S$
6:      Train source-to-target model $\Theta_{\rightarrow}$ on $T_{\rightarrow}$
7:      Use $\Theta_{\rightarrow}$ to create $S' = \{(s, \hat{t})\}$, for $s \in D^s$
8:      Let $T_{\leftarrow} = D^p \cup S'$
9: **until** convergence condition reached
Output: newly-updated models $\Theta_{\leftarrow}$ and $\Theta_{\rightarrow}$

---

the effectiveness of iterative back-translation.

4.1   Experiments on High Resource Scenario

In §3 we demonstrated that the quality of the back-translation system has significant impact on the effectiveness of the back-translation approach under high-resource data conditions such as WMT 2017 German–English. Here we ask: how much additional benefit can be realised for repeating this process? Also, do the gains for state-of-the-art systems that use deeper models, i.e., more layers in encoder and decoder (Miceli Barone et al., 2017) still apply in this setting?

We evaluate on German–English and English–German, under the same data conditions as in Section 3. We experiment with both *shallow* and *deep* stacked-layer encoder/decoder architectures.

The base translation system is trained on the parallel data only. We train a shallow system using 4-checkpoint ensembling (Chen et al., 2017). The system is used to translate the monolingual data using a beam size of 2.

The first back-translation system is trained on

German–English	Back*	Shallow	Deep	Ensemble
back-translation	23.7	32.5	35.0	35.6
re-back-translation	27.9	33.6	36.1	36.5
Best WMT 2017	-	-	-	35.1

English–German	Back*	Shallow	Deep	Ensemble
back-translation	29.1	25.9	28.3	28.8
re-back-translation	34.8	27.0	29.0	29.3
Best WMT 2017	-	-	-	28.3

Table 3: WMT News Translation Task German–English, comparing the quality of different back-translation systems with different final system architectures. *Note that the quality for the back-translation system (Back) is measured in the opposite language direction.

the parallel data and the synthetic data generated by the base translation system. For better performance, we train a deep model with 8-checkpoint ensembling; again we use a beam size of 2.

The final back-translation systems were trained using several different systems: a shallow architecture, a deep architecture, and an ensemble system of 4 independent training runs.

Across the board, the final systems with re-back-translation outperform the final systems with simple back-translation, by a margin of 0.5–1.1 BLEU.

Notably, the final deep systems trained by re-back-translation outperform the state-of-the-art established at the WMT 2017 evaluation campaign for these language pairs, by a margin of about 1 BLEU point. These are the best published results for this dataset, to the best of our knowledge.

Experimental settings For the experiments in the German–English high-resource scenario, we used the Marian toolkit (Junczys-Dowmunt et al., 2018) for training and for back-translation. The shallow systems (also used for the back-translation step) match the setup of Edinburgh's WMT 2016 system (Sennrich et al., 2016a). It is an attentional RNN (default Marian settings) with dropout of 0.2 for the RNN parameters, and 0.1 otherwise. Training is smoothed with moving average. It takes about 2–4 days.

The deep system uses matches the setup of Edinburgh's WMT 2017 system (Sennrich et al., 2017). It uses 4 encoder and 4 decoder layers (Marian setting `best-deep`) with LSTM cells.

Drop-out settings are the same as above. Decoding during test time is done with a beam size of 12, while back-translation uses only a beam size of 2. This difference is reflected in the reported BLEU score for the deep system after back-translation (35.0 for German–English, 28.3 for English–German) and the score reported for the quality of the back-translation system (34.8 (–0.2) and 27.9 (–0.4), respectively) in Table 3.

For all experiments, the true-casing model and the list of BPE operations is left constant. Both were learned from the original parallel training corpus.

4.2 Experiments on Low Resource Scenario

NMT is a data-hungry approach, requiring a large amount of parallel data to reach reasonable performance (Koehn and Knowles, 2017). In a low-resource setting, only small amount of parallel data exist. Previous work has attempted to incorporate prior or external knowledge to compensate for the lack of parallel data, e.g. injecting inductive bias via linguistic constraints (Cohn et al., 2016) or linguistic factors (Hoang et al., 2016). However, it is much cheaper and easier to obtain monolingual data in either the source or target language. An interesting question is whether the (iterative) back-translation can compensate for the lack of parallel data in such low-resource settings.

To explore this question, we conducted experiments on two datasets: A simulated low-resource setting with English–French, and a more realistic setting with English–Farsi. For the English–French dataset, we used the original WMT dataset, sub-sampled to create smaller sets of 100K and 1M parallel sentence pairs. For English–Farsi, we used the available datasets from LDC and TED Talks, totaling about 100K sentence pairs. For detailed statistics see Table 1.

Following the same experimental setup as in high-resource setting,[3] we obtain similar patterns of improvement of translation quality (Table 4).

Back-Translation Generally, it is our expectation that the back-translation approach still improves the translation accuracy in all language pairs with a low-resource setting. In the English–French experiments, large improvements over the baseline are observed in both directions, with +3.5

---

[3]The difference here is on the NMT toolkit used — we opted to use Amazon's Sockeye (Hieber et al., 2017). We used Sockeye's default configuration with dropout 0.5.

Setting	French–English		English–French		Farsi–English	English-Farsi
	100K	1M	100K	1M	100K	100K
NMT baseline	16.7	24.7	18.0	25.6	21.7	16.4
back-translation	22.1	27.8	21.5	27.0	22.1	16.7
back-translation iterative+1	22.5	-	22.7	-	22.7	17.1
back-translation iterative+2	22.6	-	22.6	-	22.6	17.2
back-translation (w/ Moses)	23.7	27.9	23.5	27.3	21.8	16.8

Table 4: Low Resource setting: Impact of the quality of the back-translation systems on the benefit of the synthetic parallel for the final system in a low-resource setting. Note that, we reported the single NMT systems in all numbers.

BLEU for English to French and +5.4 for French to English in 100K setting. In 1M setting, we also obtained a similar pattern of BLEU gains, albeit of a smaller magnitude, i.e., +1.4 BLEU for English to French and +3.1 for French to English.[4] Note that the large gains here may be due to the fact that the monolingual data is a similar domain to the test data. Inspections of the resulting translations show that the lexical choice has been improved significantly. In English-Farsi experiments shown in Table 4, we also observed BLEU gains, albeit more modest in size: +0.3 BLEU for English to Farsi and +0.4 for Farsi to English. The smaller gains may be because Farsi translation is much more difficult than French; or a result of the diverse mix of domains in the parallel training data (news with LDC and technical talks with TED) where the domain in monolingual data is entirely news, leading to much lower quality than the other datasets. Measuring the impact of iteratively back-translated data in relation to varying domain mismatch between parallel and monolingual data, is a very interesting problem which we will explore in future work; but is out of the scope for this paper.

Balance of real and synthetic parallel data In all our experiments with back-translation, in order to create synthetic parallel data, a small amount of monolingual data is randomly sampled from the big monolingual data (Table 1). As pointed out by (Sennrich et al., 2016b), the balance between the real and synthetic parallel data matters. However, there is no obvious evidence about the affect of the sample size, hence we further studied this by choosing a ratio between the real and synthetic parallel data. We opt to use different ratio (e.g., 1(real):2(synthetic) and 1(real):3(synthetic))

English–Farsi	100K
back-translation 1:1	16.7
back-translation 1:2	16.8
back-translation 1:3	16.9

Farsi-English	100K
back-translation 1:1	22.1
back-translation 1:2	22.4
back-translation 1:3	22.4

Table 5: Weighting amounts of real parallel data (1) with varying amounts of synthetic data (1-3). Larger amounts of synthetic data help.

in our experiments. Our results in Table 5 show that more synthetic parallel data seems to be useful (though not obvious), e.g., gains from 16.7 to 16.9 in English to Farsi and gain from 22.1 to 22.4 in Farsi to English.

Iterative back-translation For iterative back-translation, we obtained consistent results with the earlier findings from §4.1. In English–French tasks, we see more than +1 BLEU from a further iteration of back-translations, with little difference between 1 or 2 additional iterations. However, in English–Farsi tasks, gains are much smaller.

Comparison to back-translation with Moses We now consider the utility of creating synthetic parallel data from different sources, e.g., from a phrase-based SMT models produced by Moses (Koehn et al., 2007), a considerably faster and more scalable system than modern NMT techniques. As can be seen in Table 4, this has mixed results, being better for English–French, and worse in English–Farsi, than using neural models, although in all cases the results are not far apart.

---

[4]All the scores are statistically significant with $p < 0.01$.

Quality of the sampled monolingual data
Back-translation is dependent much on the quality of back-translated synthetic data. In our paper, repeating the back translation process in 2-3 times can lead to improved translation. However, this can be different in other language pairs and domains. Also, in our work, we sampled the monolingual data uniformly at random, so sentences may be used more than once in subsequent rounds. Its quite likely that other techniques for data sampling and selection, e.g., non-uniform sampling like transductive selection or active learning - which potentially diversifies the quality and quantity of monolingual data - would lead further improvements in translation performance. We leave this for our future work.

Efficacy on iterative back-translation The efficiency of the NMT toolkits we used (sockeye, marian-nmt) is excellent. Both support batch decoding for fast translation, e.g., with a batch-size of 200 (beam-size 5) marian-nmt can achieve over 5000 words per second on one GPU (less than 1 day for translating 4M sentences)[5]; and also this scales linearly to the number of GPUs we have. Alternatively, we can split the monolingual data into smaller parts and distribute these parts over different GPUs. This can greatly speed up the back-translation process. This leaves the problem of training the model in each iteration, which we do 2-3 times. Overall the computational complexity is not a big deal (even with larger dataset), and the iterative back translation is quite feasible with existing modern GPU servers.

5 Conclusion

We presented a simple but effective extension of the back-translation approach to training neural machine translation systems. We empirically showed that the quality of the back-translation system matters for synthetic corpus creation, and that neural machine translation performance can be improved by iterative back-translation in both high-resource and low-resource scenarios. We show empirically that this works well for both high and low resource conditions. The method is simple but highly applicable in practice.

An important avenue for future work is to unify the various approaches to learning, including back-translation (Sennrich et al., 2016b), iterative back-translation (this work), co-training, and dual learning (He et al., 2016) in a framework which can be trained in an end-to-end manner.

Acknowledgements

Most of this work took part during the 2017 JSALT Summer Workshop and we would like to thank the organizers, including our team leader George Foster for their support.

References

Dzmitry Bahdanau, Kyunghyun Cho, and Yoshua Bengio. 2015. Neural machine translation by jointly learning to align and translate. In *ICLR*.

Avrim Blum and Tom Mitchell. 1998. Combining labeled and unlabeled data with co-training. In *Proceedings of the eleventh annual conference on Computational learning theory*, pages 92–100. ACM.

Ondřej Bojar, Rajen Chatterjee, Christian Federmann, Yvette Graham, Barry Haddow, Shujian Huang, Matthias Huck, Philipp Koehn, Qun Liu, Varvara Logacheva, Christof Monz, Matteo Negri, Matt Post, Raphael Rubino, Lucia Specia, and Marco Turchi. 2017. Findings of the 2017 conference on machine translation (wmt17). In *Proceedings of the Second Conference on Machine Translation, Volume 2: Shared Task Papers*.

Ondej Bojar and Aleš Tamchyna. 2011. Improving translation model by monolingual data. In *Proceedings of the Sixth Workshop on Statistical Machine Translation*.

Hugh Chen, Scott Lundberg, and Su-In Lee. 2017. Checkpoint ensembles: Ensemble methods from a single training process. *arXiv preprint arXiv:1710.03282*.

Trevor Cohn, Cong Duy Vu Hoang, Ekaterina Vymolova, Kaisheng Yao, Chris Dyer, and Gholamreza Haffari. 2016. Incorporating structural alignment biases into an attentional neural translation model. In *Proceedings of the 2016 Conference of the North American Chapter of the Association for Computational Linguistics: Human Language Technologies*.

Anna Currey, Antonio Valerio Miceli Barone, and Kenneth Heafield. 2017. Copied monolingual data improves low-resource neural machine translation. In *Proceedings of the Second Conference on Machine Translation, Volume 1: Research Paper*.

Cyril Goutte, Nicola Cancedda, Marc Dymetman, and George Foster. 2009. *Learning Machine Translation*. The MIT Press.

Çaglar Gülçehre, Orhan Firat, Kelvin Xu, Kyunghyun Cho, Loïc Barrault, Huei-Chi Lin, Fethi Bougares,

---

[5] https://marian-nmt.github.io/features/

Holger Schwenk, and Yoshua Bengio. 2015. On using monolingual corpora in neural machine translation. *CoRR*, abs/1503.03535.

Jeremy Gwinnup, Timothy Anderson, Grant Erdmann, Katherine Young, Michaeel Kazi, Elizabeth Salesky, Brian Thompson, and Jonathan Taylor. 2017. The afrl-mitll wmt17 systems: Old, new, borrowed, bleu. In *Proceedings of the Second Conference on Machine Translation, Volume 2: Shared Task Papers*.

Di He, Yingce Xia, Tao Qin, Liwei Wang, Nenghai Yu, Tieyan Liu, and Wei-Ying Ma. 2016. Dual learning for machine translation. In D. D. Lee, M. Sugiyama, U. V. Luxburg, I. Guyon, and R. Garnett, editors, *Advances in Neural Information Processing Systems 29*, pages 820–828.

F. Hieber, T. Domhan, M. Denkowski, D. Vilar, A. Sokolov, A. Clifton, and M. Post. 2017. Sockeye: A Toolkit for Neural Machine Translation. *ArXiv e-prints*.

Cong Duy Vu Hoang, Reza Haffari, and Trevor Cohn. 2016. Improving neural translation models with linguistic factors. In *Proceedings of the Australasian Language Technology Association Workshop 2016*, pages 7–14.

Marcin Junczys-Dowmunt, Roman Grundkiewicz, Tomasz Dwojak, Hieu Hoang, Kenneth Heafield, Tom Neckermann, Frank Seide, Ulrich Germann, Alham Fikri Aji, Nikolay Bogoychev, André F. T. Martins, and Alexandra Birch. 2018. Marian: Fast neural machine translation in C++. *arXiv preprint arXiv:1804.00344*.

Philipp Koehn, Hieu Hoang, Alexandra Birch, Chris Callison-Burch, Marcello Federico, Nicola Bertoldi, Brooke Cowan, Wade Shen, Christine Moran, Richard Zens, Christopher J. Dyer, Ondřej Bojar, Alexandra Constantin, and Evan Herbst. 2007. Moses: Open source toolkit for statistical machine translation. In *Proceedings of the 45th Annual Meeting of the Association for Computational Linguistics Companion Volume Proceedings of the Demo and Poster Sessions*.

Philipp Koehn and Rebecca Knowles. 2017. Six challenges for neural machine translation. In *Proceedings of the First Workshop on Neural Machine Translation*.

Guillaume Lample, Myle Ott, Alexis Conneau, Ludovic Denoyer, and Marc'Aurelio Ranzato. 2018. Phrase-based and neural unsupervised machine translation.

Antonio Valerio Miceli Barone, Jindřich Helcl, Rico Sennrich, Barry Haddow, and Alexandra Birch. 2017. Deep architectures for neural machine translation. In *Proceedings of the Second Conference on Machine Translation, Volume 1: Research Paper*.

Rico Sennrich, Alexandra Birch, Anna Currey, Ulrich Germann, Barry Haddow, Kenneth Heafield, Antonio Valerio Miceli Barone, and Philip Williams. 2017. The university of edinburgh's neural mt systems for wmt17. In *Proceedings of the Second Conference on Machine Translation, Volume 2: Shared Task Papers*.

Rico Sennrich, Barry Haddow, and Alexandra Birch. 2016a. Edinburgh neural machine translation systems for wmt 16. In *Proceedings of the First Conference on Machine Translation*, pages 371–376, Berlin, Germany. Association for Computational Linguistics.

Rico Sennrich, Barry Haddow, and Alexandra Birch. 2016b. Improving neural machine translation models with monolingual data. In *Proceedings of the 54th Annual Meeting of the Association for Computational Linguistics (Volume 1: Long Papers)*.

Rico Sennrich, Barry Haddow, and Alexandra Birch. 2016c. Neural machine translation of rare words with subword units. In *Proceedings of the 54th Annual Meeting of the Association for Computational Linguistics (Volume 1: Long Papers)*.

Inducing Grammars with and for Neural Machine Translation

Ke Tran
Informatics Institute
University of Amsterdam
ketranmanh@gmail.com

Yonatan Bisk
Department of Computer Science
University of Washington
ybisk@cs.washington.com

Abstract

Machine translation systems require semantic knowledge and grammatical understanding. Neural machine translation (NMT) systems often assume this information is captured by an attention mechanism and a decoder that ensures fluency. Recent work has shown that incorporating explicit syntax alleviates the burden of modeling both types of knowledge. However, requiring parses is expensive and does not explore the question of what syntax a model needs during translation. To address both of these issues we introduce a model that simultaneously translates while inducing dependency trees. In this way, we leverage the benefits of structure while investigating what syntax NMT must induce to maximize performance. We show that our dependency trees are 1. language pair dependent and 2. improve translation quality.

1 Motivation

Language has syntactic structure and translation models need to understand grammatical dependencies to resolve the semantics of a sentence and preserve agreement (*e.g.*, number, gender, etc). Many current approaches to MT have been able to avoid explicitly providing structural information by relying on advances in sequence to sequence (seq2seq) models. The most famous advances include attention mechanisms (Bahdanau et al., 2015) and gating in Long Short-Term Memory (LSTM) cells (Hochreiter and Schmidhuber, 1997).

In this work we aim to benefit from syntactic structure, without providing it to the model, and to disentangle the semantic and syntactic components of translation, by introducing a gating mechanism which controls when syntax should be used.

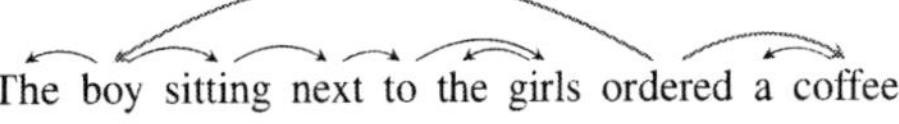

Figure 1: Our model aims to capture both: **syntactic** (verb *ordered* → subj/obj *boy, coffee*) **alignment** (noun *girls* → determiner *the*) attention.

Consider the process of translating the sentence *"The boy sitting next to the girls ordered a coffee."* (Figure 1) from English to German. In German, translating *ordered*, requires knowledge of its subject *boy* to correctly predict the verb's number *bestellte* instead of *bestellten*. This is a case where syntactic agreement requires long-distance information. On the other hand, *next* can be translated in isolation. The model should uncover these relationships and decide when and which aspects of syntax are necessary. While in principle decoders can utilize previously predicted words (*e.g.*, the translation of *boy*) to reason about subject-verb agreement, in practice LSTMs still struggle with long-distance dependencies. Moreover, Belinkov et al. (2017) showed that using attention reduces the decoder's capacity to learn target side syntax.

In addition to demonstrating improvements in translation quality, we are also interested in analyzing the predicted dependency trees discovered by our models. Recent work has begun analyzing task-specific latent trees (Williams et al., 2018). We present the first results on learning latent trees with a joint syntactic-semantic objective. We do this in the service of machine translation which inherently requires access to both aspects of a sentence. Further, our results indicate that language pairs with rich morphology require and therefore induce more complex syntactic structure.

Our use of a structured self attention encoder (§4) that predicts a non-projective dependency tree

Proceedings of the 2nd Workshop on Neural Machine Translation and Generation, pages 25–35
Melbourne, Australia, July 20, 2018. ©2018 Association for Computational Linguistics

over the source sentence provides a soft structured representation of the source sentence that can then be transferred to the decoder, which alleviates the burden of capturing target syntax on the target side.

We will show that the quality of the induced trees depends on the choice of the target language (§7). Moreover, the gating mechanism will allow us to examine which contexts require source side syntax.

In summary, in this work:

- We propose a new NMT model that discovers latent structures for encoding and when to use them, while achieving significant improvements in BLEU scores over a strong baseline.

- We perform an in-depth analysis of the induced structures and investigate where the target decoder decides syntax is required.

2   Related Work

Recent work has begun investigating what syntax seq2seq models capture (Linzen et al., 2016), but this is evaluated via downstream tasks designed to test the model's abilities and not its representation.

Simultaneously, recent research in neural machine translation (NMT) has shown the benefit of modeling syntax explicitly (Aharoni and Goldberg, 2017; Bastings et al., 2017; Li et al., 2017; Eriguchi et al., 2017) rather than assuming the model will automatically discover and encode it.

Bradbury and Socher (2017) presented an encoder-decoder architecture based on RNNG (Dyer et al., 2016). However, their preliminary work was not scaled to a large MT dataset and omits analysis of the induced trees.

Unlike the previous work on source side latent graph parsing (Hashimoto and Tsuruoka, 2017), our structured self attention encoder allows us to extract a dependency tree in a principled manner. Therefore, learning the internal representation of our model is related to work done in unsupervised grammar induction (Klein and Manning, 2004; Spitkovsky et al., 2011) except that by focusing on translation we require both syntactic and semantic knowledge.

In this work, we attempt to contribute to both modeling syntax and investigating a more interpretable interface for testing the syntactic content of a new seq2seq models' internal representation.

3   Neural Machine Translation

Given a training pair of source and target sentences $(\mathbf{x}, \mathbf{y})$ of length n and m respectively, neural machine translation is a conditional probabilistic model $p(\mathbf{y} \mid \mathbf{x})$ implemented using neural networks

$$\log p(\mathbf{y} \mid \mathbf{x};\ \boldsymbol{\theta}) = \sum_{j=1}^{m} \log p(\mathbf{y}_j \mid \mathbf{y}_{i<j}, \mathbf{x};\ \boldsymbol{\theta})$$

where $\boldsymbol{\theta}$ is the model's parameters. We will omit the parameters $\boldsymbol{\theta}$ herein for readability.

The NMT system used in this work is a seq2seq model that consists of a bidirectional LSTM encoder and an LSTM decoder coupled with an attention mechanism (Bahdanau et al., 2015; Luong et al., 2015). Our system is based on a PyTorch implementation[1] of OpenNMT (Klein et al., 2017). Let $\{\mathbf{s}_i \in \mathbb{R}^d\}_{i=1}^n$ be the output of the encoder

$$\mathbf{S} = \mathrm{BiLSTM}(\mathbf{x}) \qquad (1)$$

Here we use $\mathbf{S} = [\mathbf{s}_1; \ldots; \mathbf{s}_n] \in \mathbb{R}^{d \times n}$ as a concatenation of $\{\mathbf{s}_i\}$. The decoder is composed of stacked LSTMs with input-feeding. Specifically, the inputs of the decoder at time step t are a concatenation of the embedding of the previous generated word $\mathbf{y}_{t-1}$ and a vector $\mathbf{u}_{t-1}$:

$$\mathbf{u}_{t-1} = g(\mathbf{h}_{t-1}, \mathbf{c}_{t-1}) \qquad (2)$$

where g is a one layer feed-forward network, $\mathbf{h}_{t-1}$ is the output of the LSTM decoder, and $\mathbf{c}_{t-1}$ is a context vector computed by an attention mechanism

$$\boldsymbol{\alpha}_{t-1} = \mathrm{softmax}(\mathbf{h}_{t-1}^{\mathsf{T}} \mathbf{W}_a \mathbf{S}) \qquad (3)$$

$$\mathbf{c}_{t-1} = \mathbf{S} \boldsymbol{\alpha}_{t-1}^{\mathsf{T}} \qquad (4)$$

where $\mathbf{W}_a \in \mathbb{R}^{d \times d}$ is a trainable parameter.

Finally a single layer feed-forward network f takes $\mathbf{u}_t$ as input and returns a multinomial distribution over all the target words: $y_t \sim f(\mathbf{u}_t)$

4   Syntactic Attention Model

We propose a syntactic attention model[2] (Figure 2) that differs from standard NMT in two crucial aspects. First, our encoder outputs two sets of annotations: content annotations $\mathbf{S}$ and syntactic annotations $\mathbf{M}$ (Figure 2a). The content annotations are the outputs of a standard BiLSTM while the

<hr>

[1] http://opennmt.net/OpenNMT-py/
[2] https://github.com/ketranm/sa-nmt

syntactic annotations are produced by a head word selection layer (§4.1). The syntactic annotations $\mathbf{M}$ capture syntactic dependencies amongst the source words and enable syntactic transfer from the source to the target. Second, we incorporate the source side syntax into our model by modifying the standard attention (from target to source) in NMT such that it attends to both $\mathbf{S}$ and $\mathbf{M}$ through a *shared attention* layer. The shared attention layer biases our model toward capturing source side dependency. It produces a dependency context $\mathbf{d}$ (Figure 2c) in addition to the standard context vector $\mathbf{c}$ (Figure 2b) at each time step. Motivated by the example in Figure 1 that some words can be translated without resolving their syntactic roles in the source sentence, we include a gating mechanism that allows the decoder to decide the amount of syntax needed when it generates the next word. Next, we describe the head word selection layer and how source side syntax is incorporated into our model.

4.1 Head Word Selection

The head word selection layer learns to select a *soft* head word for each source word. This layer transforms $\mathbf{S}$ into a matrix $\mathbf{M}$ that encodes implicit dependency structure of $\mathbf{x}$ using *structured self attention*. First we apply three trainable weight matrices $\mathbf{W}_q, \mathbf{W}_k, \mathbf{W}_v \in \mathbb{R}^{d \times d}$ to map $\mathbf{S}$ to query, key, and value matrices $\mathbf{S}_q = \mathbf{W}_q \mathbf{S}, \mathbf{S}_k = \mathbf{W}_k \mathbf{S}, \mathbf{S}_v = \mathbf{W}_v \mathbf{S} \in \mathbb{R}^{d \times n}$ respectively. Then we compute the structured self attention probabilities $\beta \in \mathbb{R}^{n \times n}$ via a function *sattn*: $\beta = \text{sattn}(\mathbf{S}_q^\mathsf{T} \mathbf{S}_k / \sqrt{d})$. Finally the syntactic context $\mathbf{M}$ is computed as $\mathbf{M} = \mathbf{S}_v \beta$.

Here n is the length of the source sentence, so β captures all pairwise word dependencies. Each cell $\beta_{i,j}$ of the attention matrix β is the posterior probability $p(x_i = \text{head}(x_j) \,|\, \mathbf{x})$. The structured self attention function *sattn* is inspired by the work of (Kim et al., 2017) but differs in two important ways. First we model *non-projective dependency trees*. Second, we utilize the Kirchhoff's Matrix-Tree Theorem (Tutte, 1984) instead of the sum-product algorithm presented in (Kim et al., 2017) for fast evaluation of the attention probabilities. We note that (Liu and Lapata, 2018) were first to propose using the Matrix-Tree Theorem for evaluating the marginals in end to end training of neural networks. Their work, however, focuses on the task of natural language inference (Bowman et al., 2015) and document classification which arguably require less syntactic knowledge than machine translation.

Additionally, we will evaluate our structured self attention on datasets that are up to 20 times larger than the datasets studied in previous work.

Let $\mathbf{z} \in \{0, 1\}^{n \times n}$ be an adjacency matrix encoding a source's dependency tree. Let $\phi = \mathbf{S}_q^\mathsf{T} \mathbf{S}_k / \sqrt{d} \in \mathbb{R}^{n \times n}$ be a scoring matrix such that cell $\phi_{i,j}$ scores how likely word x_i is to be the head of word x_j. The probability of a dependency tree $\mathbf{z}$ is therefore given by

$$p(\mathbf{z} \,|\, \mathbf{x}; \phi) = \frac{\exp\left(\sum_{i,j} \mathbf{z}_{i,j} \, \phi_{i,j}\right)}{Z(\phi)} \tag{5}$$

where $Z(\phi)$ is the partition function.

In the head selection model, we are interested in the marginal $p(\mathbf{z}_{i,j} = 1 \,|\, \mathbf{x}; \phi)$

$$\beta_{i,j} = p(\mathbf{z}_{i,j} = 1 \,|\, \mathbf{x}; \phi) \;\; = \sum_{\mathbf{z} \,:\, \mathbf{z}_{i,j} = 1} p(\mathbf{z} \,|\, \mathbf{x}; \phi)$$

We use the framework presented by Koo et al. (2007) to compute the marginal of non-projective dependency structures. Koo et al. (2007) use the Kirchhoff's Matrix-Tree Theorem (Tutte, 1984) to compute $p(\mathbf{z}_{i,j} = 1 \,|\, \mathbf{x}; \phi)$ by first defining the Laplacian matrix $\mathbf{L} \in \mathbb{R}^{n \times n}$ as follows:

$$\mathbf{L}_{i,j}(\phi) = \begin{cases} \sum_{\substack{k=1 \\ k \neq j}}^{n} \exp(\phi_{k,j}) & \text{if } i = j \\ -\exp(\phi_{i,j}) & \text{otherwise} \end{cases} \tag{6}$$

Now we construct a matrix $\hat{\mathbf{L}}$ that accounts for root selection

$$\hat{\mathbf{L}}_{i,j}(\phi) = \begin{cases} \exp(\phi_{j,j}) & \text{if } i = 1 \\ \mathbf{L}_{i,j}(\phi) & \text{if } i > 1 \end{cases} \tag{7}$$

The marginals in β are then

$$\beta_{i,j} = (1 - \delta_{1,j}) \exp(\phi_{i,j}) \left[\hat{\mathbf{L}}^{-1}(\phi)\right]_{j,j} \\ - (1 - \delta_{i,1}) \exp(\phi_{i,j}) \left[\hat{\mathbf{L}}^{-1}(\phi)\right]_{j,i} \tag{8}$$

where $\delta_{i,j}$ is the Kronecker delta. For the root node, the marginals are given by

$$\beta_{k,k} = \exp(\phi_{k,k}) \left[\hat{\mathbf{L}}^{-1}(\phi)\right]_{k,1} \tag{9}$$

The computation of the marginals is fully differentiable, thus we can train the model in an end-to-end fashion by maximizing the conditional likelihood of the translation.

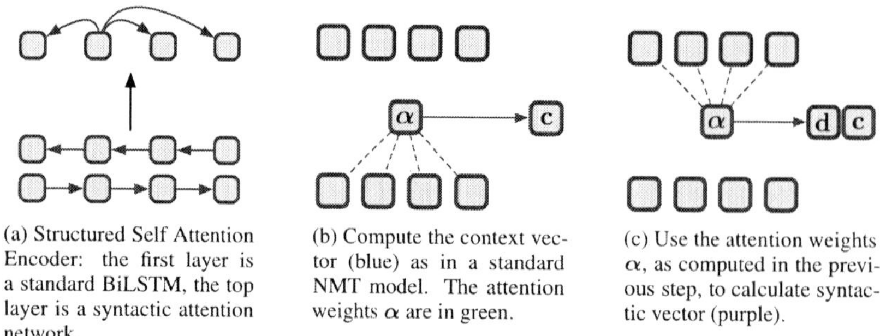

| (a) Structured Self Attention Encoder: the first layer is a standard BiLSTM, the top layer is a syntactic attention network. | (b) Compute the context vector (blue) as in a standard NMT model. The attention weights α are in green. | (c) Use the attention weights α, as computed in the previous step, to calculate syntactic vector (purple). |

Figure 2: A visual representation of our proposed mechanism for shared attention.

4.2 Incorporating Syntactic Context

Having set the annotations $\mathbf{S}$ and $\mathbf{M}$ with the encoder, the LSTM decoder can utilize this information at every generation step by means of attention. At time step t, we first compute standard attention weights $\boldsymbol{\alpha}_{t-1}$ and context vector $\mathbf{c}_{t-1}$ as in Equations (3) and (4). We then compute a weighted syntactic vector:

$$\mathbf{d}_{t-1} = \mathbf{M}\boldsymbol{\alpha}_{t-1}^{\mathsf{T}} \qquad (10)$$

Note that the syntactic vector $\mathbf{d}_{t-1}$ and the context vector $\mathbf{c}_{t-1}$ share the same attention weights $\boldsymbol{\alpha}_{t-1}$. The main idea behind sharing attention weights (Figure 2c) is that if the model attends to a particular source word x_i when generating the next target word, we also want the model to attend to the head word of x_i. We share the attention weights $\boldsymbol{\alpha}_{t-1}$ because we expect that, if the model picks a source word x_i to translate with the highest probability $\boldsymbol{\alpha}_{t-1}[i]$, the contribution of x_i's head in the syntactic vector $\mathbf{d}_{t-1}$ should also be highest. Figure 3

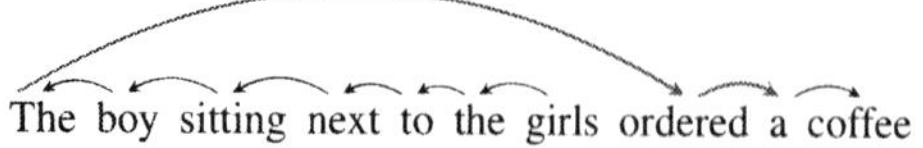

Figure 3: A latent tree learned by our model.

shows the latent tree learned by our translation objective. Unlike the gold tree provided in Figure 1, the model decided that *"the boy"* is the head of *"ordered"*. This is common in our model because the BiLSTM context means that a given word's representation is actually a summary of its local context/constituent.

It is not always useful or necessary to access the syntactic context $\mathbf{d}_{t-1}$ at every time step t. Ideally,

we should let the model decide whether it needs to use this information or not. For example, the model might decide to only use syntax when it needs to resolve long distance dependencies on the source side. To control the amount of source side syntactic information, we introduce a gating mechanism:

$$\hat{\mathbf{d}}_{t-1} = \mathbf{d}_{t-1} \odot \sigma(\mathbf{W}_g \mathbf{h}_{t-1}) \qquad (11)$$

The vector $\mathbf{u}_{t-1}$ from Eq. (2) now becomes

$$\mathbf{u}_{t-1} = g(\mathbf{h}_{t-1}, \mathbf{c}_{t-1}, \hat{\mathbf{d}}_{t-1}) \qquad (12)$$

Another approach to incorporating syntactic annotations $\mathbf{M}$ in the decoder is to use a separate attention layer to compute the syntactic vector $\mathbf{d}_{t-1}$ at time step t:

$$\boldsymbol{\gamma}_{t-1} = \mathrm{softmax}(\mathbf{h}_{t-1}^{\mathsf{T}} \mathbf{W}_m \mathbf{M}) \qquad (13)$$
$$\mathbf{d}_{t-1} = \mathbf{M}\boldsymbol{\gamma}_{t-1}^{\mathsf{T}} \qquad (14)$$

We will provide a comparison to this approach in our results.

4.3 Hard Attention over Tree Structures

Finally, to simulate the scenario where the model has access to a dependency tree given by an external parser we report results with hard attention. Forcing the model to make hard decisions during training mirrors the extraction and conditioning on a dependency tree (§7.1). We expect this technique will improve the performance on grammar induction, despite making translation lossy. A similar observation has been reported in (Hashimoto and Tsuruoka, 2017) which showed that translation performance degraded below their baseline when they provided dependency trees to the encoder.

Recall the marginal $\beta_{i,j}$ gives us the probability that word x_i is the head of word x_j. We convert these soft weights to hard ones $\bar{\beta}$ by

$$\bar{\beta}_{k,j} = \begin{cases} 1 & \text{if } k = \arg\max_i \beta_{i,j} \\ 0 & \text{otherwise} \end{cases} \qquad (15)$$

We train this model using the straight-through estimator (Bengio et al., 2013). In this setup, each word has a parent but there is no guarantee that the structure given by hard attention will result in a tree (*i.e.*, it may contain cycle). A more principled way to enforce a tree structure is to decode the best tree $\mathcal{T}$ using the maximum spanning tree algorithm (Chu and Liu, 1965; Edmonds, 1967) and to set $\bar{\beta}_{k,j} = 1$ if the edge $(x_k \to x_j) \in \mathcal{T}$. Maximum spanning tree decoding can be prohibitively slow as the Chu-Liu-Edmonds algorithm is not GPU friendly. We therefore greedily pick a parent word for each word x_j in the sentence using Eq. (15). This is actually a principled simplification as greedily assigning a parent for each word is the first step in Chu-Liu-Edmonds algorithm.

5 Experiments

Next we will discuss our experimental setup and report results for English↔German (En↔De), English↔Russian (En↔Ru), and Russian→Arabic (Ru→Ar) translation models.

5.1 Data

We use the WMT17 (Bojar et al., 2017) data in our experiments. Table 1 shows the statistics of the data. For En↔De, we use a concatenation of Europarl, Common Crawl, Rapid corpus of EU press releases, and News Commentary v12. We use *newstest2015* for development and *newstest2016, newstest2017* for testing. For En↔Ru, we use Common Crawl, News Commentary v12, and Yandex Corpus. The development data comes from *newstest2016* and *newstest2017* is reserved for testing. For Ru→Ar, we use the data from the six-way sentence-aligned subcorpus of the United Nations Parallel Corpus v1.0 (Ziemski et al., 2016). The corpus also contains the official development and test data. Our lan-

	Train	Valid	Test	Vocabulary
En↔De	5.9M	2,169	2,999 / 3,004	36,251 / 35,913
En↔Ru	2.1M	2,998	3,001	34,872 / 34,989
Ru→Ar	11.1M	4,000	4,000	32,735 / 32,955

Table 1: Statistics of the data.

guage pairs were chosen to compare results across

and between morphologically rich and poor languages. This will prove particularly interesting in our grammar induction results where different pairs must preserve different amounts of syntactic agreement information.

We use BPE (Sennrich et al., 2016) with 32,000 merge operations. We run BPE for each language instead of using BPE for the concatenation of both source and target languages.

5.2 Baselines

Our baseline is an NMT model with input-feeding (§3). As we will be making several modifications from the basic architecture in our proposed structured self attention NMT (SA-NMT), we will verify each choice in our architecture design empirically. First we validate the structured self attention module by comparing it to a self-attention module (Lin et al., 2017; Vaswani et al., 2017). Self attention computes attention weights β simply as $\beta = \text{softmax}(\phi)$. Since self-attention does not assume any hierarchical structure over the source sentence, we refer it as flat-attention NMT (FA-NMT). Second, we validate the benefit of using two sets of annotations in the encoder. We combine the hidden states of the encoder $\mathbf{h}$ with syntactic context $\mathbf{d}$ to obtain a single set of annotation using the following equation:

$$\bar{\mathbf{s}}_i = \mathbf{s}_i + \sigma(\mathbf{W}_g \mathbf{s}_i) \odot \mathbf{d}_i \qquad (16)$$

Here we first down-weight the syntactic context $\mathbf{d}_i$ before adding it to $\mathbf{s}_i$. The sigmoid function $\sigma(\mathbf{W}_g \mathbf{s}_i)$ decides the weight of the head word of x_i based on whether translating x_i needs additionally dependency information. We refer to this baseline as SA-NMT-1set. Note that in this baseline, there is only one attention layer from the target to the source $\bar{\mathbf{S}} = \{\bar{\mathbf{s}}_i\}_1^n$.

In all the models, we share the weights of target word embeddings and the output layer as suggested by Inan et al. (2017) and Press and Wolf (2017).

5.3 Hyper-parameters and Training

For all the models, we set the word embedding size to 1024, the number of LSTM layers to 2, and the dropout rate to 0.3. Parameters are initialized uniformly in $(-0.04, 0.04)$. We use the Adam optimizer (Kingma and Ba, 2015) with an initial learning rate of 0.001. We evaluate our models on development data every 10,000 updates for De–En and Ru→Ar, and 5,000 updates for Ru–En. If the validation perplexity increases, we decay the learning rate by 0.5. We stop training after decaying the learning rate five times as suggested by Denkowski and Neubig (2017). The mini-batch size is 64 in Ru→Ar experiments and 32 in the rest. Finally, we report BLEU scores computed using the standard `multi-bleu.perl` script.

In our experiments, the SA-NMT models are twice slower than the baseline NMT measuring by the number of target words generated per second.

5.4 Translation Results

Table 2 shows the BLEU scores in our experiments. We test statistical significance using bootstrap resampling (Riezler and Maxwell, 2005). Statistical significances are marked as $^{\dagger}p < 0.05$ and $^{\ddagger}p < 0.01$ when compared against the baselines. Additionally, we also report statistical significances $^{\triangle}p < 0.05$ and $^{\blacktriangle}p < 0.01$ when comparing against the FA-NMT models that have two separate attention layers from the decoder to the encoder. Overall, the SA-NMT (shared) model performs the best gaining more than 0.5 BLEU De→En on *wmt16*, up to 0.82 BLEU on En→De *wmt17* and 0.64 BLEU En→Ru direction over a competitive NMT baseline. The gain of the SA-NMT model on Ru→Ar is small (0.45 BLEU) but significant. The results show that structured self attention is useful when translating from English to languages that have long-distance dependencies and complex morphological agreements. We also see that the gain is marginal compared to self-attention models (FA-NMT-shared) and not significant. Within FA-NMT models, sharing attention is helpful. Our results also confirm the advantage of having two separate sets of annotations in the encoder when modeling syntax. The hard structured self attention model (SA-NMT-hard) performs comparably to the baseline. While this is a somewhat expected result from the hard attention model, we will show in Section 7 that the quality of induced trees from hard attention is often far better than those from soft attention.

6 Gate Activation Visualization

As mentioned earlier, our models allow us to ask the question: When does the target LSTM need to access source side syntax? We investigate this by analyzing the gate activations of our best model, SA-NMT (shared). At time step t, when the model is about to predict the target word y_t, we compute

the norm of the gate activations

$$z_t = \|\sigma(\mathbf{W}_g \mathbf{h}_{t-1})\|_2 \qquad (17)$$

The activation norm z_t allows us to see how much syntactic information flows into the decoder. We observe that z_t has its highest value when the decoder is about to generate a verb while it has its lowest value when the end of sentence token </s> is predicted. Figure 4 shows some examples of German target sentences. The darker colors represent higher activation norms.

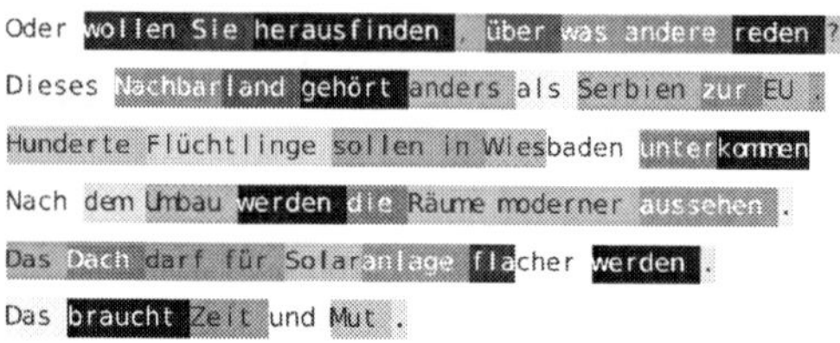

Figure 4: Visualization of gate norm. Darker means the model is using more syntactic information.

It is clear that translating verbs requires structural information. We also see that after verbs, the gate activation norms are highest at nouns Zeit (*time*), Mut (*courage*), Dach (*roof*) and then tail off as we move to function words which require less context to disambiguate. Below are the frequencies with which the highest activation norm in a sentence is applied to a given part-of-speech tag on *newstest2016*. We include the top 7 most common activations. We see that while nouns are often the most common tag in a sentence, syntax is disproportionately used for translating verbs.

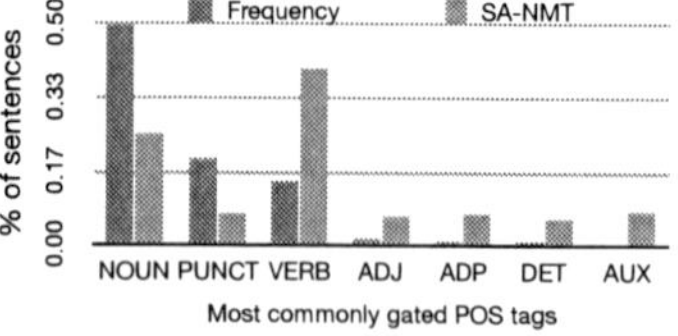

7 Grammar Induction

NLP has long assumed hierarchical structured representations are important to understanding language. In this work, we borrowed that intuition to inform the construction of our model. We investigate whether the internal latent representations discovered by our models share properties previously identified within linguistics and if not, what important differences exist. We investigate the interpretability of our model's representations by: 1)

Model	Shared	De→En		Ru→En	En→De		En→Ru	Ru→Ar
		wmt16	*wmt17*	*wmt17*	*wmt16*	*wmt17*	*wmt17*	*un-test*
NMT	-	33.16	28.94	30.17	29.92	23.44	26.41	37.04
FA-NMT	yes	33.55	29.43	30.22	30.09	24.03	26.91	37.41
	no	33.24	29.00	30.34	29.98	23.97	26.75	37.20
SA-NMT-1set	-	33.51	29.15	30.34	$30.29^{\dagger}$	24.12	26.96	37.34
SA-NMT-hard	yes	33.38	28.96	29.98	29.93	23.84	26.71	37.33
SA-NMT	yes	$33.73^{\ddagger\triangle}$	$29.45^{\ddagger\blacktriangle}$	**30.41**	30.22	$24.26^{\ddagger\triangle}$	$27.05^{\ddagger}$	$37.49^{\ddagger\triangle}$
	no	33.18	29.19	30.15	30.17	23.94	27.01	37.22

Table 2: Results for translating En↔De, En↔Ru, and Ru→Ar. Statistical significances are marked as $^{\dagger}p < 0.05$ and $^{\ddagger}p < 0.01$ when compared against the baselines and $^{\triangle}/^{\blacktriangle}$ when compared against the FA-NMT (no-shared). The results indicate the strength of our proposed *shared-attention* for NMT.

	FA		SA			Baseline		
	no-shared	shared	no-shared	shared	hard	L	R	Un
EN (→DE)	17.0/25.2	27.6/41.3	23.6/33.7	27.8/42.6	**31.7/45.6**	34.0	7.8	40.9
EN (→RU)	35.2/48.5	**36.5**/48.8	12.8/25.5	33.1/**48.9**	33.7/46.0			
DE (→EN)	21.1/33.3	20.1/33.6	12.8/22.5	21.5/38.0	**26.3/40.7**	34.4	8.6	41.5
RU (→EN)	19.2/33.2	20.4/34.9	19.3/34.4	**24.8/41.9**	23.2/33.3	32.9	15.2	47.3
RU (→AR)	21.1/41.1	22.2/42.1	11.6/21.4	28.9/50.4	**30.3/52.0**			

Table 3: Directed and Undirected (DA/UA) model accuracy (without punctuation) compared to branching baselines: left (L), right (R) and undirected (Un). Our results show an intriguing effect of the target language on induction. Note the accuracy discrepancy between translating RU to EN versus AR.

A quantitative attachment accuracy and 2) A qualitative look at its output.

Our results corroborate and refute previous work (Hashimoto and Tsuruoka, 2017; Williams et al., 2018). We provide stronger evidence that syntactic information can be discovered via latent structured self attention, but we also present preliminary results indicating that conventional definitions of syntax may be at odds with task specific performance.

Unlike in the grammar induction literature our model is not specifically constructed to recover traditional dependency grammars nor have we provided the model with access to part-of-speech tags or universal rules (Naseem et al., 2010; Bisk and Hockenmaier, 2013). The model only uncovers the syntactic information necessary for a given language pair, though future work should investigate if structural linguistic constraints benefit MT.

7.1 Extracting a Tree

For extracting non-projective dependency trees, we use Chu-Liu-Edmonds algorithm (Chu and Liu, 1965; Edmonds, 1967). First, we must collapse BPE segments into words. Assume the k-th word corresponds to BPE tokens from index u to v. We obtain a new matrix $\hat{\phi}$ by summing over $\phi_{i,j}$ that are the corresponding BPE segments.

$$
\hat{\phi}_{i,j} =
\begin{cases}
\phi_{i,j} & \text{if } i \notin [u,v] \wedge j \notin [u,v] \\
\sum_{l=u}^{v} \phi_{i,l} & \text{if } j = k \wedge i \notin [u,v] \\
\sum_{l=u}^{v} \phi_{l,j} & \text{if } i = k \wedge j \notin [u,v] \\
\sum_{l,h=u}^{v} \phi_{l,h} & \text{otherwise}
\end{cases}
$$

7.2 Grammatical Analysis

To analyze performance we compute unlabeled directed and undirected attachment accuracies of our predicted trees on gold annotations from the Universal Dependencies (UD version 2) dataset.[3] We chose this representation because of its availability in many languages, though it is atypical for grammar induction. Our five model settings in addition to left and right branching baselines are presented in Table 3. The results indicate that the target language effects the source encoder's induction performance and several settings are competitive with branching baselines for determining headedness. Recall that syntax is being modeled on the source language so adjacent rows are comparable.

We observe a huge boost in DA/UA scores for EN and RU in FA-NMT and SA-NMT-shared models when the target languages are morphologically

---

[3] http://universaldependencies.org

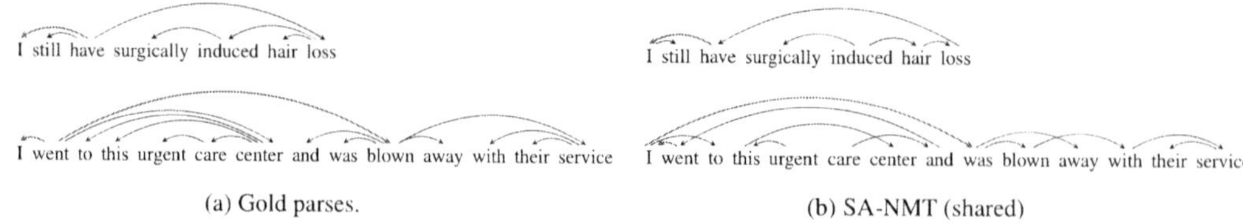

(a) Gold parses. (b) SA-NMT (shared)

Figure 6: Samples of induced trees for English by our (En→Ru) model. Notice the red arrows from *subject↔verb* which are necessary for translating Russian verbs.

rich (RU and AR respectively). In comparison to previous work (Belinkov et al., 2017; Shi et al., 2016) on an encoder's ability to capture source side syntax, we show a stronger result that even when the encoders are designed to capture syntax explicitly, the choice of the target language influences the amount of syntax learned by the encoder.

We also see gains from hard attention and several models outperform baselines for undirected dependency metrics (UA). Whether hard attention helps in general is unclear. It appears to help when the target languages are morphologically rich.

Successfully extracting linguistic structure with hard attention indicates that models can capture interesting structures beyond semantic co-occurrence via discrete actions. Our approach also outperforms (Hashimoto and Tsuruoka, 2017) despite lacking access to additional resources like POS tags.[4]

7.3 Dependency Accuracies & Discrepancies

While the SA-NMT-hard model gives the best directed attachment scores on EN→DE, DE→EN and RU→AR, the BLEU scores of this model are below other SA-NMT models as shown in Table 2. The lack of correlation between syntactic performance and NMT contradicts the intuition of previous work and suggests that useful structures learned in service of a task might not necessarily benefit from or correspond directly to known linguistic formalisms. We want to raise three important differences between these induced structures and UD.

First, we see a blurred boundary between dependency and constituency representations. As noted earlier, the BiLSTM provides a local summary. When the model chooses a head word, it is actually choosing hidden states from a BiLSTM and therefore gaining access to a constituent or region. This means there is likely little difference between attending to the noun vs the determiner in

a phrase (despite being wrong according to UD). Future work might force this distinction by replacing the BiLSTM with a bag-of-words but this will likely lead to substantial losses in MT performance.

Second, because the model appears to use syntax for agreement, often verb dependencies link to subjects directly to capture predicate argument structures like those in CCG or semantic role labeling. UD instead follows the convention of attaching all verbs that share a subject to one another or their conjunctions. We have colored some subject–verb links in Figure 6: *e.g.*, between *I, went* and *was*.

Finally, the model's notion of headedness is atypical as it roughly translates to "helpful when translating". The head word gets incorporated into the shared representation which may cause the arrow to flip from traditional formalisms. Additionally, because the model can turn on and off syntax as necessary, it is likely to produce high confidence treelets rather than complete parses. This means arcs produced from words with weak gate activations (Figure 4) are not actually used during translation and likely not-syntactically meaningful.

We will not speculate if these are desirable properties or issues to address with constraints, but the model's decisions appear well motivated and our formulation allows us to have the discussion.

8 Conclusion

We have proposed a structured self attention encoder for NMT. Our models show significant gains in performance over a strong baseline on standard WMT benchmarks. The models presented here do not access any external information such as parse-trees or part-of-speech tags yet appear to use and induce structure when given the opportunity. Finally, we see our induction performance is language pair dependent, which invites an interesting research discussion as to the role of syntax in translation and the importance of working with morphologically rich languages.

---

[4]The numbers are not directly comparable since they use WSJ corpus to evaluate the UA score.

Acknowledgments

We thank Joachim Daiber, Ekaterina Garmash, and Julia Kiseleva for helping with German and Russian examples. We are grateful to Arianna Bisazza, Miloš Stanojević, and Raquel Garrido Alhama for providing feedback on the draft. The second author was supported by Samsung Research.

References

Roee Aharoni and Yoav Goldberg. 2017. Towards string-to-tree neural machine translation. In *Proceedings of the 55th Annual Meeting of the Association for Computational Linguistics (Volume 2: Short Papers)*, pages 132–140, Vancouver, Canada. Association for Computational Linguistics.

Dzmitry Bahdanau, Kyunghyun Cho, and Yoshua Bengio. 2015. Neural machine translation by jointly learning to align and translate. In *ICLR 2015*, San Diego, CA, USA.

Joost Bastings, Ivan Titov, Wilker Aziz, Diego Marcheggiani, and Khalil Simaan. 2017. Graph convolutional encoders for syntax-aware neural machine translation. In *Proceedings of the 2017 Conference on Empirical Methods in Natural Language Processing*, pages 1947–1957. Association for Computational Linguistics.

Yonatan Belinkov, Nadir Durrani, Fahim Dalvi, Hassan Sajjad, and James Glass. 2017. What do neural machine translation models learn about morphology? In *Proceedings of the 55th Annual Meeting of the Association for Computational Linguistics (Volume 1: Long Papers)*, pages 861–872. Association for Computational Linguistics.

Yoshua Bengio, Nicholas Léonard, and Aaron Courville. 2013. Estimating or propagating gradients through stochastic neurons for conditional computation. *ArXiv e-prints*.

Yonatan Bisk and Julia Hockenmaier. 2013. An HDP Model for Inducing Combinatory Categorial Grammars. *Transactions of the Association for Computational Linguistics*, pages 75–88.

Ondřej Bojar, Rajen Chatterjee, Christian Federmann, Yvette Graham, Barry Haddow, Shujian Huang, Matthias Huck, Philipp Koehn, Qun Liu, Varvara Logacheva, Christof Monz, Matteo Negri, Matt Post, Raphael Rubino, Lucia Specia, and Marco Turchi. 2017. Findings of the 2017 conference on machine translation (wmt17). In *Proceedings of the Second Conference on Machine Translation*, pages 169–214, Copenhagen, Denmark. Association for Computational Linguistics.

Samuel R. Bowman, Gabor Angeli, Christopher Potts, and Christopher D. Manning. 2015. A large annotated corpus for learning natural language inference. In *Proceedings of the 2015 Conference on Empirical Methods in Natural Language Processing*, pages 632–642. Association for Computational Linguistics.

James Bradbury and Richard Socher. 2017. Towards neural machine translation with latent tree attention. In *Proceedings of the 2nd Workshop on Structured Prediction for Natural Language Processing*, pages 12–16, Copenhagen, Denmark. Association for Computational Linguistics.

Y. J. Chu and T. H. Liu. 1965. On the shortest arborescence of a directed graph. *Science Sinica*, 14.

Michael Denkowski and Graham Neubig. 2017. Stronger baselines for trustable results in neural machine translation. In *Proceedings of the First Workshop on Neural Machine Translation*, pages 18–27, Vancouver. Association for Computational Linguistics.

Chris Dyer, Adhiguna Kuncoro, Miguel Ballesteros, and Noah A. Smith. 2016. Recurrent neural network grammars. In *Proceedings of the 2016 Conference of the North American Chapter of the Association for Computational Linguistics: Human Language Technologies*, pages 199–209, San Diego, California. Association for Computational Linguistics.

Jack Edmonds. 1967. Optimum Branchings. *Journal of Research of the National Bureau of Standards*, 71B:233–240.

Akiko Eriguchi, Yoshimasa Tsuruoka, and Kyunghyun Cho. 2017. Learning to parse and translate improves neural machine translation. In *Proceedings of the 55th Annual Meeting of the Association for Computational Linguistics (Volume 2: Short Papers)*, pages 72–78. Association for Computational Linguistics.

Kazuma Hashimoto and Yoshimasa Tsuruoka. 2017. Neural machine translation with source-side latent graph parsing. In *Proceedings of the 2017 Conference on Empirical Methods in Natural Language Processing*, pages 125–135. Association for Computational Linguistics.

Sepp Hochreiter and Jürgen Schmidhuber. 1997. Long short-term memory. *Neural Computation*, 9(8):1735–1780.

Hakan Inan, Khashayar Khosravi, and Richard Socher. 2017. Tying word vectors and word classifiers: A loss framework for language modeling. In *ICLR*.

Yoon Kim, Carl Denton, Luong Hoang, and Alexander M. Rush. 2017. Structured attention networks. In *ICLR*.

Diederik Kingma and Jimmy Ba. 2015. Adam: A method for stochastic optimization. In *Proceedings of ICLR*, San Diego, CA, USA.

Dan Klein and Christopher D Manning. 2004. Corpus-based induction of syntactic structure: Models of dependency and constituency. In *Proceedings of the*

42nd Meeting of the Association for Computational Linguistics (ACL'04), Main Volume, pages 478–485, Barcelona, Spain.

Guillaume Klein, Yoon Kim, Yuntian Deng, Jean Senellart, and Alexander Rush. 2017. Opennmt: Opensource toolkit for neural machine translation. In *Proceedings of ACL 2017, System Demonstrations*, pages 67–72, Vancouver, Canada. Association for Computational Linguistics.

Terry Koo, Amir Globerson, Xavier Carreras, and Michael Collins. 2007. Structured prediction models via the matrix-tree theorem. In *EMNLP*, pages 141–150, Prague, Czech Republic. Association for Computational Linguistics.

Junhui Li, Deyi Xiong, Zhaopeng Tu, Muhua Zhu, Min Zhang, and Guodong Zhou. 2017. Modeling source syntax for neural machine translation. In *Proceedings of the 55th Annual Meeting of the Association for Computational Linguistics (Volume 1: Long Papers)*, pages 688–697. Association for Computational Linguistics.

Zhouhan Lin, Minwei Feng, Cicero Nogueira dos Santos, Mo Yu, Bing Xiang, Bowen Zhou, and Yoshua Bengio. 2017. A structured self-attentive sentence embedding. In *ICLR*.

Tal Linzen, Emmanuel Dupoux, and Yoav Goldberg. 2016. Assessing the ability of lstms to learn syntax-sensitive dependencies. *Transactions of the Association for Computational Linguistics*, 4:521–535.

Yang Liu and Mirella Lapata. 2018. Learning structured text representations. *Transactions of the Association for Computational Linguistics*, 6:63–75.

Thang Luong, Hieu Pham, and Christopher D. Manning. 2015. Effective approaches to attention-based neural machine translation. In *Proceedings of the 2015 Conference on Empirical Methods in Natural Language Processing*, pages 1412–1421, Lisbon, Portugal. Association for Computational Linguistics.

Tahira Naseem, Harr Chen, Regina Barzilay, and Mark Johnson. 2010. Using universal linguistic knowledge to guide grammar induction. In *Proceedings of the 2010 Conference on Empirical Methods in Natural Language Processing*, pages 1234–1244, Cambridge, MA.

Ofir Press and Lior Wolf. 2017. Using the output embedding to improve language models. In *Proceedings of the 15th Conference of the European Chapter of the Association for Computational Linguistics: Volume 2, Short Papers*, pages 157–163. Association for Computational Linguistics.

Stefan Riezler and John T. Maxwell. 2005. On some pitfalls in automatic evaluation and significance testing for mt. In *Proceedings of the ACL Workshop on Intrinsic and Extrinsic Evaluation Measures for Machine Translation and/or Summarization*, pages

57–64, Ann Arbor, Michigan. Association for Computational Linguistics.

Rico Sennrich, Barry Haddow, and Alexandra Birch. 2016. Neural machine translation of rare words with subword units. In *Proceedings of the 54th Annual Meeting of the Association for Computational Linguistics (Volume 1: Long Papers)*, pages 1715–1725, Berlin, Germany. Association for Computational Linguistics.

Xing Shi, Inkit Padhi, and Kevin Knight. 2016. Does string-based neural mt learn source syntax? In *Proceedings of the 2016 Conference on Empirical Methods in Natural Language Processing*, pages 1526–1534, Austin, Texas. Association for Computational Linguistics.

Valentin I Spitkovsky, Hiyan Alshawi, Angel X Chang, and Daniel Jurafsky. 2011. Unsupervised dependency parsing without gold part-of-speech tags. In *Proceedings of the 2011 Conference on Empirical Methods in Natural Language Processing*, pages 1281–1290, Edinburgh, Scotland, UK. Association for Computational Linguistics.

W. T Tutte. 1984. *Graph theory*. Cambridge University Press.

Ashish Vaswani, Noam Shazeer, Niki Parmar, Jakob Uszkoreit, Llion Jones, Aidan N Gomez, Ł ukasz Kaiser, and Illia Polosukhin. 2017. Attention is all you need. In I. Guyon, U. V. Luxburg, S. Bengio, H. Wallach, R. Fergus, S. Vishwanathan, and R. Garnett, editors, *Advances in Neural Information Processing Systems 30*, pages 6000–6010. Curran Associates, Inc.

Adina Williams, Andrew Drozdov, and Samuel R. Bowman. 2018. Do latent tree learning models identify meaningful structure in sentences? *Transactions of the Association for Computational Linguistics*.

Michał Ziemski, Marcin Junczys-Dowmunt, and Bruno Pouliquen. 2016. The united nations parallel corpus v1.0. In *Proceedings of the Tenth International Conference on Language Resources and Evaluation (LREC 2016)*, Paris, France. European Language Resources Association (ELRA).

A   Attention Visualization

Figure 7 shows a sample visualization of structured attention models trained on En→De data. It is worth noting that the shared SA-NMT model (Figure 7a) and the hard SA-NMT model (Figure 7b) capture similar structures of the source sentence. We hypothesize that when the objective function requires syntax, the induced trees are more consistent unlike those discovered by a semantic objective (Williams et al., 2018). Both models correctly identify that the verb is the head of pronoun (hope→I,

said→she). While intuitively it is clearly beneficial
to know the subject of the verb when translating
from English into German, the model attention is
still somewhat surprising because long distance dependency phenomena are less common in English,
so we would expect that a simple content based addressing (*i.e.*, standard attention mechanism) would
be sufficient in this translation

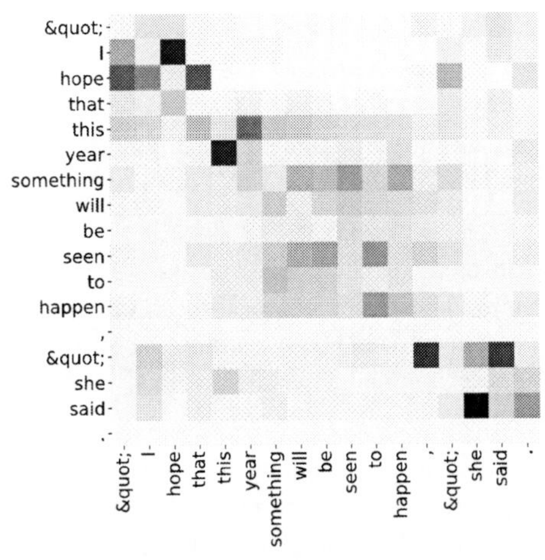

(a) SA-NMT (shared) attention.

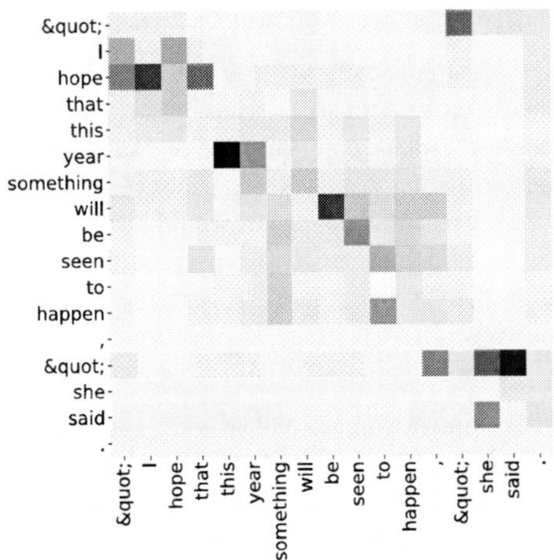

(b) SA-NMT with hard structured attention.

Figure 7: A visualization of attention distributions
over head words (on y-axis).

Regularized Training Objective for Continued Training
for Domain Adaptation in Neural Machine Translation

Huda Khayrallah   Brian Thompson   Kevin Duh   Philipp Koehn
Department of Computer Science
Johns Hopkins University
{huda, brian.thompson}@jhu.edu, {kevinduh, phi}@cs.jhu.edu

Abstract

Supervised domain adaptation—where a large generic corpus and a smaller in-domain corpus are both available for training—is a challenge for neural machine translation (NMT). Standard practice is to train a generic model and use it to initialize a second model, then continue training the second model on in-domain data to produce an in-domain model. We add an auxiliary term to the training objective during continued training that minimizes the cross entropy between the in-domain model's output word distribution and that of the out-of-domain model to prevent the model's output from differing too much from the original out-of-domain model. We perform experiments on EMEA (descriptions of medicines) and TED (rehearsed presentations), initialized from a general domain (WMT) model. Our method shows improvements over standard continued training by up to 1.5 BLEU.

1   Introduction

Neural Machine Translation (NMT) (Bahdanau et al., 2015) is currently the state-of-the art paradigm for machine translation. It dominated the recent WMT shared task (Bojar et al., 2017), and is used commercially (Wu et al., 2016; Crego et al., 2016; Junczys-Dowmunt et al., 2016).

Despite their successes, NMT systems require a large amount of training data and do not perform well in low resource and domain adaptation scenarios (Koehn and Knowles, 2017). Domain adaptation is required when there is sufficient data to train an NMT system in the desired language pair, but the *domain* (the topic, genre, style or level of

formality) of this large corpus differs from that of the data that the system will need to translate at test time.

In this paper, we focus on the supervised domain adaptation problem, where in addition to a large out-of-domain corpus, we also have a smaller in-domain parallel corpus available for training.

A technique commonly applied in this situation is continued training (Luong and Manning, 2015), where a model is first trained on the out-of-domain corpus, and then that model is used to initialize a new model that is trained on the in-domain corpus.

This simple method leads to empirical improvements on in-domain test sets. However, we hypothesize that some knowledge available in the out-of-domain data—which is not observed in the smaller in-domain data but would be useful at test time—is being forgotten during continued training, due to overfitting. (This phenomena can be viewed as a version of catastrophic forgetting (Goodfellow et al., 2013)).

For this reason, we add an additional term to the loss function of the NMT training objective during continued training. In addition to minimizing the cross entropy between the model's output word distribution and the reference translation, the additional term in the loss function minimizes the cross entropy between the model's output word distribution and that of the out-of-domain model.[1] This prevents the distribution of words produced from differing too much from the original distribution.

We show that this method improves upon standard continued training by as much as 1.5 BLEU.

---

[1] The code is available:
github.com/khayrallah/OpenNMT-py-reg

Proceedings of the 2nd Workshop on Neural Machine Translation and Generation, pages 36–44
Melbourne, Australia, July 20, 2018. ©2018 Association for Computational Linguistics

2   Method

In this work, we focus on the following scenario: we assume there is a model that was trained on a large, general (out-of-domain) corpus in the language pair of interest, and there is a new domain, along with a small in-domain training set, for which we would like to build a model. We begin by initializing the weights of the in-domain model with the weights of the out-of-domain model, and then continue training the new model on the in-domain data, using the modified training objective to prevent the model from differing too much from the original out-of-domain model.

Before describing our method in detail, we first review the general framework of neural machine translation and the standard continued training approach.

2.1   NMT Objective

Encoder-decoder neural machine translation with attention (Bahdanau et al., 2015) consists of: an *encoder*—a bidirectional recurrent neural network that encodes the source sentence as vectors; and a *decoder*—a recurrent neural network that conditions each output word on the previous output and a weighted average of the encoder states (*attention*).[2]

The standard training criteria in NMT, for the ith target word, is:

$$\mathcal{L}_{\text{NLL}}(\theta) = -\sum_{v \in \mathcal{V}} \left(\mathbb{1}\{y_i = v\} \right. \tag{1}$$
$$\left. \times \ \log \ p(y_i = v \,|\, x; \theta; y_{j<i}) \right)$$

where $\mathcal{V}$ is the vocabulary, $\mathbb{1}\{\cdot\}$ is the indicator function, and p is the output distribution of the model (parameterized by θ).

This objective minimizes the cross-entropy between the gold-standard distribution $\mathbb{1}\{y_i = v\}$ (which is simply a one-hot vector that indicates if the correct word was produced), and the model's distribution $p(y_i = v \,|\, x; \theta; y_{j<i})$.

2.2   Continued Training

Continued training is a simple yet effective technique for domain adaptation. It consists of three steps:

1. Train a model until convergence on large out-of-domain bitext using $\mathcal{L}_{\text{NLL}}$ as the training objective.

2. Initialize a new model with the final parameters of Step 1.

3. Train the model from Step 2 until convergence on in-domain bitext, again using $\mathcal{L}_{\text{NLL}}$ as objective.

In other words, continued training initializes an in-domain model training process with parameters from an out-of-domain model. The hope is that the out-of-domain model provides a reasonable starting point and is better than random initialization.

In our proposal in the next section, we will replace $\mathcal{L}_{\text{NLL}}$ in Step 3 by a interpolated regularized objective. All other steps remain the same.

2.3   Regularized NMT Objective

We use the output distribution of the trained out-of-domain model to regularize the training of our in-domain model as we perform continued training to adapt to a new domain.

We add an additional regularization (*reg*) term to incorporate information from an auxiliary (*aux*) out-of-domain model into the training objective:

$$\mathcal{L}_{\text{reg}}(\theta) = -\sum_{v \in \mathcal{V}} \left(p_{aux}(y_i = v \,|\, x; \theta_{aux}; y_{j<i}) \right.$$
$$\tag{2}$$
$$\left. \times \ \log \ p(y_i = v \,|\, x; \theta; y_{j<i}) \right)$$

where p_{aux} is the output distribution from the auxiliary out-of-domain model, parameterized by θ_{aux},[3] and p is the output distribution from the in-domain model being trained, parameterized by θ.

The regularization objective (Eq. 2) minimizes the cross-entropy between the out-of-domain model distribution $p_{\text{out}}(y_i = v \,|\, x; \theta; y_{j<i})$ and the in-domain model distribution $p(y_i = v \,|\, x; \theta; y_{j<i})$. We interpolate this with the standard training objective (Eq. 1) to obtain the final training objective:

$$\mathcal{L}(\theta) = (1 - \alpha) \, \mathcal{L}_{\text{NLL}}(\theta) + \alpha \, \mathcal{L}_{\text{reg}}(\theta) \tag{3}$$

The added regularization term is formulated in the spirit of knowledge distillation (Kim and Rush,

---

[2] For a detailed explanation of attention based NMT see Bahdanau et al. (2015) (the original paper), or for a gentle introduction see the textbook chapter by Koehn (2017).

[3] The out-of-domain model is fixed while training the in-domain model.

2016), where a student model is trained to match the output distribution of a parent model. In word-level knowledge distillation, the student model's output distribution is trained on the same data that the parent model was trained. In contrast, our domain specific model (which replaces the student) is trained with a loss term that encourages it to match the out-of-domain model (which replaces the parent) on in-domain training data that the out-of-domain model was not trained on.

3 Experiments

3.1 Data

For our large, out-of-domain corpus we utilize bi-text from WMT2017 (Bojar et al., 2017),[4] which contains data from several sources: Europarl parliamentary proceedings (Koehn, 2005),[5] News Commentary (political and economic news commentary),[6] Common Crawl (web-crawled parallel corpus), and the EU Press Releases.

We use `newstest2015` as the out-of-domain development set and `newstest2016` as the out-of-domain test set. These consist of professionally translated news articles released by the WMT shared task.

We perform adaptation into two different domains: EMEA (descriptions of medicines) and TED Talks (rehearsed presentations). For EMEA, we use the data split from (Koehn and Knowles, 2017),[7] which was extracted from from OPUS (Tiedemann, 2009, 2012).[8] For TED, we use the data split from the Multitarget TED Talks Task (MTTT) (Duh, 2018).[9] which was extracted from WIT[3] (Cettolo et al., 2012).[10] Tables 1–3 give the number of words and sentences of each of the corpora in the train, dev, and test sets, respectively.

In addition to experiments on the full training sets, we also conduct experiments adapting to each given domain using only the first 2,000 sentences of each in-domain training set to simulate adaptation into a low-resource domain.

For all experiments we translate from English to German as well as from German to English.

corpus	de words	en words	sentences
EMEA	13,572,552	14,774,808	1,104,752
TED	2,966,837	3,161,544	152,609
WMT	139,449,418	146,569,151	5,919,142

Table 1: Tokenized training set sizes.

corpus	de words	en words	sentences
EMEA	26479	28838	2000
TED	37509	38717	1958
newstest15	44869	47569	2169

Table 2: Tokenized development set sizes.

corpus	de words	en words	sentences
EMEA	31737	33884	2000
TED	35516	36857	1982
newstest16	64379	65647	2999

Table 3: Tokenized test set sizes.

3.2 NMT settings

Our neural machine translation systems are trained using a modified version of OpenNMT-py (Klein et al., 2017).[11] We build RNN-based encoder-decoder models with attention (Bahdanau et al., 2015), and use a bidirectional-RRN for the encoder. The encoder and decoder both have 2 layers with LSTM hidden sizes of 1024. Source and target word vectors are of size 500. We apply dropout with 30% probability. We use stochastic gradient descent as the optimizer, with an initial learning rate at 1 and a decay of 0.5. We use a batch size of 64. We keep the model parameters settings constant for all experiments.

We train byte pair encoding segmentation models (BPE) (Sennrich et al., 2016) on the out-of-domain training corpus. We train separate BPE models for each language, each with a vocab size of $50,000$ and then apply those models to each corpus, including the in-domain ones. This setup allows us to mimic the realistic setting where the computationally-expensive-to-train generic model is trained once, and when there is a new domain that needs translating the existing model is adapted to that domain without retraining on the out-of-domain corpus.

We train our out-of-domain models on the WMT corpora and use the WMT development

---

[4] statmt.org/wmt17
[5] statmt.org/europarl
[6] casmacat.eu/corpus/news-commentary.html
[7] github.com/khayrallah/domain-adaptation-data
[8] opus.nlpl.eu/EMEA.php
[9] cs.jhu.edu/ kevinduh/a/multitarget-tedtalks
[10] wit3.fbk.eu

[11] github.com/khayrallah/OpenNMT-py-reg

training condition	De-En		En-De	
	EMEA-test	TED-test	EMEA-test	TED-test
out-of-domain	30.8	29.8	25.1	25.9
in-domain	43.2	31.4	37.0	25.1
continued-train w/o regularization	48.5	36.4	41.0	30.8
continued-train w/ regularization	49.3 (+0.8)	36.9 (+0.5)	42.5 (+1.5)	30.8 (+0.0)

Table 4: BLEU score improvements over continued training. We compare to the out-of-domain baseline and the in-domain baseline. We also compare to continued training without the additional regularization term.

training condition	De-En		En-De	
	EMEA-test	TED-test	EMEA-test	TED-test
out-of-domain	30.8	29.8	25.1	25.9
continued-train w/o regularization	34.3	33.4	30.0	28.1
continued-train w/ regularization	35.2 (+0.9)	33.6 (+0.2)	30.2 (+0.2)	28.4 (+0.3)

Table 5: BLEU score improvements over continued training using the $2,000$ sentence subsets as the in-domain corpus. We compare to the out-of-domain baseline and continued training without the additional regularization term.

set (`newstest15`) to select the best epoch as our out-of-domain model. When training our domain specific models, we use the in-domain development set to select the best epoch. When we switch to the in-domain training corpus, we reset the learning rate to 1, with a decay of 0.5, and continue to apply dropout with 30% probability.

4   Results

Table 4 shows the in-domain and out-of-domain baselines, the improvement provided by continued training, and the added improvement of regularization during continued training on the entire in-domain datasets.[12]

When translating the De-En EMEA test set, the out-of-domain model obtains 30.8 BLEU and the in-domain model (trained on EMEA training data) obtains 43.2 BLEU. As expected, standard continued training (without regularization) outperforms both baselines, achieving 48.5 BLEU. This is an improvement of 5.3 BLEU over the in-domain model. Our proposed regularization method further improves this by 0.8, to 49.3 BLEU.

The trends are similar in all four test conditions: Continued training significantly outperforms both baselines, beating the stronger of the two by be-

tween 4.0 and 5.3 BLEU points. Our regularization method provides additional improvement over continued training by up to to 1.5 BLEU. There is one setting (En-De Ted) where there is no change.

We also repeat the experiment for cases where the in-domain training data is smaller, which corresponds to a more challenging (yet realistic) domain adaptation scenario. Table 5 shows the results of adaptation when only $2,000$ sentences of in-domain parallel text are available. This amount of data is insufficient to train an in-domain NMT model; however, standard continued training is able to improve upon the out-of-domain baseline by 2.2 to 4.9 BLEU. Adding our additional regularization term improves performance by an additional 0.2 to 0.9 BLEU.

In both Table 4 and Table 5, we confirm previous research findings that continued training is effective, and demonstrate that our regularized objective adds further gains. Furthermore, as shown in Section 5, it is straightforward to choose the interpolation weight, α.

5   Analysis

In this section, we perform more detailed analysis of our method. Our research questions are as follows:

---

[12]For the regularized results, α is selected to maximize BLEU on the dev set. See Section 5 for more details.

training condition	De-En		En-De	
	EMEA-test	TED-test	EMEA-test	TED-test
out-of-domain	30.8	29.9	25.1	25.9
in-domain	43.2	31.4	37.0	25.1
in-domain w/ regularization	45.5 (+2.3)	31.2 (+0.2)	38.8 (+1.8)	26.0 (+0.9)

Table 6: Analysis of BLEU score improvements without continued training. We compare to the out-of-domain baseline and the in-domain baseline.

training domain	testset	Baseline		Regularized Continued Training (α)			
		in-domain	out-of-domain	0	0.001	0.01	0.1
EMEA	EMEA-dev	49.6	31.4	53.2	53.1	53.4	52.9
	EMEA-test	43.2	30.8	48.5	48.5	49.3	48.1
	newstest2016	5.5	33.8	23.6	23.8	24.1	27.0
	TED-test	4.6	29.8	19.2	19.2	19.7	22.3
TED	TED-dev	27.1	27.1	31.8	31.9	32.2	32.1
	TED-test	27.1	29.8	36.4	36.7	36.9	36.7
	newstest2016	17.0	33.8	30.6	30.9	30.9	31.6
	EMEA-test	8.7	30.8	23.8	23.3	23.5	25.7

Table 7: Analysis of the sensitivity of BLEU scores on the domain-specific sets and `newstest2016` to the interpolation parameter (α) for De-En. Continued training with an $\alpha = 0$ is standard continued training, without regularization. Performance on the in-domain test sets is best with an interpolation weight of .01 in this language pair, while performance on the out-of-domain test sets is better with an interpolation weight of .1, the highest value we search over.

Is the additional training objective transferring general knowledge to the in-domain model? We hypothesize that the regularization term presents knowledge from the out-of-domain model to the continued training model while the later adapts. This allows the domain-adapted model to retain knowledge from the original (out-of-domain) model that is useful and would otherwise be lost while training continues on the in-domain data, due so the sparsity of the smaller in-domain dataset.

If this is true, using the additional regularization term should improve performance of an in-domain model (that does not use continued training), since our technique should transfer general domain knowledge learned from the out-of-domain corpus.

To test this idea, we train an in-domain model from scratch (as opposed to initializing with the out-of-domain model) using our regularization term. The results are shown in Table 6. In this setting, the only out-of-domain information is coming from the additional term in the loss function. Our method provides an improvement of up to 2.8 BLEU over the in-domain model, though in

De-En TED performance degrades by 0.3 BLEU. While none of these experiments outperform continued training, the large improvements suggest the method is effective at transferring general domain knowledge into the domain specific model.

Additionally, these experiments suggest our method could be beneficial in situations where continued training is not an option. For example, the out-of-domain model might be much larger or perhaps a completely different architecture than the in-domain model; as long as it provides a distribution over the same vocabulary as the in-domain model, it can be used as the auxiliary model in the training objective.

How does this method impact performance on the original domain? To examine how well general domain knowledge is retained by the adapted models, we evaluate the domain specific models on a more general domain test set (`newstest2016`),[13] as well as on the other domain's test set (i.e. performance of the TED model

---

[13]Note that this analysis is complicated by the fact that the WMT task is, in fact, a domain adaptation task, since the WMT test set consists of news articles, while the training data includes parliamentary text, political and economic commentary and press releases.

OOV Types   OOV Tokens

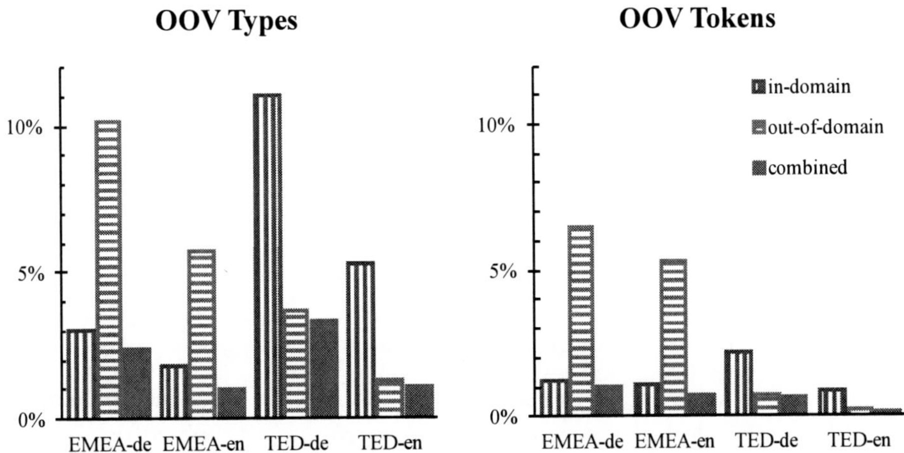

Figure 1: Percentage of out-of-vocabulary words by (a) *type* and (b) *token*.

on the EMEA test set and vice-versa). We report the results for De-En in Table 7. In each case, as regularization increases, both general-domain and cross-domain performance increase. Continued training for a particular domain harms performance on the other domains when compared to the original out-of-domain model.

This suggests that there is some amount of general information about translating between the two languages that is being forgotten by the network during continued training, and the regularization term helps remember it.

Why does EMEA show larger improvements? Throughout our experiments, we observe larger improvements for EMEA than we do for for TED. For TED, performance is similar for both the in-domain and out-of-domain baselines (the in- and out-of-domain baselines are within 1.6 BLEU of each other for TED, whereas for EMEA the in-domain model is over 11 BLEU better in both directions—see Table 4 for full results).

We hypothesize that this is because TED is actually similar in domain to our 'out-of-domain' training set. In particular, we suspect that TED talks are similar to parliamentary speech, which is a portion of the WMT training data—both are oral presentations that cover a variety of topics.

In contrast, EMEA focuses on a single topic (descriptions of medicines) and contains specialized medical terminology throughout.

The out-of-vocabulary rates (OOV) are consistent with this hypothesis (see Figures 1a and 1b for OOV rates by type and token, respectively). For EMEA, the OOV rate is lower for the in-domain training set compared to the out-of-domain training set while for TED, the opposite is true: the OOV rate is lower for the out-of-domain training set compared to the in-domain training set. This suggests that the EMEA domain has a unique vocabulary that needs to be adapted to, while TED covers a wide variety of topics, and requires a large corpus to cover its vocabulary, and the adaptation problem is more about the style of the corpus.

This contrast between a very homogeneous domain and a heterogeneous one is typically not made: both are typically described as "domain adaptation." However, perhaps future work should approach these problems differently.

What value should α be set to? We perform a linear search over α, the interpolation parameter between NLL and our regularization term. We run experiments with α values of $0.001, 0.01, 0.1$, and select the best model based on in-domain development set performance. Table 7 shows the development and test scores when translating into English (the trend is similar going into German, and is thus not shown here). In general, we see the best in-domain performance with α set to 0.01 or 0.1. It is likely possible to make further improvements by searching over a more fine-grained range of α values, but we refrain from using this approach due to the additional compute resources it would require.

41

6 Related Work

Prior work has included the use of similar techniques to solve problems different than ours, as well as different approaches to solve the same problem.

6.1 Regularization Techniques

We draw inspiration from a number of prior works including Yu et al. (2013), which introduces Kullback-Leibler (KL) divergence between the model being trained and an out-of-domain model as a regularization scheme for speaker adaptation. Their work adapts a context dependent deep neural network hidden Markov model (CD-DNN-HMM) using the KL-divergence between the softmax outputs (modeling tied-triphone states) of a network trained on a large, speaker independent (SI) corpus the model being adapted to a specific speaker, initialized with the SI model. Our technique can also be viewed as an extension of label smoothing (Szegedy et al., 2016; Vaswani et al., 2017; Pereyra et al., 2017), where instead of a simple uniform or unigram word distribution, we use the distribution of an auxiliary NMT model.

6.2 Continued Training

Since Luong and Manning (2015) introduced continued training[14] in NMT, it has become the de facto standard for domain adaptation. The method has been surprisingly robust, and in-domain gains have been shown with as few as tens of in-domain training sentences (Miceli Barone et al., 2017).

Despite the success of continued training, several studies have noted that a model trained via continued training tends to significantly underperform the original model on the original domain. (This is an instance of catastrophic forgetting where the subsequent task is highly related, but still different than, the initial task.[15]) Freitag and Al-Onaizan (2016) found that that ensembling an out-of-domain model with a model trained via continued training can significantly reduce the performance drop on the original domain compared to the continued training model alone. In contrast,

our work focuses on further improving in-domain results.

Chu et al. (2017) present mixed fine-tuning. They begin by training an out-of-domain NMT model but they continue training on a mix of in-domain and out-of-domain data (with the in-domain data oversampled). They also experiment with tagging each sentence with the domain it comes from, allowing a single system to adapt to multiple domains. In contrast, our method does not require further training on (or even access to) the very large general domain dataset while adapting the model to the new domain.

6.3 Regularizing Continued Training

Miceli Barone et al. (2017) share our goal of improving in-domain results and compare three methods of regularization to improve leaning during continued training: 1) Bayesian dropout 2) L2 regularization, and 3) *tuneout*, which is similar to Bayesian dropout but instead of setting weights to zero, they are set to the value of the out-of-domain model. They report small gains (≈ 0.3 BLEU) with Bayesian dropout and L2, but tuneout results are inconsistent and mostly hurt BLEU. In contrast to all three methods, which regularize the weights of the model, our work regularizes only the output distribution and does not directly control the weights.

The work of Dakwale and Monz (2017) is very similar to ours but focuses on retaining out-of-domain performance during continued training, instead of in-domain gains. They perform multi-objective learning with most of the weight (90%) on the auxiliary objective. By contrast, our training emphasizes the in-domain training objective (weighting the auxiliary objective 0.1% to 10%) and we show much larger in-domain gains.

7 Conclusion and Future Work

In this work, we focus on the following scenario: we assume there is a model that has been trained in the language pair of interest, and we now have a new domain for which we would like to build a model using some additional training data. We add an additional term to the NMT training objective that minimizes the cross-entropy between the model output vocabulary distribution and an auxiliary model's output vocabulary distribution. We begin by initializing with the out-of-domain model, and then continue training on the

---

[14]This is also often referred to as *fine tuning*, we use the term *continued training* to distinguish from the framework of Hinton and Salakhutdinov (2006), which uses supervised learning to fine tune features obtained through unsupervised learning.

[15]See Kirkpatrick et al. (2017) for a recent approach in this space which deals with independent problems.

in-domain data, using the modified training objective to prevent the model from differing too much from the original out-of-domain model. We report potential improvements of up to 1.5 BLEU over a strong baseline of continued training when using the full domain adaptation corpora, and up to 0.9 BLEU over continued training in our extremely low resource domain adaptation setting.

Our work can be viewed as multi-objective learning with both regular word-level NLL loss and word-level auxiliary loss. Kim and Rush (2016) presented gains using novel sequence-level Knowledge distillation that may be useful to incorporate in future work.

We kept the model hyperparameters fixed for all experiments, and only tuned the regularization coefficient. Future work should explore the interaction between continued training, regularization, and other hyperparameters.

Acknowledgements

This material is based upon work supported in part by DARPA LORELEI and by the Department of Defense through the National Defense Science & Engineering Graduate Fellowship (NDSEG) Program.

References

Dzmitry Bahdanau, Kyunghyun Cho, and Yoshua Bengio. 2015. Neural Machine Translation by Jointly Learning to Align and Translate. Proceedings of the International Conference on Learning Representations (ICLR).

Ondřej Bojar, Rajen Chatterjee, Christian Federmann, Yvette Graham, Barry Haddow, Shujian Huang, Matthias Huck, Philipp Koehn, Qun Liu, Varvara Logacheva, Christof Monz, Matteo Negri, Matt Post, Raphael Rubino, Lucia Specia, and Marco Turchi. 2017. Findings of the 2017 conference on machine translation (wmt17). In *Proceedings of the Second Conference on Machine Translation, Volume 2: Shared Task Papers*, pages 169–214, Copenhagen, Denmark. Association for Computational Linguistics.

Mauro Cettolo, Christian Girardi, and Marcello Federico. 2012. Wit^3: Web inventory of transcribed and translated talks. In *Proceedings of the 16th Conference of the European Association for Machine Translation (EAMT)*, pages 261–268, Trento, Italy.

Chenhui Chu, Raj Dabre, and Sadao Kurohashi. 2017. An empirical comparison of domain adaptation methods for neural machine translation. In *Proceedings of the 55th Annual Meeting of the Association for Computational Linguistics (Volume 2: Short Papers)*, pages 385–391. Association for Computational Linguistics.

Josep Maria Crego, Jungi Kim, Guillaume Klein, Anabel Rebollo, Kathy Yang, Jean Senellart, Egor Akhanov, Patrice Brunelle, Aurelien Coquard, Yongchao Deng, Satoshi Enoue, Chiyo Geiss, Joshua Johanson, Ardas Khalsa, Raoum Khiari, Byeongil Ko, Catherine Kobus, Jean Lorieux, Leidiana Martins, Dang-Chuan Nguyen, Alexandra Priori, Thomas Riccardi, Natalia Segal, Christophe Servan, Cyril Tiquet, Bo Wang, Jin Yang, Dakun Zhang, Jing Zhou, and Peter Zoldan. 2016. Systran's pure neural machine translation systems. *CoRR*, abs/1610.05540.

Praveen Dakwale and Christof Monz. 2017. Fine-tuning for neural machine translation with limited degradation across in-and out-of-domain data. *Proceedings of the XVI Machine Translation Summit*, page 117.

Kevin Duh. 2018. The multitarget ted talks task. http://www.cs.jhu.edu/~kevinduh/a/multitarget-tedtalks/.

Markus Freitag and Yaser Al-Onaizan. 2016. Fast Domain Adaptation for Neural Machine Translation. *CoRR*, abs/1612.06897.

Ian J Goodfellow, Mehdi Mirza, Da Xiao, Aaron Courville, and Yoshua Bengio. 2013. An empirical investigation of catastrophic forgetting in gradient-based neural networks. *arXiv preprint arXiv:1312.6211*.

G. E. Hinton and R. R. Salakhutdinov. 2006. Reducing the dimensionality of data with neural networks. *Science*, 313(5786):504–507.

Marcin Junczys-Dowmunt, Tomasz Dwojak, and Hieu Hoang. 2016. Is Neural Machine Translation Ready for Deployment? A Case Study on 30 Translation Directions. In *Proceedings of the 9th International Workshop on Spoken Language Translation (IWSLT)*, Seattle, WA.

Yoon Kim and Alexander M. Rush. 2016. Sequence-level knowledge distillation. In *Proceedings of the 2016 Conference on Empirical Methods in Natural Language Processing*, pages 1317–1327, Austin, Texas. Association for Computational Linguistics.

James Kirkpatrick, Razvan Pascanu, Neil Rabinowitz, Joel Veness, Guillaume Desjardins, Andrei A. Rusu, Kieran Milan, John Quan, Tiago Ramalho, Agnieszka Grabska-Barwinska, Demis Hassabis, Claudia Clopath, Dharshan Kumaran, and Raia Hadsell. 2017. Overcoming catastrophic forgetting in neural networks. *Proceedings of the National Academy of Sciences*, 114(13):3521–3526.

Guillaume Klein, Yoon Kim, Yuntian Deng, Jean Senellart, and Alexander M. Rush. 2017. Opennmt: Open-source toolkit for neural machine translation. In *Proc. ACL*.

Philipp Koehn. 2005. Europarl: A parallel corpus for statistical machine translation. In *Proceedings of the Tenth Machine Translation Summit (MT Summit X)*, Phuket, Thailand.

Philipp Koehn. 2017. Neural machine translation. *CoRR*, abs/1709.07809.

Philipp Koehn and Rebecca Knowles. 2017. Six Challenges for Neural Machine Translation. In *Proceedings of the 1st Workshop on Neural Machine Translation (and Generation) at ACL*. Association for Computational Linguistics.

Minh-Thang Luong and Christopher D. Manning. 2015. Stanford Neural Machine Translation Systems for Spoken Language Domain. In *International Workshop on Spoken Language Translation*, Da Nang, Vietnam.

Antonio Valerio Miceli Barone, Barry Haddow, Ulrich Germann, and Rico Sennrich. 2017. Regularization techniques for fine-tuning in neural machine translation. In *Proceedings of the 2017 Conference on Empirical Methods in Natural Language Processing*, pages 1489–1494, Copenhagen, Denmark. Association for Computational Linguistics.

Gabriel Pereyra, George Tucker, Jan Chorowski, Łukasz Kaiser, and Geoffrey Hinton. 2017. Regularizing neural networks by penalizing confident output distributions. *arXiv preprint arXiv:1701.06548*.

Rico Sennrich, Barry Haddow, and Alexandra Birch. 2016. Neural Machine Translation of Rare Words with Subword Units. In *Proceedings of the 54th Annual Meeting of the Association for Computational Linguistics*, Berlin, Germany. Association for Computational Linguistics.

Christian Szegedy, Vincent Vanhoucke, Sergey Ioffe, Jon Shlens, and Zbigniew Wojna. 2016. Rethinking the inception architecture for computer vision. In *Proceedings of the IEEE Conference on Computer Vision and Pattern Recognition*, pages 2818–2826.

Jörg Tiedemann. 2009. News from OPUS - A collection of multilingual parallel corpora with tools and interfaces. In N. Nicolov, K. Bontcheva, G. Angelova, and R. Mitkov, editors, *Recent Advances in Natural Language Processing*, volume V. John Benjamins, Amsterdam/Philadelphia, Borovets, Bulgaria.

Jörg Tiedemann. 2012. Parallel Data, Tools and Interfaces in OPUS. In *Proceedings of the 8th International Conference on Language Resources and Evaluation*.

Ashish Vaswani, Noam Shazeer, Niki Parmar, Jakob Uszkoreit, Llion Jones, Aidan N Gomez, Łukasz Kaiser, and Illia Polosukhin. 2017. Attention is all you need. In *Advances in Neural Information Processing Systems*, pages 6000–6010.

Yonghui Wu, Mike Schuster, Zhifeng Chen, Quoc V. Le, Mohammad Norouzi, Wolfgang Macherey, Maxim Krikun, Yuan Cao, Qin Gao, Klaus Macherey, Jeff Klingner, Apurva Shah, Melvin Johnson, Xiaobing Liu, Lukasz Kaiser, Stephan Gouws, Yoshikiyo Kato, Taku Kudo, Hideto Kazawa, Keith Stevens, George Kurian, Nishant Patil, Wei Wang, Cliff Young, Jason Smith, Jason Riesa, Alex Rudnick, Oriol Vinyals, Greg Corrado, Macduff Hughes, and Jeffrey Dean. 2016. Google's neural machine translation system: Bridging the gap between human and machine translation. *CoRR*, abs/1609.08144.

Dong Yu, Kaisheng Yao, Hao Su, Gang Li, and Frank Seide. 2013. Kl-divergence regularized deep neural network adaptation for improved large vocabulary speech recognition. In *2013 IEEE International Conference on Acoustics, Speech and Signal Processing*, pages 7893–7897.

Controllable Abstractive Summarization

Angela Fan   David Grangier   Michael Auli

Facebook AI Research
Menlo Park, California, USA

Abstract

Current models for document summarization disregard user preferences such as the desired length, style, the entities that the user might be interested in, or how much of the document the user has already read. We present a neural summarization model with a simple but effective mechanism to enable users to specify these high level attributes in order to control the shape of the final summaries to better suit their needs. With user input, our system can produce high quality summaries that follow user preferences. Without user input, we set the control variables automatically – on the full text CNN-Dailymail dataset, we outperform state of the art abstractive systems (both in terms of F1-ROUGE1 40.38 vs. 39.53 F1-ROUGE and human evaluation).

1   Introduction

Summarization condenses a document into a short paragraph or a single sentence while retaining core information. Summarization algorithms are either extractive or abstractive. Extractive algorithms form summaries by pasting together relevant portions of the input, while abstractive algorithms may generate new text that is not present in the initial document (Das and Martins, 2007; Nenkova et al., 2011).

This work focuses on abstractive summarization and, in contrast to previous work, describes mechanisms that enable the reader to control important aspects of the generated summary. The reader can select the desired *length* of the summary depending on how detailed they would like the summary to be. The reader can require the text to focus on *entities* they have a particular interest in. We let the reader choose the *style* of the summary based on their favorite source of information, e.g., a particular news source. Finally, we allow the reader to specify that they only want to summarize a portion of the article, for example the *remaining* paragraphs they haven't read.

Our work builds upon sequence-to-sequence models (Sutskever et al., 2014; Bahdanau et al., 2015), which have been extensively applied to abstractive summarization (Rush et al., 2015; Chopra et al., 2016; Nallapati et al., 2016; See et al., 2017; Paulus et al., 2017). These conditional language models use an encoder network to build a representation of the input document and a decoder network to generate a summary by attending to the source representation (Bahdanau et al., 2015).

We introduce a straightforward and extensible controllable summarization model to enable personalized generation and fully leverage that automatic summaries are generated at the reader's request. We show that (1) our generated summaries follow the specified preferences and (2) these control variables guide the learning process and improve generation even when they are set automatically during inference. Our comparison with state-of-the-art models on the standard CNN/DailyMail benchmark (Nallapati et al., 2016), a multi-sentence summarization news corpus, highlights the advantage of our approach. On both the entity-anonymized (+0.76 F1-ROUGE1) and full text versions (+0.85 F1-ROUGE1) of the dataset, we outperform previous pointer-based models trained with maximum likelihood despite the relative simplicity of our model. Further, we demonstrate in a blind human evaluation study that our model generates summaries preferred by human readers.

2   User Controllable Summarization

We introduce our summarization model and describe the control variables users can modify.

2.1   Convolutional Sequence-to-Sequence

Our approach builds upon the convolutional model of Gehring et al. (2017). The encoder and decoder

45

Proceedings of the 2nd Workshop on Neural Machine Translation and Generation, pages 45–54
Melbourne, Australia, July 20, 2018. ©2018 Association for Computational Linguistics

are deep convolutional networks (LeCun et al., 1990). Both start with a word embedding layer followed by alternating convolutions with Gated Linear Units (GLU) (Dauphin et al., 2017). The decoder is connected to the encoder through attention modules (Bahdanau et al., 2015) that performs a weighted sum of the encoder outputs. The weights are predicted from the current decoder states, allowing the decoder to emphasize the parts of the input document which are the most relevant for generating the next token. We use multi-hop attention, i.e. attention is applied at each layer of the decoder.

In addition to attending over encoder states (Bahdanau et al., 2015), we also use intra-attention in the decoder to enable the model to refer back to previously generated words. This allows the decoder to keep track of its progress and reduces the generation of repeated information (Vaswani et al., 2017; Paulus et al., 2017). To combine encoder and decoder attention, we alternate between each type of attention at every layer.

Much prior work on the CNN-Dailymail benchmark employed pointer networks to copy rare entities from the input (Nallapati et al., 2016), which introduces additional complexity to the model. Instead, we rely on sub-word tokenization and weight sharing. We show this simple approach is very effective. Specifically, we use byte-pair-encoding (BPE) for tokenization, a proven strategy that has been shown to improve the generation of proper nouns in translation (Sennrich et al., 2016b). We share the representation of the tokens in the encoder and decoder embeddings and in the last decoder layer.

2.2 Length-Constrained Summarization

Summarization allows a reader with limited time to quickly comprehend the essence of a document. Controlling summary length enables reading with different time budgets: a document might be summarized as a five-word headline, a single sentence or a paragraph, each providing more and more detail.

To enable the user to control length, we first quantize summary length into discrete bins, each representing a size range. Length bins are chosen so that they each contain roughly an equal number of training documents. We then expand the input vocabulary with special word types to indicate the length bin of the desired summary, which allows generation to be conditioned upon this discrete length variable. For training, we prepend the input of our summarizer with a marker that indicates the length of the ground-truth summary.

At test time, we control the length of generated text by prepending a particular length marker token. Our experiments (§5.2) provide quantitative and qualitative evidence that the model effectively uses this variable: output length is easily controlled by changing the length marker and supplying ground truth markers drastically improves summary quality. We compare our method to Kikuchi et al. (2016) and demonstrate that our straightforward length control strategy is more effective.

2.3 Entity-Centric Summarization

The reader might be interested in a document to learn about specific entities, such as people or locations. For example, a sports fan reading about a recent game might want to focus the summary on the performance of their favorite player. To enable entity-centric summaries, we first anonymize entities by replacing all occurrences of a given entity in a document by the same token. For training, we also anonymize the corresponding reference summary. For a (document, summary) pair, each entity is replaced with a token from the set (@entity0, ..., @entityN). This abstracts away the surface form, allowing our approach to scale to many entities and generalize to unseen ones.

We then express that an entity should be present in the generated summary by prepending the entity token to the input — prepending @entity3 expresses that the model should generate a summary where @entity3 is present. In effect, this instructs the model to focus on sentences that mention the marked entities.

At training time, we prepend each document with markers referring to an entity from the ground-truth summary. To ensure the entity request is informative, we provide an entity that is present in the ground-truth but not present in the summary generated by the baseline model. At test time, we may specify any entity marker that we wish the summary to contain. Our experiments (§5.2) evaluate the effect of prepending different markers to the input. We show that higher accuracy is achieved when we specify entities from the first few sentences of a document or if we supply markers taken from the reference summary to illustrate specific user preferences. We extend this approach to multiple entity markers and experiment with appending all ground-truth entities for training and provide all entities from Lead-3 at test time. We show that providing more entities improves summarization quality.

2.4 Source-Specific Summarization

Text sources such as newspapers and magazines often have specific style guidelines to provide a consistent experience. Readers are accustomed to the styles of their favorite sources. Therefore, we enable users to specify a preferred source style for a summary. Similar to length and entities, we introduce special marker tokens (@genSource0, ..., @genSourceN) to express source desiderata. For training, we preprend the input with the marker corresponding to the ground-truth source. At inference, we control the style of generated summary by prepending different markers. Our experiments (§4) evaluate whether providing the true source-style produces summaries that are closer to the reference summary. We additionally provide examples of distinct summaries resulting from changing source-style conditioning.

2.5 Remainder Summarization

Beyond reading summaries of full documents, readers may want the flexibility of only summarizing certain portions of a document. For example, a reader who has read the first few paragraphs would want a summary of the remaining text to cover what they missed.

Training and evaluating remainder summarization requires specific data, namely a dataset of full documents with position markers separating the already read portion from the remainder part along with the corresponding summaries. Such a dataset is not readily available and would be challenging to collect. To enable remainder summarization without such data, we align summaries to full documents. Our procedure matches each reference summary sentence to its best matching document sentence based on ROUGE-L. For any position in the document, we remove sentences aligned before this point from the full summary and consider this shorter summary as the summary of the remainder. In our experiment, we consider as read portions all article positions located at the middle of two alignment points, except for alignment points separated by less than 2 sentences.

We consider the following methods:
(1) **full summary baseline:** the baseline model predicts a full summary, disregarding the separation of the read portion from the remainder.
(2) **post-inference alignment:** a full summary is generated from the baseline model and the summary is shortened with our alignment procedure. The decoded summary sentences that align to the remainder portion compose the summary of the remainder.
(3) **remainder only**: the model is trained to map the document remainders to the remainder summaries on pre-aligned training data. This model is not given the read portion of the article.

(4) **read and remainder**: the model receives both read portion of the article and the remainder separated by a special token. It is trained to predict the remainder summary. We distinguish the read and remainder part of the article by using distinct sets of position embeddings.

We compare these methods in Section 4 and show the advantage of the model that receives both the user-read portion and the remainder of the document.

3 Related Work

3.1 Sequence-to-Sequence for Summarization

Automatic summarization has been an active research field for 60 years (Luhn, 1958). Extractive and abstractive methods have benefited from advances in natural language processing, pattern recognition, and machine learning (Nenkova et al., 2011). Recently, sequence-to-sequence neural networks (Sutskever et al., 2014) have been applied to abstractive summarization (Nallapati et al., 2016; See et al., 2017; Paulus et al., 2017) following their success in translation (Bahdanau et al., 2015; Luong et al., 2015b), parsing (Luong et al., 2015a) and image captioning (Vinyals et al., 2015b). Neural abstractive summarization has built upon advances from machine translation and related fields: attention (Bahdanau et al., 2015) enables generation to focus on parts of the source document while pointers (Vinyals et al., 2015a) help abstractive summarization to copy entities from the input (See et al., 2017; Paulus et al., 2017; Nallapati et al., 2016).

However, summarization also has distinct challenges. The generation of multi-sentence summaries differs from single sentence translation: left-to-right decoders need to be aware of their previous generation at a larger time scale, otherwise models tend to produce repeated text. To address this impediment, (See et al., 2017) introduce coverage modeling, (Paulus et al., 2017) propose intra-decoder attention, and (Suzuki and Nagata, 2017) equip the decoder with an estimator of unigram frequency. Previous work has also explored learning objectives: (Paulus et al., 2017) investigates replacing maximum likelihood training with Reinforcement Learning (RL) to optimize ROUGE, the most common automatic metric to assess summarization. Combining both strategies is found to perform best in human evaluations, as training with RL alone often produces non-grammatical text.

Our work builds upon prior research: like (Gehring et al., 2017), we rely on convolutional networks, which enable faster training. This contrasts with prior work using recurrent networks (Nallapati et al., 2016; See et al., 2017; Paulus et al., 2017). We borrow intra-attention from (Paulus et al., 2017) and expand it to multi-hop intra-attention inspired by multi-hop source attention from (Gehring et al., 2017). To facilitate copying input entities, we share the word representations between encoder and decoder (Paulus et al., 2017), and also rely on BPE tokenization (Sennrich et al., 2016b). This combination allows us to forgo an additional pointer mechanism unlike (Paulus et al., 2017; See et al., 2017; Nallapati et al., 2016). Unlike (Paulus et al., 2017), we did not explore training objectives and maximized the likelihood of the training summaries given the source document. Our model is amenable to RL, but this aspect is largely orthogonal to our main goal, i.e. controllable summarization.

3.2 Controllable Text Generation

Text generation is an established research area (McKeown, 1992). The field follows recent advances in generative models, such as the introduction of variational auto-encoders (Kingma and Welling, 2013) and adversarial networks (Goodfellow et al., 2014). This is exemplified by work focusing on natural language generation such as (Bowman et al., 2016; Yu et al., 2017; Zhao et al., 2017; Rajeswar et al., 2017).

Building upon unconditioned generation, controllable generation is an emerging research field. Research in computer vision includes style transfer (Gatys et al., 2015) or controllable image generation (Lample et al., 2017). Text generation work focuses on controlling tense or sentiment with variational auto-encoders (Hu et al., 2017). Shen et al. (2017) relies on adversarial training for manipulating sentence sentiment and Sennrich et al. (2016a) propose using side constraints for polite neural machine translation models. Takeno et al. (2017) extend the side constraints to control further aspects of translation output, such as length. Others have worked on style, for example Ficler and Goldberg (2017) propose using a conditional language model to generate text with stylistic requirements and Kobus et al. (2017) propose using tokens and additional features to translate text in different domains. Filippova (2017) proposes controlling length for generating answers in a question answering task. Kikuchi et al. (2016) explores length control for sentence compression using decoding-time restrictions and training-time length token embeddings.

Motivated by simplicity, our work relies on conditional language modeling and does not require adversarial training, latent variable models such as variational auto-encoders, or pointer networks. While latent variable models are popular for the generation of continuous outputs such as images, (conditional) language models are flexible enough to capture the multimodal nature of the data. We leave the assessment of how additional latent variables might improve upon our results to future work.

4   Experimental Setup

Dataset: We use the CNN-Dailymail dataset (Hermann et al., 2015; Nallapati et al., 2016). It consists of news articles along with multi-sentence summaries, with a total of 287k train, 13k valid and 11k test articles. On average, the articles are 758 token long, and the summaries are 55 token long. Most of our experiments are performed with articles truncated at 400 tokens, as suggested by (See et al., 2017). We evaluate on two versions of the data: the entity anonymized version (Hermann et al., 2015; Nallapati et al., 2016; Paulus et al., 2017) and the full text version (See et al., 2017). We use BPE with 30K types (Sennrich et al., 2016b) for most experiments. For non-BPE models, input and output vocabularies have resp. 47k and 21k word types, corresponding to types with more than 20 train occurrences.

Further, we compare length control with (Kikuchi et al., 2016) on DUC-2004 single-sentence summarization task. We train on English Gigaword following the protocol of Rush et al. (2015). The data consist of 3.6 million pairs (first sentence, headline of news articles). Following (Kikuchi et al., 2016), we evaluate on the 500 documents in the DUC2004 task-1. We use a source and target vocabulary of 30k words.

Architecture, Training, and Generation: We implement models with the fairseq library[1]. For CNN-Dailymail, our model has 8 layers in the encoder and decoder, each with kernel width 3. We use 512 hidden units for each layer, embeddings of size 340, and dropout 0.2. For DUC, we have 6 layers in the encoder and decoder with 256 hidden units.

Similar to Gehring et al. (2017), we train using Nesterov accelerated gradient method (Sutskever et al., 2013) with gradient clipping 0.1 (Pascanu et al., 2013), momentum 0.99, and learning rate 0.2. We reduce the learning rate by an order of magnitude when the validation perplexity ceases to improve, and end training when the learning rate drops below 10^{-5}. Summaries are generated using beam search

---

[1] github.com/facebookresearch/fairseq

with beam size 5. To avoid repetition, we prevent the decoder from generating the same trigram more than once, following Paulus et al. (2017).

Evaluation: On the CNN-Dailymail benchmark, our **automatic evaluation** reports F1-ROUGE scores for ROUGE-1, ROUGE-2, and ROUGE-L (Lin, 2004). We compare to existing abstractive baselines (Nallapati et al., 2016; See et al., 2017; Paulus et al., 2017). We also compare with Lead-3 which selects the first three sentences of the article as the summary. Note that, although simple, this baseline is not outperformed by all models.

For **human evaluation**, we conduct a human evaluation study using Amazon Mechanical Turk and the test set generation output of See et al. (2017). 500 articles from the test set were randomly selected and evaluated by 5 raters. The raters were presented with the first 400 words of each news article and asked to select the summarization output they preferred.

For the DUC-2004, we report recall ROUGE for ROUGE-1, ROUGE-2, and ROUGE-L at 30, 50, and 75 byte lengths following Kikuchi et al. (2016).

5 Results

We evaluate the design choices of our model and the impact of manipulating the control variables. We analyze the performance of the remainder summarization task and demonstrate the advantage of modeling both the read and remainder portions of the document.

5.1 Convolutional Summarization

Table 1 details the effect of our design choices for our baseline. Adding a constraint to avoid repeated trigrams at generation time improves F1-ROUGE1 by +2.86. Adding intra-attention to enable the model to examine past generations over long distances improves the accuracy obtained with the trigram constraint by a further 0.51 F1-ROUGE1. The modest improvement is likely because the two features address a similar problem of avoiding repeated generations. Switching tokenization from word to BPE gives another +0.79 F1-ROUGE1. BPE improves the ability to copy proper nouns and rare inflections, both of which are difficult to model in word-based vocabularies. This agrees with translation results (Sennrich et al., 2016b). Lastly, we find tuning the min/max length on the validation set and applying the constraints to the test set improves F1-ROUGE1 by 0.25.

Model	ROUGE		
	1	**2**	**L**
fairseq	33.32	12.64	30.57
+ trigram decoding	36.18	14.10	33.18
+ intra-attention	36.69	14.28	33.47
+ BPE	37.48	15.12	34.16
+ tuning min/max len	37.73	15.03	34.49

Table 1: Baseline without control variables. Each row add a feature on top of the previous row features.

Model	ROUGE		
	1	**2**	**L**
baseline, no control	37.73	15.03	34.49
Length constraint	39.16	15.54	35.94
Entity centric	38.17	15.16	34.92
Source specific	37.68	15.16	34.40
Length+Entity+Source	39.61	15.83	36.48

Table 2: Summarization with oracle control to simulate user preference.

Model	ROUGE		
	1	**2**	**L**
Lead-3			
Nallapati et al. (2017)	**39.2**	**15.7**	35.5
Maximum Likelihood			
Nallapati et al. (2016)	35.46	13.30	32.65
Paulus et al. (2017)	37.86	14.69	34.99
Paulus et al. + intra-attn	38.30	14.81	35.49
fairseq no control (ours)	37.48	15.12	34.16
+ fixed control	**38.68**	**15.40**	35.47
+ Lead-3 ent	**39.06**	**15.38**	**35.77**
Reinforcement Learning			
Paulus et al. (2017)	**39.87**	**15.82**	**36.90**

Table 3: Fixed control variables on entity-anonymized text. Even with fixed variables, the controllable model improves ROUGE compared to ML alternatives.

5.2 Controllable Summarization

Our summarizer lets users control the length of the generated summary, entities on which it focuses on, and source style it imitates (see§2). We first evaluate the effect of providing the oracle reference variables at decoding time. This simulates a user setting their preferences to specific values. We then assess the effect of providing non-reference control variables.

Table 2 reports our results for each variable and their combined effect. All control variables improve the summary quality, but length control has the most

Model	ROUGE		
	1	**2**	**L**
Lead-3	**40.34**	**17.70**	**36.57**
Maximum Likelihood			
See et al. (2017)	39.53	17.28	36.38
fairseq no control (ours)	38.23	16.68	34.77
+ fixed control	**39.75**	17.29	**36.54**
+ Lead-3 ent	**40.38**	**17.44**	**37.15**

Table 4: Summarization with fixed control variables on original text. Even with a fixed setting, the controlled summarization model improves ROUGE.

impact, followed by entity control and source style. Further, the advantages of each control variable cumulatively produce an even stronger summary: we obtain +2.2 F1-ROUGE1 when combining control variables.

Length control improves accuracy by 1.68 F1-ROUGE1 (Table 2). This improvement is due to two effects: length mismatch is heavily penalized by F1-ROUGE. Moreover, the baseline struggles at predicting correct lengths. The latter is due to large uncertainty in summary length, i.e. even humans have difficulty predicting the correct length.

Figure 1 reports the average summary length when decoding all examples in the test set using each of the 10 possible length markers. The model is shown to respect length markers. Table 8 demonstrates the effect of the length marker on a specific example.

Entity control has less impact on ROUGE compared to length control at +0.69 vs. +1.68 F1-ROUGE1 (Table 2). This is mainly because our summaries often already contain most entities from the ground-truth without the need for additional instruction. Table 6 further analyzes entity control for 100 test documents. We decode repeatedly requiring each entity from lead-3. We then repeat the experiment with each entity from the full article. We report how often the entity-centric model generates a summary that actually contains the requested entity. For Lead-3 entities, the model mentions the requested entity 61% of the time, while for all entities from the input, the model mentions required entities 34% of the time. In both settings, these rates are much higher than the baseline. The model has difficulty generating summaries with entities which are unlikely to appear in the human references, e.g. unimportant entities far from the beginning of the article.

Source-style control is the least impactful control in terms of ROUGE, we report +0.2 F1-ROUGE1 in Table 2. Changing the source style variable changes the summary as shown in Table 8. Generally, we observe that generated summaries in the Dailymail-style are more repetitive and slightly longer than the CNN-style summaries. This matches the differences between the two sources in the reference text. The impact of style requests might be greater with a richer set of styles — in future work, we plan to evaluate on datasets where varied styles are available.

5.3 Summarization with Automatic Control

Our primary objective is to allow readers to control the attributes of generated summaries. However, we can also set the control variables automatically in absence of reader desiderata. For length and source-style, we set the variable to a constant value that maximizes ROUGE on the validation set. For entity control, we randomly sample an entity that appears in lead-3 and provide it as the entity of interest.

Table 3 reports results on the entity-anonymized version of the dataset like (Nallapati et al., 2016; Paulus et al., 2017) and Table 4 reports results on the full text data like (See et al., 2017). In both cases, our method is advantageous over alternatives. Further, providing all of the entities at training time and only lead-3 entities at test time improves quality. On the original text, we report 40.38 F1-ROUGE1 as opposed to 39.53 for (See et al., 2017). On the entity-anonymized text, we report 39.06 F1-ROUGE1 as opposed to 38.30 for the best maximum likelihood setting of (Paulus et al., 2017). We hypothesize that providing all lead-3 entities encourages copying from lead-3. Our model does not outperform the reinforcement learning model of (Paulus et al., 2017) which optimizes ROUGE. However, training objectives are orthogonal to our work on control variables and we expect reinforcement learning to equally benefit our model.

Table 5 compares results on DUC-2004 to the best method presented by (Kikuchi et al., 2016). We find that adding length embedding improves the ROUGE-1 and ROUGE-L scores for 30, 50, and 75 byte evaluation. Notably, ROUGE improves more for shorter text evaluation, likely because requesting a shorter document allows the model to plan its generation. Comparing to Kikuchi et al. (2016), our results are stronger while our method is very simple – (Kikuchi et al., 2016) explore embedding the remaining length at each timestep during decoding and creating a separate memory cell to control length. In contrast, we simply provide the desired length as a special token and show this simple approach is effective. Lastly, we note that length-control has less effect on DUC-2004 compared

Model	30 byte			50 byte			75 byte		
	1	**2**	**L**	**1**	**2**	**L**	**1**	**2**	**L**
$LenInit_{(0,L)}$ (Kikuchi et al., 2016)	14.31	3.27	13.19	20.87	6.16	19.00	25.87	8.27	23.24
Baseline without control	21.47	**7.63**	20.71	25.07	**8.49**	22.97	29.88	**10.37**	26.29
+ fixed length (ours)	**21.81**	7.51	**21.05**	**25.39**	8.38	**23.37**	**30.00**	10.27	**26.43**

Table 5: ROUGE for fixed length control variable on DUC-2004 Task 1.

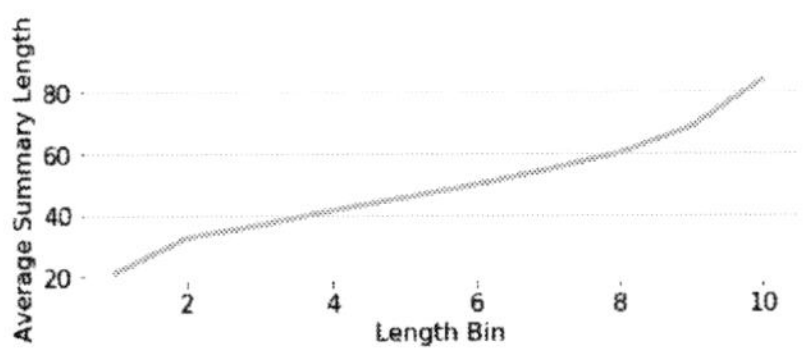

Figure 1: Length control vs summary length. Length control can take 10 discrete values.

	Baseline	Entity-centric
Lead-3	15.28	**61.15**
Full input	7.64	**33.76**

Table 6: Fraction of requested entity actually occurring in decoded summaries. Entities originate either from lead-3 or from the full document.

to CNN-Dailymail since truncated recall-ROUGE evaluation does not penalize length mismatch strongly.

Overall, the improvements from automatic control show that a better model can be obtained by providing additional information during training – we present the first model trained with maximum likelihood to match the strong Lead-3 baseline. When the model is not required to predict the summary length or the entities of interest, it can assign more capacity to generating text conditioned on these variables. This is particularly useful for variables which are hard to predict from the input due to intrinsic uncertainty like length. In subsequent work, we plan to explore architectures to explicitly divide the prediction of control variables and sequence-to-sequence mapping.

Model	ROUGE		
	1	**2**	**L**
Full summary	28.12	9.46	18.81
Post-inference align.	27.13	7.68	27.45
Remainder only	30.30	11.44	27.46
Read + remainder	**30.54**	**11.60**	27.67
Read + rem. + length	**30.70**	11.52	**27.78**

Table 7: Remainder Summarization.

5.4 Remainder Summarization

Summarizing the remainder of an article helps the reader to quickly grasp what they have not yet read. Table 7 presents our results relying on aligned data introduced in §2.5. Generally, this task is more difficult than summarizing the entire article. First, the length of both read portions and summaries varies greatly. It is difficult for the model to distinguish information specific to the remaining portion of the document from the general point of the article. Despite this, when models trained on summarizing the remainder are tasked with summarizing only full documents, the performance is not much worse (37.02 F1-ROUGE1 compared to 37.73 F1-ROUGE1 of the baseline in Table 1).

Our baseline always presents the full summary, regardless of the portion of the article presented as input. It achieves an F1-ROUGE1 score of 28.12. Among our three proposed methods, forming the remainder summaries post-inference performs poorly as it depends largely on alignment quality. The news articles are repetitive, so one summary sentence can align to multiple locations in the source. Training the model to perform remainder summarization significantly improves our results. Models that receive only the remainder and produce a summary achieve F1-ROUGE1 of 30.30, while models that receive both the read and remainder portions are slightly better (F1-ROUGE1 30.54). We hypothesize that presenting the read portion of the article improves the quality as the model can focus on the new information in the remainder. An explicit method for eliminating redundancy between the read and the remainder is relevant future work.

Remainder summary length is particularly difficult to predict. We therefore rely on length control: we split the validation dataset into 10 partitions based on how far in the article the remainder begins and determine the best length setting for each partition. We decode the test data with this setting which provides an additional improvement, 30.70 F1-ROUGE1. However, partitioning is not an accurate length model and we hypothesize that length control could provide a greater improvement with a better model.

a. Summary with Length Control

Requesting Length 2: @entity0 [Easter] is over for the wild rabbits of greater @entity2 [Sydney] as councils and parks prepare another attempt to kill them off with a deadly virus. It comes after over 30 government bodies scattered carrots laced with calicivirus.

Requesting Length 6: @entity0 [Easter] is over for the wild rabbits of greater @entity2 [Sydney] as councils and parks prepare another attempt to kill them off with a deadly virus. This year, because of really high summer rainfall - which led to great food availability - there has been a big surge in the rabbit population in @entity2 [Sydney].

Requesting Length 10: @entity0 [Easter] is over for the wild rabbits of greater @entity2 [Sydney] as councils and parks prepare another attempt to kill them off with strategically placed carrots that have been laced with a deadly virus. This year,because of really high summer rainfall - which led to great food availability - there has been a big surge in the rabbit population in @entity2 [Sydney]. It comes after over 30 government bodies scattered carrots laced with calicivirus around public areas in March.

b. Summary with Entity Control   *blue highlights requested entity*

Requesting @entity17 [Route 5]: @entity1 [Linda MacDonald], 55 , was arrested for driving under the influence of alcohol Monday night in @entity4 [Dummerston], @entity5 [Vermont]. Police say the woman from @entity15 [Shelburne], @entity16 [Massachusetts] was driving drunk around 10:30pm when she ran off @entity17 [Route 5] in @entity4 [Dummerston].

Requesting @entity20 [MacDonald]: @entity1 [Linda MacDonald], 55 , was arrested for driving under the influence of alcohol Monday night in @entity4 [Dummerston], @entity5 [Vermont]. @entity20 [MacDonald] told officers that she crashed while talking on the phone and trying to take directions down on a legal note pad in her car. But when officers smelled alcohol on @entity20 [MacDonald], they administered a breathalyzer test and she posted a .10 blood-alcohol content.

c. Summary with Source-Style Control   *blue highlights different text*

Requesting CNN-Style: Officer @entity6 [Jared Forsyth], 33, had been a member of the @entity7 [Ocala Police Department] since 2012. He was wearing bulletproof vest, but round entered in his arm and went through his chest. @entity6 [Jared Forsyth] was rushed to hospital in critical condition.

Requesting DailyMail-Style: Officer @entity6 [Jared Forsyth], 33, had been a member of the @entity7 [Ocala Police Department] since 2012. He was rushed to @entity26 [Ocala Regional Medical Center] in critical condition and was taken into surgery. Police say the incident occurred about 3.30pm at a gun range at the @entity13 [Lowell Correctional Institution].

d. Remainder Summary

Full Article: @entity4 [Harry Potter] star says he has no plans to fritter his cash away on fast cars, drink and celebrity parties. @entity3 [Daniel Radcliffe]'s earnings from the first five @entity4 [Harry Potter] films have been held in a trust fund which he has not been able to touch.

After 8 sentences: He'll be able to gamble in a casino, buy a drink in a pub or see the horror film. @entity3 [Daniel Radcliffe]'s earnings from first five @entity4 [Harry Potter] films have been held in trust fund .

After 12 sentences: @entity3 [Daniel Radcliffe]'s earnings from first five @entity4 [Harry Potter] films have been held in trust fund .

Table 8: Summaries with various settings for user control variables and remainder summarization.

	ROUGE1	Human Pref.
(See et al., 2017)	39.53	41.04%
fixed ctrl+Lead-3 ent.	**40.38**	**58.99%**

Table 9: Human evaluation: 59% of ratings prefer our summaries (500 CNN-DM test articles, 5 raters each).

5.5 Human Evaluation

Our study compares summarization with fixed value control variables on full text CNN-Dailymail with (See et al., 2017). Table 9 shows that human raters prefer our model about 59% of the time based 2.5k judgments. Our model can therefore improve summary quality in a discernible way. As an aside, we find that ROUGE and ratings agree in two-thirds of the cases, where at least four out of five humans agree.

6 Conclusion

We proposed a controllable summarization model to allow users to define high-level attributes of generated summaries, such as length, source-style, entities of interest, and summarizing only remaining portions of a document. We simulate user preferences for these variables by setting them to oracle values and show large ROUGE gains. The control variables are effective without user input which we demonstrate by assigning them fixed values tuned on a held-out set. This outperforms comparable state of the art summarization models for both ROUGE and human evaluation.

Acknowledgments We thank Yann Dauphin for helpful discussions. We thanks Abigail See for sharing her summaries and Romain Paulus for clarifying their setup. We thank Jonas Gehring and Denis Yarats for writing the fairseq toolkit used for these experiments.

References

Dzmitry Bahdanau, Kyunghyun Cho, and Yoshua Bengio. 2015. Neural machine translation by jointly learning to align and translate. *International Conference on Learning Representation (ICLR)* .

Samuel R. Bowman, Luke Vilnis, Oriol Vinyals, Andrew M. Dai, Rafal Józefowicz, and Samy Bengio. 2016. Generating sentences from a continuous space. In *CoNLL*.

Sumit Chopra, Michael Auli, and Alexander M Rush. 2016. Abstractive sentence summarization with attentive recurrent neural networks. *Conference of the North American Chapter of the Association for Computational Linguistics (NAACL)* .

Dipanjan Das and André FT Martins. 2007. A survey on automatic text summarization. *Literature Survey for the Language and Statistics II course at CMU* 4:192–195.

Yann N. Dauphin, Angela Fan, Michael Auli, and David Grangier. 2017. Language modeling with gated convolutional networks .

Jessica Ficler and Yoav Goldberg. 2017. Controlling linguistic style aspects in neural language generation. *Workshop on Stylistic Variations* abs/1707.02633.

Katja Filippova. 2017. Sentence and passage summarization for question answering. Talk given at EMNLP 2017 Workshop on New Frontiers in Summarization.

Leon A Gatys, Alexander S Ecker, and Matthias Bethge. 2015. A neural algorithm of artistic style. *arXiv preprint arXiv:1508.06576* .

Jonas Gehring, Michael Auli, David Grangier, Denis Yarats, and Yann Dauphin. 2017. Convolutional sequence to sequence learning .

Ian J. Goodfellow, Jean Pouget-Abadie, Mehdi Mirza, Bing Xu, David Warde-Farley, Sherjil Ozair, Aaron C. Courville, and Yoshua Bengio. 2014. Generative adversarial nets. In *NIPS*.

Karl Moritz Hermann, Tomáš Kočiský, Edward Grefenstette, Lasse Espeholt, Will Kay, Mustafa Suleyman, and Phil Blunsom. 2015. Teaching machines to read and comprehend. In *Neural Information Processing Systems (NIPS)*.

Zhiting Hu, Zichao Yang, Xiaodan Liang, Ruslan Salakhutdinov, and Eric P. Xing. 2017. Toward controlled generation of text. In *ICML*.

Yuta Kikuchi, Graham Neubig, Ryohei Sasano, Hiroya Takamura, and Manabu Okumura. 2016. Controlling output length in neural encoder-decoders. *arXiv preprint arXiv:1609.09552* .

Diederik P. Kingma and Max Welling. 2013. Auto-encoding variational bayes. *Arxiv* abs/1312.6114.

Catherine Kobus, Josep Crego, and Jean Senellart. 2017. Domain control for neural machine translation. In *Proceedings of the International Conference Recent Advances in Natural Language Processing, RANLP 2017*. INCOMA Ltd., Varna, Bulgaria, pages 372–378.

Guillaume Lample, Neil Zeghidour, Nicolas Usunier, Antoine Bordes, Ludovic Denoyer, and Marc'Aurelio Ranzato. 2017. Fader networks: Manipulating images by sliding attributes. *Arxiv* abs/1706.00409.

Yann LeCun, Bernhard E Boser, John S Denker, Donnie Henderson, Richard E Howard, Wayne E Hubbard, and Lawrence D Jackel. 1990. Handwritten digit recognition with a back-propagation network. In *Advances in neural information processing systems (NIPS)*. pages 396–404.

Chin-Yew Lin. 2004. Rouge: A package for automatic evaluation of summaries. In *Workshop on Text Summarization Branches Out*.

H. P. Luhn. 1958. The automatic creation of literature abstracts. *IBM Journal of Research and Development* 2(2).

Minh-Thang Luong, Quoc V. Le, Ilya Sutskever, Oriol Vinyals, and Lukasz Kaiser. 2015a. Multi-task sequence to sequence learning. *Arxiv* abs/1511.06114.

Thang Luong, Hieu Pham, and Christopher D. Manning. 2015b. Effective approaches to attention-based neural machine translation. In *Conference on Empirical Methods in Natural Language Processing (EMNLP)*.

Kathleen McKeown. 1992. *Text generation*. Cambridge University Press.

Ramesh Nallapati, Feifei Zhai, and Bowen Zhou. 2017. Summarunner: A recurrent neural network based sequence model for extractive summarization of documents. *Conference of the Association for the Advancement of Artificial Intelligence (AAAI)* .

Ramesh Nallapati, Bowen Zhou, Caglar Gulcehre, Bing Xiang, et al. 2016. Abstractive text summarization using sequence-to-sequence rnns and beyond. *Conference of the Association for the Advancement of Artificial Intelligence (CONLL)* .

Ani Nenkova, Kathleen McKeown, et al. 2011. Automatic summarization. *Foundations and Trends® in Information Retrieval* 5(2–3):103–233.

Razvan Pascanu, Tomas Mikolov, and Yoshua Bengio. 2013. On the difficulty of training recurrent neural networks. In *ICML*.

Romain Paulus, Caiming Xiong, and Richard Socher. 2017. A deep reinforced model for abstractive summarization. *arXiv preprint arXiv:1705.04304* .

Sai Rajeswar, Sandeep Subramanian, Francis Dutil, Christopher Joseph Pal, and Aaron C. Courville. 2017. Adversarial generation of natural language. *Workshop on Representation Learning for NLP* .

Alexander M Rush, SEAS Harvard, Sumit Chopra, and Jason Weston. 2015. A neural attention model for sentence summarization. *Conference on Empirical Methods in Natural Language Processing (EMNLP)* .

Abigail See, Peter J Liu, and Christopher D Manning. 2017. Get to the point: Summarization with pointer-generator networks. *Annual Meeting of the Association for Computational Linguistics (ACL)* .

Rico Sennrich, Barry Haddow, and Alexandra Birch. 2016a. Controlling politeness in neural machine translation via side constraints. In *Proceedings of the 2016 Conference of the North American Chapter of the Association for Computational Linguistics: Human Language Technologies*. Association for Computational Linguistics, San Diego, California, pages 35–40.

Rico Sennrich, Barry Haddow, and Alexandra Birch. 2016b. Neural machine translation of rare words with subword units. *Annual Meeting of the Association for Computational Linguistics (ACL)* .

Tianxiao Shen, Tao Lei, Regina Barzilay, and Tommi S. Jaakkola. 2017. Style transfer from non-parallel text by cross-alignment. *Arxiv* abs/1705.09655.

Ilya Sutskever, James Martens, George E. Dahl, and Geoffrey E. Hinton. 2013. On the importance of initialization and momentum in deep learning. In *ICML*.

Ilya Sutskever, Oriol Vinyals, and Quoc V Le. 2014. Sequence to sequence learning with neural networks. In *Neural Information Processing Systems (NIPS)*.

Jun Suzuki and Masaaki Nagata. 2017. Cutting-off redundant repeating generations for neural abstractive summarization. In *European Conference of the Association of Computer Linguists (EACL)*.

Shunsuke Takeno, Masaaki Nagata, and Kazuhide Yamamoto. 2017. Controlling target features in neural machine translation via prefix constraints. In *Proceedings of the 4th Workshop on Asian Translation (WAT2017)*. Asian Federation of Natural Language Processing, Taipei, Taiwan, pages 55–63.

Ashish Vaswani, Noam Shazeer, Niki Parmar, Jakob Uszkoreit, Llion Jones, Aidan N Gomez, Lukasz Kaiser, and Illia Polosukhin. 2017. Attention is all you need. *arXiv preprint arXiv:1706.03762* .

Oriol Vinyals, Meire Fortunato, and Navdeep Jaitly. 2015a. Pointer networks. In *Conference on Advances in Neural Information Processing Systems (NIPS)*.

Oriol Vinyals, Alexander Toshev, Samy Bengio, and Dumitru Erhan. 2015b. Show and tell: A neural image caption generator. *Conference on Computer Vision and Pattern Recognition (CVPR)* .

Lantao Yu, Weinan Zhang, Jun Wang, and Yong Yu. 2017. Seqgan: Sequence generative adversarial nets with policy gradient. In *AAAI*.

Junbo Zhao, Y. Kim, K. Zhang, A. M. Rush, and Y. LeCun. 2017. Adversarially Regularized Autoencoders for Generating Discrete Structures. *ArXiv* 1706.04223.

Enhancement of Encoder and Attention
Using Target Monolingual Corpora in Neural Machine Translation

Kenji Imamura, Atsushi Fujita, and **Eiichiro Sumita**
National Institute of Information and Communications Technology
3-5 Hikaridai, Seika-cho, Soraku-gun, Kyoto 619-0289, Japan
{kenji.imamura,atsushi.fujita,eiichiro.sumita}@nict.go.jp

Abstract

A large-scale parallel corpus is required to train encoder-decoder neural machine translation. The method of using synthetic parallel texts, in which target monolingual corpora are automatically translated into source sentences, is effective in improving the decoder, but is unreliable for enhancing the encoder. In this paper, we propose a method that enhances the encoder and attention using target monolingual corpora by generating multiple source sentences via sampling. By using multiple source sentences, diversity close to that of humans is achieved. Our experimental results show that the translation quality is improved by increasing the number of synthetic source sentences for each given target sentence, and quality close to that using a manually created parallel corpus was achieved.

1 Introduction

In recent years, neural machine translation (NMT) based on encoder-decoder models (Sutskever et al., 2014; Bahdanau et al., 2014) has become the mainstream approach for machine translation. In this method, the encoder converts an input sentence into numerical vectors called "states," and the decoder generates a translation on the basis of these states. Although the encoder-decoder models can generate high-quality translations, they require large amounts of parallel texts for training.

On the other hand, monolingual corpora are readily available in large quantities. Sennrich et al. (2016a) proposed a method using synthetic parallel texts, in which target monolingual corpora are translated back into the source language (Figure 1). The advantage of this method is that the de-coder is accurately trained because the target side of the synthetic parallel texts consists of manually created (correct) sentences. Consequently, this method provides steady improvements. However, this approach may not contribute to the improvement of the encoder because the source side of the synthetic parallel texts are automatically generated.

In this paper, we extend the method proposed by Sennrich et al. (2016a) to enhance the encoder and attention using target monolingual corpora. Our proposed method generates multiple source sentences by sampling when each target sentence is translated back. By using multiple source sentences, we aim to achieve the following.

- To average errors in individual synthetic sentences and reduce their harmful effects.

- To ensure diversity as human translations. This is a countermeasure against machine-translated sentences that have less variety.

The remainder of this paper is organized as follows. Section 2 provides an overview of related work that uses monolingual corpora in NMT. Section 3 describes the proposed method, and Section 4 evaluates the proposed method through experiments. In addition, Section 5 proposes the application of our method as a self-training approach. Finally, Section 6 concludes the paper.

2 Related Work

One approach of using target monolingual corpora is to construct a recurrent neural network language model and combine the model with the decoder (Gülçehere et al., 2015; Sriram et al., 2017). Similarly, there is a method of training language models, jointly with the translator, using multi-task learning (Domhan and Hieber, 2017). These

55

Proceedings of the 2nd Workshop on Neural Machine Translation and Generation, pages 55–63
Melbourne, Australia, July 20, 2018. ©2018 Association for Computational Linguistics

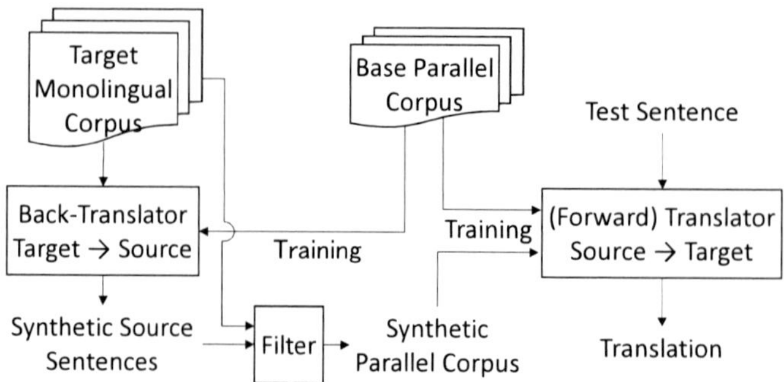

Figure 1: Flow of Our Approach

methods only enhance the decoder and require a modification of the NMT.

Another approach of using monolingual corpora of the target language is to learn models using synthetic parallel sentences. The method of Sennrich et al. (2016a) generates synthetic parallel corpora through back-translation and learns models from such corpora. Our proposed method is an extension of this method. Currey et al. (2017) generated synthetic parallel sentences by copying target sentences to the source. This method utilizes a feature in which some words, such as named entities, are often identical across the source and target languages and do not require translation. However, this method provides no benefits to language pairs having different character sets, such as English and Japanese.

On the other hand, the basis of source monolingual corpora, a pre-training method based on an autoencoder has been proposed to enhance the encoder (Zhang and Zong, 2016). However, the decoder is not enhanced by this method. Cheng et al. (2016) trained two autoencoders using source and target monolingual corpora, while translation models are trained using a parallel corpus. This method enhances both the encoder and decoder, but it requires two monolingual corpora, respectively. Our proposed method enhances not only the decoder but also the encoder and attention using target monolingual corpora.

3 Proposed Method

3.1 Synthetic Source Sentences

The back-translator used in this study is an NMT trained on a small parallel corpus (hereinafter referred to as the base parallel corpus). Each sentence in a target monolingual corpus is translated

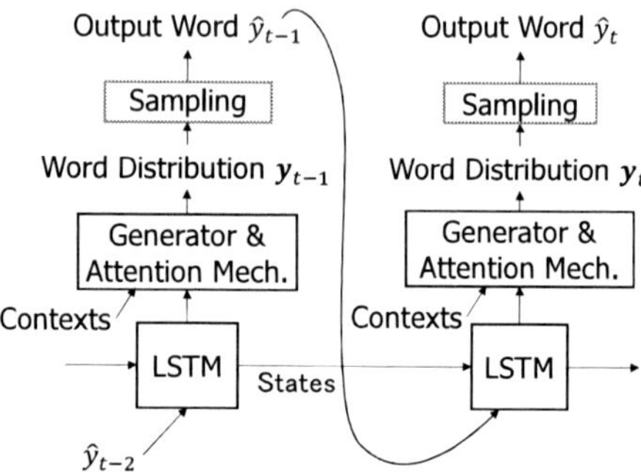

Figure 2: Decoding Process of Back-Translator

by the back-translator to generate synthetic source sentences. The back-translator does not output only high-likelihood sentences but generates sentences by random sampling.

Figure 2 illustrates the decoding process of the back-translator. When the decoder generates a sentence word-by-word, it also generates the posterior probability distribution of an output word $\Pr(y_t)$ through the decoding process. We call this a word distribution. In a usual decoding process, the output word $\hat{y}_t$ is determined by selecting a word with the highest probability (if the decoder outputs 1-best translation by greedy search). [1]

$$\hat{y}_t = \underset{y_t}{\operatorname{argmax}} \Pr(y_t|\boldsymbol{y}_{<t}, \boldsymbol{x}), \qquad (1)$$

where $\boldsymbol{y}_{<t}$ and $\boldsymbol{x}$ are the history of the output words and the input word sequence, respectively.

In contrast, the back-translator in this paper determines the output word by sampling based on the

---

[1] In translation, an output sentence is generally generated from multiple hypotheses using beam search. However, it is the same that the beam search selects high-likelihood words.

Log-likelihood	Synthetic Source Sentence
-2.25	what should i do when i get injured or sick in japan ?
-2.38	what should i do *if* i get injured or sick in japan ?
-5.20	what should i do *if* i get injured or *illness* in japan ?
-5.52	what should *we* do when *we* get injured or sick in japan ?
-13.87	*if i get injured or a sickness in japan , what shall i do ?*
Target Sentence	日本 で 怪我 や 病気 を し た とき は どう すれ ば いい の でしょう か ？
Manual Back-Translation	what should i do when i get injured or sick in japan ?

Table 1: Examples of Synthetic Source Sentences (English-Japanese Translation): The italicized words indicate differences with the manual back-translation.

word distribution.

$$\hat{y}_t = \operatorname*{sampling}_{y_t}(\Pr(y_t|\boldsymbol{y}_{<t}, \boldsymbol{x})), \qquad (2)$$

where $\operatorname{sampling}_y(P)$ denotes the sampling operation of y based on the probability distribution P. The decoding continues until the end-of-sentence symbol is generated.[2] We repeat the above process to generate multiple synthetic sentences. Note that this generation method is the same as that of the minimum risk training (Shen et al., 2016).

In NMT, even if a low-probability word is selected by the sampling, the subsequent word would become fluent because it is conditioned by the history. Table 1 presents examples of the synthetic source sentences produced by the back-translator. Most of the synthetic source sentences are identical, or close to, the manual back-translation (i.e., the reference translation). On the other hand, the last example is quite different from the perspective of word order because the clauses are inverted. Such a synthetic sentence is usually not produced by the n-best translation because of the low likelihood. However, it is possible to generate diverse source sentences by sampling.

The sampling occasionally generates identical sentences as a result. However, we did not remove the duplication to reflect the original probability distribution.

3.2 Training

The synthetic source sentences are paired with the target sentences to construct the synthetic parallel corpus. The NMT model is trained on a mixture of the synthetic corpus and the base parallel corpus.

In the training, we must deal with the two different types of sentence pairs. In addition, if we use multiple source sentences for a given target sentence, the model will be biased toward the synthetic corpus. To avoid this problem, we adjust the learning rate according to the size of the corpora. Specifically, we first configure two mini-batch sets each from the base and synthetic corpora. Thereafter, the learning rate η/N is applied to the mini-batches of the synthetic corpus, in contrast to the learning rate η for those of the base corpus, where N denotes the number of synthetic source sentences per target sentence. Finally, the two sets are shuffled and used for training.

The training time increases along with the increase of data. However, the translation speed does not change because the model structure is not changed.

It must be noted that if the domains of the base parallel and the target monolingual corpora are different, it is better to perform "further training" using the base parallel corpus for domain adaptation (Freitag and Al-Onaizan, 2016; Servan et al., 2016). [3]

3.3 Filtering of Synthetic Parallel Sentences

The synthetic source sentences contain errors. A direct approach to reduce such errors involves filtering the sentence pairs according to their quality. In this paper, we consider the following three methods.

3.3.1 Likelihood Filtering

The first method is filtering by the likelihood output from the back-translator. We consider the likelihood as an indicator of translation quality, and low-likelihood synthetic sentences are filtered

---

[2] The back-translator does not use the beam search because the sampling is independently performed for each word.

[3] We did not perform "further training" in this paper.

out. Note that the likelihood is corrected with the length of the synthetic source sentence. We call this the length biased log-likelihood ll_{len} (Oda et al., 2017).

$$ll_{\text{len}}(\boldsymbol{y}|\boldsymbol{x}) = \sum_t \log \Pr(y_t|\boldsymbol{x}, \boldsymbol{y}_{<t}) + WP{\cdot}T, \quad (3)$$

where the first term on the right-hand side is the log-likelihood, WP denotes the word penalty ($WP \geq 0$), and T denotes the number of words in the synthetic source sentence.

NMTs tend to generate shorter translations than the expectation (Morishita et al., 2017). The word penalty works to increase the likelihood of long hypotheses when it is set to a positive value. With an appropriate value, we can obtain synthetic sentences that are almost of the same length as the manual back-translation. We set the word penalty such that the lengths of the translation and reference translation on the development set are approximately equal, using line search.

3.3.2 Confidence Filtering

The second method involves filtering with the confidence of translation used in the translation quality estimation task. We use the data provided by Fujita and Sumita (2017), which is a collection of manual labels indicating whether the translation is acceptable or not. We train the support vector machines (SVMs) on the sentence-level data and regard the classifier's score as the confidence score.

The features of the SVM classifier include the 17 basic features of QuEst++ (Specia et al., 2015).[4] They are roughly categorized into the following two types.

- Language model features of each of the source and target sentences.

- Features based on the parallel sentences such as the average number of translation hypotheses per word.

In addition, we add the source and target word embeddings. The sentence features are computed by averaging all word embeddings (Shah et al., 2016). The hyperparameters for the training are set using the grid search on the development set.

In the expriments of Section 4, features are extracted from the base parallel corpus.

	Type	# Sentences
Parallel	Base	400,000
	Development	2,000
	Test	2,000
Monolingual	GCP Corpus	1,552,475
(Japanese)	BCCWJ	4,791,336

Table 2: Corpus Statistics

3.3.3 Random Filtering

The third method is random filtering. This is identical to the reduction of the number of synthetic source sentences to be generated.

4 Experiments

4.1 Experimental Settings

Corpora The corpus sizes used here are shown in Table 2. We used the global communication plan corpus (the GCP corpus, (Imamura and Sumita, 2018)), which is an in-house parallel corpus of daily life conversations and consists of Japanese (Ja), English (En), and Chinese (Zh). The experiments were performed on English-to-Japanese and Chinese-to-Japanese translation tasks. We randomly selected 400K sentences for the base parallel corpus, and the remaining (1.55M sentences) were used as the Japanese monolingual corpus. The reason for dividing the parallel corpus into two corpora is to measure the upper-bound of quality improvement by using existing parallel texts on the same domain as the manual back-translation.

We also used the Balanced Corpus of Contemporary Written Japanese (BCCWJ)[5] as a monolingual corpus from a different domain. We used approximately 4.8M sentences, each of which contains less than 1024 characters. We assume practical situations in which the domains of parallel and monolingual corpora are not identical.

All sentences were segmented into words using an in-house word segmenter. The words were further segmented into 16K sub-words based on the byte-pair encoding rules (Sennrich et al., 2016b) acquired from the base parallel corpus for each language independently.

Translation System The translation system used in this study was OpenNMT (Klein et al., 2017). We modified it to accept Sections 3.1 and 3.2.

---

[4]http://www.quest.dcs.shef.ac.uk/

[5]http://pj.ninjal.ac.jp/corpus_center/bccwj/en/

The encoder was comprised of a two-layer Bi-LSTM (500 + 500 units), the decoder included a two-layer LSTM (1,000 units), and the stochastic gradient descent was used for optimization. The learning rate for the base parallel corpus was 1.0 for the first 14 epochs, followed by the annealing of 6 epochs while decreasing the learning rate by half. The mini-batch size was 64.

At the translation stage, we generated 10-best translations and selected the best among them on the basis of the length reranking (Morishita et al., 2017). Equation 3 was used as the score function for the reranking. By correcting the translation length, the translation quality can be compared without the effect of the brevity penalty of the BLEU score.

The back-translator was comprised of the same system. We generated 10 synthetic source sentences per target sentence using the method described in Section 3.1, and filtered them to create synthetic parallel sentences.

Competing Methods In this paper, we consider the case in which only the base parallel corpus is used as the baseline, and the case in which the manual back-translation of the GCP corpus is added as the upper-bound of the translation quality. Thereafter, we compare the following methods and settings:

- Various numbers of synthetic source sentences for a given target sentence
- The methods for generating synthetic source sentences: sampling vs. n-best generation
- The three filtering methods described in Section 3.3

Evaluation BLEU (Papineni et al., 2002) was used for the evaluation. The multeval tool (Clark et al., 2011)[6] was used for statistical testing at a significance level of 5% ($p < 0.05$).

4.2   Results with GCP Corpus

Figures 3 and 4 depict the relationship between the number of synthetic source sentences and the BLEU score on the GCP corpus of En-Ja and Zh-Ja translation tasks, respectively. The graphs and tables in the figures present the same data for overviews and for analyzing the data in detail. Note that the method of Sennrich et al. (2016a) corresponds to the case of one synthetic source

sentence of the n-best generation (i.e., 1-best generation).

In both En-Ja and Zh-Ja translation, the score was improved when multiple synthetic sentences were given. Even though the method of Sennrich et al. (2016a) achieved improvements of +2.42 and +2.38 BLEU points from the base corpus only for En-Ja and Zh-Ja translations, respectively, further improvements were observed by using multiple synthetic sentences. Since the target sentences were the same in all cases except for the base corpus only, we can conclude that providing multiple source sentences is effective for improving the encoder and attention.[7]

The improvements from the base corpus only to the manual back-translation reached +4.86 and +5.29 BLEU points in En-Ja and Zh-Ja translations, respectively. When we focus on the case in which the number of synthetic source sentences is 6, for example, the improvements in the proposed methods (the likelihood, confidence, and random filtering) were achieved at least +4.08 and +5.01 BLEU points. This means that more than 80% of improvements with the manual back-translation were achieved using only monolingual corpora. Nevertheless, all methods did not reach the BLEU score of the manual back-translation; thus, we cannot substitute parallel corpora with monolingual corpora.

When we compared the three filtering methods, the BLEU scores were almost equivalent in most cases. In fact, there were no significant differences among filtering methods in all cases of Zh-Ja translation. In En-Ja translation, there were some significantly different cases, but the significance was not consistently derived.

When the synthetic source generation was changed to the n-best generation, the BLEU scores were visibly degraded relative to the proposed method (i.e., sampling). We speculate that the likelihood and confidence filtering were ineffective because of the high-quality back-translator, and the diversity of the synthetic source sentences contributed considerably to quality improvement.

4.3   Results with BCCWJ

Table 3 shows the results using BCCWJ as a monolingual corpus (the results of the GCP cor-

---

[6]https://github.com/jhclark/multeval

[7]Unfortunately, it is unknown in this experiment whether the encoder or attention were enhanced. We plan to investigate which module is enhanced by freezing parameters (Zoph et al., 2016) of the encoder and attention through the training.

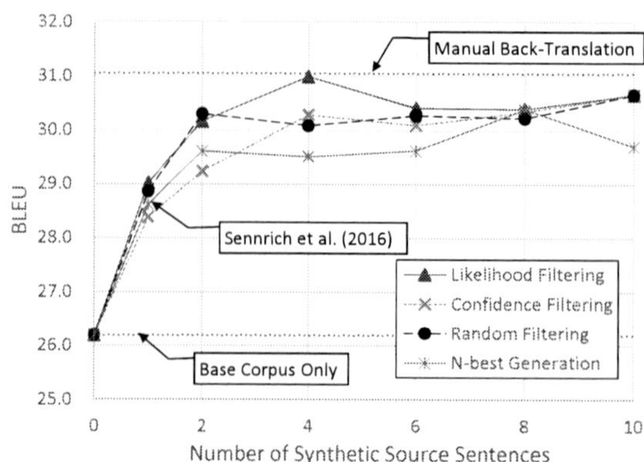

| # of Synthetic | En-Ja | | | |
Sentences	Likelihood Filtering	Confidence Filtering	Random Filtering	N-best Generation
Base Corpus Only	26.19			
Sennrich et al. (2016a)	28.61 (+2.42)			
1	29.01 (+2.82)	28.49 (+2.30)	28.85 (+2.66)	28.61 (+2.42)
2	30.16 (+3.97)	29.26 (+3.07)	30.30 (+4.11)	29.61 (+3.42)
4	30.99 (+4.80)	30.26 (+4.07)	30.08 (+3.89)	29.51 (+3.32)
6	30.41 (+4.22)	30.59 (+4.40)	30.27 (+4.08)	29.62 (+3.43)
8	30.39 (+4.20)	30.53 (+4.34)	30.22 (+4.03)	30.39 (+4.20)
10	30.66 (+4.47)	30.66 (+4.47)	30.66 (+4.47)	29.70 (+3.51)
Manual Back-Translation	31.05 (+4.86)			

Figure 3: The BLEU scores using the GCP corpus (English-Japanese translation) represented by a graph and table. The bracketed values of the table indicate differences from those of the base corpus only.

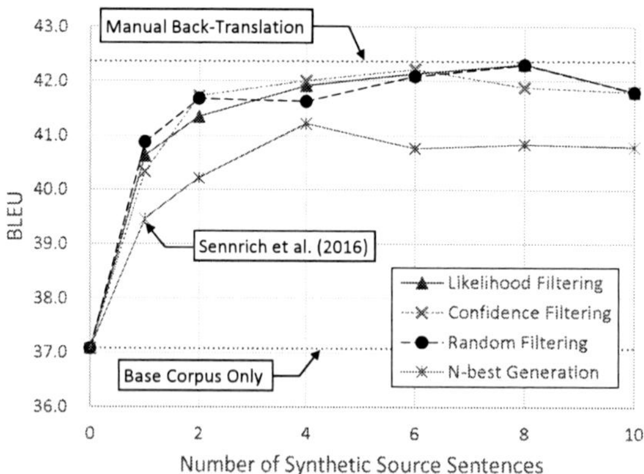

| # of Synthetic | Zh-Ja | | | |
Sentences	Likelihood Filtering	Confidence Filtering	Random Filtering	N-best Generation
Base Corpus Only	37.08			
Sennrich et al. (2016a)	39.46 (+2.38)			
1	40.63 (+3.55)	40.34 (+3.26)	40.88 (+3.80)	39.46 (+2.38)
2	41.35 (+4.27)	41.73 (+4.65)	41.68 (+4.60)	40.22 (+3.14)
4	41.92 (+4.84)	42.01 (+4.93)	41.63 (+4.55)	41.22 (+4.14)
6	42.14 (+5.06)	42.22 (+5.14)	42.09 (+5.01)	40.77 (+3.69)
8	42.31 (+5.23)	41.89 (+4.81)	42.30 (+5.22)	40.84 (+3.76)
10	41.80 (+4.72)	41.80 (+4.72)	41.80 (+4.72)	40.79 (+3.71)
Manual Back-Translation	42.37 (+5.29)			

Figure 4: The BLEU scores using the GCP corpus (Chinese-Japanese translation) represented by a graph and table. The bracketed values of the table indicate differences from those of the base corpus only.

# of Synthetic Source Sentences	BCCWJ BLEU	GCP Corpus BLEU
0 (Base Corpus Only)	26.19	
1	29.84	29.01
2	29.94	30.16
4	30.66	30.99
Manual Back-Translation	-	31.05

Table 3: The BLEU scores of the BCCWJ and GCP corpora according to the number of synthetic source sentences (En-Ja, the random filtering).

	Sampling	N-best Gen.
BLEU	15.05	21.55
Edit Distance		
A) between SYN and MAN	9.73	8.52
B) among SYNs	9.34	3.90

Table 4: The BLEU scores and the edit distances of synthetic source sentences based on 10 synthetic sentences and manual back-translation for the same 1,000 target sentences in the GCP corpus.

pus are also shown for reference). In this study, we only performed random filtering experiments on En-Ja translation due to resource limitations.

In the case of BCCWJ, the BLEU scores increased with the number of synthetic source sentences, similar to the GCP corpus. We cannot directly compare the scores of the two corpora; however, similar improvement was achieved when we used a several-fold size of the different domain monolingual corpus.

4.4 Analysis

The above experiments consider diversity under the following two assumptions.

- The number of synthetic source sentences indicates the diversity.

- The diversity of the synthetic sentences by sampling is higher than that of the n-best generation.

In this section, we quantify the diversity using the edit distance among the systhetic source sentences to compare the generation methods.

We sampled 1,000 Japanese sentences from the GCP corpus in En-Ja translation with their ten corresponding back-translations generated by each method. Table 4 shows the results. The BLEU scores were computed regarding the 10,000 sentences as a document. The edit distances were

computed for the following two cases, setting the insertion, deletion, and substitution costs to 1.0.

A) The average distance between a synthetic sentence (SYN) and the manual back-translation (MAN; i.e., reference translation). Note that this value also indicates translation quality because it is a source for computing the word error rate (smaller value represents better quality).

B) The average distance among synthetic source sentences of a target sentence ($_{10}C_2 = 45$ combinations per target sentence).

As for the BLEU scores in Table 4, the sampling method achieved a lower score than that of the n-best generation. Similarly, the edit distance A of the sampling had a larger value than that of the n-best generation. These results imply that the sampling generates poor synthetic sentences. However, these scores are influenced by the diversity because they naturally become worse along with the variety of synthetic sentences when they are computed using a single reference.

On the other hand, as for edit distance B, the distance of the n-best generation was less than half of that of the sampling, even though sentences of the sampling generation can include identical sentences. Intuitively, the n-best generation generates similar sentences where only few words are different. As shown in Table 4, the distances of the synthetic sentences by sampling were almost the same as those from the manual back-translation, and the distances by the n-best generation were not. This result verifies that the generation by sampling increases the diversity of the synthetic source sentences.

5 Application to Self-Training Using Parallel Corpora

In this paper, we enhanced the encoder and attention using target monolingual corpora. Our proposed method can be applied to a self-training method only using parallel corpora. Specifically, we train a back-translator using a given parallel corpus, and the target side of the parallel corpus is translated into the source. Then, the original and synthetic parallel corpora are mixed. We finally train the forward translator using this corpus to enhance the encoder.

# of Source Sentences	BLEU
1 (Manual Bitexts Only)	31.05
2 (Manual Bitexts + 1 Syn. Sentence)	31.29
4 (Manual Bitexts + 3 Syn. Sentences)	31.65
6 (Manual Bitexts + 5 Syn. Sentences)	31.75
8 (Manual Bitexts + 7 Syn. Sentences)	32.25
10 (Manual Bitexts + 9 Syn. Sentences)	32.28

Table 5: The effect of self-training (En-Ja translation)

5.1 Settings

We confirm whether the quality can be improved from the upper-bound of the experiments in Section 4.

The experimental settings were the same as those of Section 4 except for the corpora. We considered the mixture of the base and GCP corpora (including the manual back-translation) in Table 2 as the original parallel corpus, with 1.95M sentences. The monolingual corpus was the target side of the entire parallel corpus. The back-translator generated nine synthetic source sentences, and they were randomly filtered. The original and synthetic parallel corpora were concatenated to train the forward translator. Namely, the number of source sentences per target sentence was at most ten.

In this experiment, we used the learning rate η for the original parallel corpus and η/N for the synthetic parallel corpus, where N denotes the number of synthetic source sentences per target sentence. The learning rate was $\eta = 0.5$, which means 1.0 for a target sentence in total.

5.2 Results

Table 5 shows the BLEU scores in the En-Ja translation according to the number of source sentences. Similar to the results in Section 4, the BLEU scores increased along with the increase in the number of source sentences. When we added nine synthetic source sentences, the BLEU score was improved by $+1.23$ points in comparison to the manual bitext only. Therefore, by increasing the diversity of the manual translation using synthetic sentences, we can further enhance the encoder and attention.

6 Conclusions

In this paper, we enhanced the encoder and attention by using multiple synthetic source sentences, in which target monolingual corpora were trans-lated by sampling. During the training, we used different learning rates for the base and synthetic parallel corpora to avoid overfitting to the synthetic corpus. As a result, the translation quality was improved by increasing the number of synthetic source sentences for a given target sentence, and the quality approached that of the manual back-translation. In addition, we confirmed the generation by sampling synthesized diverse source sentences and consequently improved the translation quality in comparison with the n-best generation. We also attempted some filtering methods on the synthetic source sentences to obtain improved parallel sentences, but we could not confirm their effectiveness in our experiments.

Our future work is to clarify the other conditions where the proposed method is effective, such as the relationship between qualities of the backward and forward translations, experiments on public data sets, and comparison with the number of synthetic sentences and monolingual corpus size at the same training time. In addition, we plan to consider other applications, such as applying our methods to smaller parallel corpora and using source monolingual corpora.

Acknowledgments

The authors appreciate anonymous reviewers for their helpful comments.

This work was supported by "Promotion of Global Communications Plan — Research and Development and Social Demonstration of Multilingual Speech Translation Technology," a program of the Ministry of Internal Affairs and Communications, Japan.

References

Dzmitry Bahdanau, Kyunghyun Cho, and Yoshua Bengio. 2014. Neural machine translation by jointly learning to align and translate. *CoRR*, abs/1409.0473.

Yong Cheng, Wei Xu, Zhongjun He, Wei He, Hua Wu, Maosong Sun, and Yang Liu. 2016. Semi-supervised learning for neural machine translation. In *Proceedings of the 54th Annual Meeting of the Association for Computational Linguistics (Volume 1: Long Papers)*, pages 1965–1974, Berlin, Germany.

Jonathan H. Clark, Chris Dyer, Alon Lavie, and Noah A. Smith. 2011. Better hypothesis testing for statistical machine translation: Controlling for optimizer instability. In *Proceedings of the 49th Annual Meeting of the Association for Computational*

Linguistics: Human Language Technologies, pages 176–181, Portland, Oregon, USA.

Anna Currey, Antonio Valerio Miceli Barone, and Kenneth Heafield. 2017. Copied monolingual data improves low-resource neural machine translation. In *Proceedings of the Second Conference on Machine Translation*, pages 148–156, Copenhagen, Denmark.

Tobias Domhan and Felix Hieber. 2017. Using target-side monolingual data for neural machine translation through multi-task learning. In *Proceedings of the 2017 Conference on Empirical Methods in Natural Language Processing*, pages 1500–1505, Copenhagen, Denmark.

Markus Freitag and Yaser Al-Onaizan. 2016. Fast domain adaptation for neural machine translation. *CoRR*, abs/1612.06897.

Atsushi Fujita and Eiichiro Sumita. 2017. Japanese to English/Chinese/Korean datasets for translation quality estimation and automatic post-editing. In *Proceedings of the 4th Workshop on Asian Translation (WAT2017)*, pages 79–88, Taipei, Taiwan.

Çaglar Gülçehere, Orhan Firat, Kelvin Xu, Kyunghyun Cho, Loïc Barrault, Huei-Chi Ling, Fethi Bougares, Holger Schwenk, and Yoshua Bengio. 2015. On using monolingual corpora in neural machine translation. In *CoRR, abs/1503.03535*.

Kenji Imamura and Eiichiro Sumita. 2018. Multilingual parallel corpus for global communication plan. In *Proceedings of the Eleventh International Conference on Language Resources and Evaluation (LREC 2018)*, pages 3453–3458, Miyazaki, Japan.

Guillaume Klein, Yoon Kim, Yuntian Deng, Jean Senellart, and Alexander M. Rush. 2017. OpenNMT: Open-source toolkit for neural machine translation. In *Proceedings of ACL 2017, System Demonstrations*, pages 67–72, Vancouver, Canada.

Makoto Morishita, Jun Suzuki, and Masaaki Nagata. 2017. NTT neural machine translation systems at WAT 2017. In *Proceedings of the 4th Workshop on Asian Translation (WAT2017)*, pages 89–94, Taipei, Taiwan.

Yusuke Oda, Katsuhito Sudoh, Satoshi Nakamura, Masao Utiyama, and Eiichiro Sumita. 2017. A simple and strong baseline: NAIST-NICT neural machine translation system for WAT2017 English-Japanese translation task. In *Proceedings of the 4th Workshop on Asian Translation (WAT2017)*, pages 135–139, Taipei, Taiwan.

Kishore Papineni, Salim Roukos, Todd Ward, and Wei-Jing Zhu. 2002. Bleu: a method for automatic evaluation of machine translation. In *Proceedings of the 40th Annual Meeting of the Association for Computational Linguistics (ACL)*, pages 311–318, Philadelphia, Pennsylvania, USA.

Rico Sennrich, Barry Haddow, and Alexandra Birch. 2016a. Improving neural machine translation models with monolingual data. In *Proceedings of the 54th Annual Meeting of the Association for Computational Linguistics (ACL-2016, Volume 1: Long Papers)*, pages 86–96, Berlin, Germany.

Rico Sennrich, Barry Haddow, and Alexandra Birch. 2016b. Neural machine translation of rare words with subword units. In *Proceedings of the 54th Annual Meeting of the Association for Computational Linguistics (Volume 1: Long Papers)*, pages 1715–1725, Berlin, Germany.

Christophe Servan, Josep Maria Crego, and Jean Senellart. 2016. Domain specialization: a post-training domain adaptation for neural machine translation. *CoRR*, abs/1612.06141.

Kashif Shah, Fethi Bougares, Loïc Barrault, and Lucia Specia. 2016. Shef-lium-nn: Sentence level quality estimation with neural network features. In *Proceedings of the First Conference on Machine Translation*, pages 838–842, Berlin, Germany.

Shiqi Shen, Yong Cheng, Zhongjun He, Wei He, Hua Wu, Maosong Sun, and Yang Liu. 2016. Minimum risk training for neural machine translation. In *Proceedings of the 54th Annual Meeting of the Association for Computational Linguistics (Volume 1: Long Papers)*, pages 1683–1692, Berlin, Germany.

Lucia Specia, Gustavo Paetzold, and Carolina Scarton. 2015. Multi-level translation quality prediction with quest++. In *Proceedings of ACL-IJCNLP 2015 System Demonstrations*, pages 115–120, Beijing, China.

Anuroop Sriram, Heewoo Jun, Sanjeev Satheesh, and Adam Coates. 2017. Cold fusion: Training seq2seq models together with language models. *CoRR*, abs/1708.06426.

Ilya Sutskever, Oriol Vinyals, and Quoc V. Le. 2014. Sequence to sequence learning with neural networks. In *Proceedings of Advances in Neural Information Processing Systems 27 (NIPS 2014)*, pages 3104–3112.

Jiajun Zhang and Chengqing Zong. 2016. Exploiting source-side monolingual data in neural machine translation. In *Proceedings of the 2016 Conference on Empirical Methods in Natural Language Processing (EMNLP-2016)*, pages 1535–1545, Austin, Texas.

Barret Zoph, Deniz Yuret, Jonathan May, and Kevin Knight. 2016. Transfer learning for low-resource neural machine translation. In *Proceedings of the 2016 Conference on Empirical Methods in Natural Language Processing*, pages 1568–1575, Austin, Texas.

Document-Level Adaptation for Neural Machine Translation

Sachith Sri Ram Kothur[*]
Dept. of Computer Science
Johns Hopkins University
kothursachith@gmail.com

Rebecca Knowles[*]
Dept. of Computer Science
Johns Hopkins University
rknowles@jhu.edu

Philipp Koehn
Dept. of Computer Science
Johns Hopkins University
phi@jhu.edu

Abstract

It is common practice to adapt machine translation systems to novel domains, but even a well-adapted system may be able to perform better on a particular document if it were to learn from a translator's corrections within the document itself. We focus on adaptation within a single document – appropriate for an interactive translation scenario where a model adapts to a human translator's input over the course of a document. We propose two methods: *single-sentence adaptation* (which performs online adaptation one sentence at a time) and *dictionary adaptation* (which specifically addresses the issue of translating novel words). Combining the two models results in improvements over both approaches individually, and over baseline systems, even on short documents. On WMT news test data, we observe an improvement of +1.8 BLEU points and +23.3% novel word translation accuracy and on EMEA data (descriptions of medications) we observe an improvement of +2.7 BLEU points and +49.2% novel word translation accuracy.

1 Introduction

The challenge of adapting to a new domain is a well-studied problem in machine translation research. But even within a particular domain, each new document may pose unique challenges due to novelty of vocabulary, word senses, style, and more.[1] It stands to reason that fine-grained adaptation using sentences from within a document (for example, as it is being translated by a human translator in a computer aided translation (CAT) environment) could provide the added benefit of a closer in-domain match than existing approaches that use data from other documents within the same domain. We propose two complementary approaches to the treatment of novel words and fine-grained document-level adaptation of machine translation systems, and show that the combination of approaches outperforms each approach individually, resulting in BLEU point improvements of +1.8 and +2.7 across two domains, in addition to demonstrating improvements in novel word translation accuracy.

As Carpuat (2009) observed, there is a tendency for translators to produce translations such that the "one translation per discourse" hypothesis holds within a particular document.[2] That is, human translators tend to prefer consistent translations of individual terms throughout a document. Other work on "translationese" has also found that translations show regularities in syntax and punctuation (Baroni and Bernardini, 2005). Thus, even expanding beyond words with multiple senses, we expect that learning from the translator's lexical, syntactic, and stylistic choices at the beginning of a document should result in a well-tailored system that is better at translating subsequent sentences. We can think of fine-grained adaptation over a document as producing a document-specific machine translation system that encodes or highlights document context.

Continued training of neural machine translation (NMT) systems has been shown to be an effective and efficient way to tune them for a specific target domain (Luong and Manning, 2015). One such technique is incremental updating – comparing the system's predicted translation of an input sentence to a reference translation and then updat-

---

[*]These authors contributed equally to this work.

[1]Carpuat et al. (2012) decompose errors into seen, sense, score, and search; the first two are most relevant to our work.

[2]This work follows from "one sense per discourse" (Gale et al., 1992), which found that the vast majority of polysemous words share only one sense within a given document.

Proceedings of the 2nd Workshop on Neural Machine Translation and Generation, pages 64–73
Melbourne, Australia, July 20, 2018. ©2018 Association for Computational Linguistics

Source	Reference	Baseline MT Output
Ambirix (Ambi/rix)	Ambirix (Ambi/rix)	Hampshire, Glaurix, Tandemrix, ...
Prepandemic (Prep/an/demic)	Präpandemischer (Prä/pandem/ischer)	Proteasehemmer
Cataplexy (Cat/ap/lex/y)	Kataplexie (Kat/ap/lex/ie)	Cataplexy
hormone-dependent (hormon/e-/dependent)	hormonabhängig (hormon/abhängig)	hormonell

Table 1: Examples of novel words and their mistranslations. The subword segmentation (in parentheses) is indicated by "/" for the source and reference.

ing the model parameters to improve future predictions. Though this is typically done in batches during training, a single sentence pair or even a word and its translation can be treated as a training instance.

Computer aided translation provides an ideal use case for exploring model adaptation at such a fine granularity. As a human translator works, each sentence that they translate (or each novel word for which they provide a translation) can then be used as a new training example for a neural machine translation system. In an interactive translation setting or a post-editing scenario, rapid incremental updating of the neural model will allow the neural system to adapt to an individual translator, a particular new domain, or novel vocabulary over the course of a document.

In an open-vocabulary NMT system that uses byte-pair encoding (Sennrich et al., 2016b), tokens that were never seen in training data are represented as sequences of known subword units. These may sometimes be successfully translated (or copied, subword by subword, when appropriate) on the first try, but sometimes systems generate incorrect translations or even nonsensical words. Table 1 shows example mistranslations of novel words.

We test our two complementary approaches to document-level NMT adaptation (dictionary training and single-sentence adaptation) on two very different domains: news and formal descriptions of medications, each of which provide their own challenges. In our datasets, just under 80% of news documents and just over 90% of medical documents contain at least one word that was unobserved in the training data. In the news documents, 12.8% of lines contain at least one novel word, whereas in the medical data, 38.3% of lines contain at least one novel word. We show that models can learn to correctly translate novel vocabulary items and can adapt to document-specific terminology usage and style, even in short documents.

2   Related Work

This work relates closely to three lines of research on neural machine translation models: rare word translation, copying mechanisms, and domain adaptation. Concerns about rare words and copying mechanisms are closely linked; words that need to be copied (or nearly copied) are often proper names or technical vocabulary, which may be infrequent or unobserved in training data.

Arthur et al. (2016) propose to improve the translation of rare (low-frequency) content words through the use of translation probabilities from discrete lexicons. Nguyen and Chiang (2018) propose to train a feed-forward neural network to generate a target word based directly on a source word. Both then weight these probabilities using the attention mechanism and combine them with the standard translation approach. Gu et al. (2016) propose a (monolingual) sequence-to-sequence model, COPYNET, that can select input sequences to copy to the output within the course of generating a single sequence. All of these approaches require modifications to the neural network architecture. Additionally, some require knowledge of the rare words during training, meaning they are inapplicable to novel words.

By modifying the available training data rather than the neural architecture, Currey et al. (2017) find that training a neural machine translation system to do both translation and copying of target language text improves results on low-resource neural machine translation and learns to pass untranslated words through to the target. They do this by mixing monolingual target data (as source-target pairs) with parallel training data. In contrast, Khayrallah and Koehn (2018) find that this dramatically hurts performance (in a higher-resource setting). Ott et al. (2018) provide additional analysis of copying behavior. Fadaee et al. (2017) propose to learn better translations of rare words by generating new sentences that include them to add to the training data.

Domain adaptation has long been an area of interest for researchers in the machine translation community and is relevant both to the translation of new words and to more general improvements in translation quality. Recent work (Freitag and Al-Onaizan, 2016; Luong and Manning, 2015) has proposed to do domain adaptation for NMT systems by training a general system then fine-tuning by continuing to train using only in-domain data (typically a smaller dataset). Wang et al. (2017) present a similar approach where they weight each source-target sentence pair during training based on scores from in-domain and out-of-domain language models. Kobus et al. (2017) use special tokens to indicate domain. Chu et al. (2017) compare the approaches. These approaches typically use larger amounts of in-domain data to do adaptation, far greater than the amounts that might be available in a CAT setting. Cettolo et al. (2014) proposed adapting statistical phrase-based machine translation systems to particular projects (multiple documents) and Peris and Casacuberta (2018) propose adapting neural machine translation systems in CAT settings. Neither explore very small amounts of data at the sub-document level.

Two recent papers have tried a domain adaptation approach using very small data sizes, ranging from 1 sentence to 128 sentences (Farajian et al., 2017; Li et al., 2016). They adapt models for new sentences by training on sentence pairs from a training corpus (or translation memory) that are similar to the new sentence, which means they cannot adapt to novel vocabulary.

3 Approaches

We propose two complementary approaches for adapting an NMT model over the course of a single document's translation and the combination of the two. For each approach, adaptation is done at a document level and the model is reset to baseline between documents.[3]

3.1 Single-Sentence Adaptation

In this approach, the model is iteratively adapted over the previous translated sentence (and its reference), then the updated model is used to translate the next sentence. Thus, line n of the document is translated by a model which has been incrementally adapted to all previous lines (1 through $n-1$)

---

[3]In cases where the domain is fairly homogeneous, it may be beneficial *not* to reset the model between documents, while in heterogeneous domains it may be desirable to do so always. We leave this issue to future work.

of the document. See Algorithm 1 for details. Such an approach could be applied in a computer aided translation tool, which would allow the machine translation system to adapt to translator corrections as produced by post-editing or through an interactive translation prediction interface (Wuebker et al., 2016; Knowles and Koehn, 2016). Single-sentence adaptation allows the model to learn the translator's preferred translations, which may be specific to the particular document. For example, the system might initially produce a valid translation for a word in the document, while the translator prefers an alternate translation; after single-sentence adaptation, the system can learn to produce the translator's preferred translation in future sentences.

Algorithm 1 Single-Sentence Adaptation

1: M : Baseline Model
2: D : Set of Documents
3: **for** $d \in D$ **do**
4:     $\triangleright\, ref$: reference translation of d
5:     $\triangleright\, m_i$: model trained through i^{th} sentence
6:     $\triangleright\, d_i$: i^{th} line in d
7:     $\triangleright\, ref_i$: i^{th} line in ref
8:     $result \leftarrow \{\}$
9:     $m_0 \leftarrow M$
10:     **for** $i \leftarrow 1, \text{NUMLINES}(d)$ **do**
11:        $result_i \leftarrow \text{INFER}(m_{i-1}, d_i)$
12:        $m_i \leftarrow \text{ADAPT}(m_{i-1}, (d_i, ref_i))$
13:     **end for**
14:     $baseHyp \leftarrow \text{INFER}(M, d)$
15:     $baseScore \leftarrow \text{BLEU}(baseHyp, ref)$
16:     $adaptScore \leftarrow \text{BLEU}(result, ref)$
17: **end for**
18: $\triangleright$ We compare $baseScore$ and $adaptScore$

3.2 Dictionary Training

This approach aims to adapt models with the specific goal of better translating novel words. Given a new document to translate, we identify words that are novel (have not appeared in any training or adaptation data). Next, we obtain a single translation for each of these words (in a computer aided translation setting, this might consist of asking a human translator to provide translations; along the lines of terminology curation). In this work, we simulate the collection of such dictionaries (or terminology banks) using the reference. We then treat the list of novel words and their respective translations as bitext and continue model training, producing a model specifically adapted to this document's novel vocabulary, which we can then use to decode the complete document. Note that this is a very small bitext to train on, and each line of the bitext contains a single word (segmented into multiple tokens by byte-pair encoding).

To simulate a translator-produced dictionary, we build a dictionary of novel word translations from the source and reference. First we run fast-align (Dyer et al., 2013) over the byte-pair encoded representations of the source and reference sentences.[4] The target-side token whose subword segments most frequently align to the subword segments of the source-side token is selected as a candidate translation, and a single final translation is selected based on the most common candidate translation within the document.[5]

3.3 Single-Sentence Adaptation with Dictionary Training

Dictionary training and sentence adaptation offer distinct benefits when adapting over a document. Dictionary training helps the model learn the right translations for novel words and single-sentence adaptation can provide a more general adaptation. The latter can also learn correct translations of repeated novel words, but may require multiple instances to do so. Doing dictionary adaptation beforehand could ensure that the novel terminology is correctly and consistently translated from the beginning of the document, which could eliminate a pain point for human translators. In this combined approach, we begin with the document's dictionary trained model and use that as the initial model for single-sentence adaptation.

4 Data and Models

We use two distinct datasets and baseline models to evaluate our approaches, translating from English into German. We evaluate on WMT news data and EMEA medical data using baseline WMT and EMEA domain adapted models, respectively. The different domains (news vs. medical) allow us to evaluate our approaches in different scenarios.

4.1 WMT

WMT Data: We test on the full WMT 2017 news translation test set, splitting it into 130 unique documents (derived from the document splits in the original SGM file). Each document is a short news story. These stories are drawn from a number of news sources, covering a wide range of topics. While all documents are in the "news" domain, this is a fairly heterogeneous dataset. The documents range in length from 2 to 64 lines, with an average length of 22.1 lines (median 20).

We used the first 20 documents from the 2016 WMT news translation test set as a development set for selecting training parameters for dictionary training experiments, and a subset of 8 of these documents for selecting parameters for the single-sentence training experiments. The development set documents had a similar range of lengths (3 lines to 62 lines, with an average of 19.0).

The number of novel word types per document in our test set ranged from 0 (no novel words; no dictionary adaptation) to 15 novel words. There are 295 novel types (across all documents combined) and 442 novel tokens. Across the test set, 12.8% of lines contain at least one novel word. In some cases, up to 75% of the lines within a single document contain at least one novel word.

WMT Baseline Model: We use a publicly available English-German model.[6] The model is trained using Nematus (Sennrich et al., 2017) on the WMT parallel text, supplemented by synthetic back-translated data as described in Edinburgh's WMT 2016 submission (Sennrich et al., 2016a). They use byte-pair encoding (Sennrich et al., 2016b) to allow for (near) open-vocabulary NMT. The model uses 512 length word-embeddings with an hidden layer size of 1024. As this was trained for the 2016 WMT evaluation, both the 2016 and 2017 test sets can be safely used for development and testing, respectively, as they were not included in training data.

4.2 EMEA

EMEA Data: We use a subset[7] of the European Medicines Agency (EMEA) parallel corpus.[8] It consists of sentence-aligned documents focusing

---

[4]The fast-align model is trained over the byte-pair encoded representations of the full training data: WMT data, backtranslations released by Sennrich et al. (2016b), and EMEA data used for adaptation.

[5]Note that, particularly for words with morphological variants in the target language, there may have been more than one correct translation. We account for this in evaluation, but only train on one translation option.

[6]`data.statmt.org/rsennrich/wmt16_systems`

[7]We select only those documents labeled as "humandocs" and filter out documents that contain only or primarily highly-repetitive dosage information.

[8]`http://opus.lingfil.uu.se/EMEA.php`

on medical products (Tiedemann, 2009). The corpus contains high levels of domain-specific terminology and repetition, making it appropriate for this task. Each document describes a new medication, meaning that new documents contain novel vocabulary. The medication name is typically repeated frequently within the document. Other novel vocabulary items include highly-specific medical terminology; these tend to appear fewer times within the document.

We divide the documents into training, development, and test sets such that all documents about a particular medication are in the same set. Thus most novel medication names in the development and test data will have been unobserved in the training data. We use four splits of the data: 500 document pairs (375K sentence pairs) for training a baseline EMEA-adapted model, 22 document pairs (5K sentence pairs) as validation for that training, 5 document pairs (285 sentence pairs) for a small grid search over parameters, and 47 documents (2,755 sentence pairs) for testing.

Test documents ranged in length from 48 lines to 95 lines. In general, the EMEA documents have a greater variation in length than this (with some having 1000 or more lines). For data with 200 or more lines, considerable BLEU improvements have been documented with online adaptation and continued training. However, we seek to demonstrate that adaptation can be done with even shorter documents, and so focus this test set on documents with fewer than 100 lines.

The number of novel types per document in our test set ranged from 0 (no novel words; no dictionary adaptation) to 10 novel words. There are a total of 151 novel types (all documents combined) and 1,129 novel tokens. Across the test set, 38.3% of lines contain at least one novel word. In some cases, up to 63.5% of the lines within a single document contain at least one novel word. Some novel word types occurred more than 30 times within a single document.

EMEA Baseline Model: The WMT model is trained on data which is significantly different from the EMEA data's medical domain. We see considerable differences including vocabulary and sentence lengths. If we were to use the unadapted WMT model as our baseline, we might expect high gains from very small amounts of data due to the domain differences. Instead, in order to determine what marginal gains are possible in a real-life use scenario where a client already has access to a domain-specific model, we first adapt the WMT model on the EMEA train data so that it is familiar with the general style and vocabulary of the new dataset. Thus, improvements are attributable to document-specific adaptation rather than general domain adaptation.

We use the 375K sentence pair training set, validating on the 5K sentence pair development set, to perform continued training (Freitag and Al-Onaizan, 2016; Luong and Manning, 2015). We use the same subword vocabulary and preprocessing pipeline as the WMT model. We clip sentence lengths to 50 tokens and train with a batch size of 80 over 15 epochs. We use a learning rate of 0.001 with the Adam optimizer (Kingma and Ba, 2014).

While training, external validation is done every 1,000 batches and models are saved accordingly. We choose the model that gives the best validation score over the development set. Results are consistent with prior work: performance on the new domain peaks around the first few epochs and then tails off (Freitag and Al-Onaizan, 2016; Luong and Manning, 2015).

The performance of the baseline WMT model on the EMEA development set gives a BLEU score of 18.2. Our best adapted model gives a BLEU of 51.5. With over 30 points increase in BLEU, the adapted model is well-tuned to the EMEA corpus. We use this adapted model as the baseline for further document-level adaptation.

5 Experiments

The two domains and their respective baseline models provide us two distinct scenarios to evaluate our methodology. Both simulate a relatively data-rich realistic setting in which translators have completed translations of in-domain data and continue to work on new documents (with novel terminology) within that domain. Each domain provides its own challenges: the WMT data covers a wide range of topics and sources of news stories, while the EMEA data includes highly technical medical vocabulary, presented in fairly consistent ways. Due to the way our EMEA data splits were produced, this in particular means that the new EMEA documents will likely contain novel vocabulary (such as names of medications and other specific terminology). Similarly, we expect news stories to cover new names, locations, and more as news breaks over time.

Source	Breast-feeding should be stopped while taking Siklos .
Reference	Das Stillen sollte während der Behandlung mit Siklos eingestellt werden .
Baseline	Während der Einnahme von Xenlos sollte abgestillt werden .
Dict.-Adapt.	Während der Einnahme von Siklos sollte abgestillt werden .
Single-Sent.-Adapt.	Während der Behandlung mit Ivlos sollte abgestillt werden .
Dict.+Single-Sent.-Adapt.	Während der Behandlung mit Siklos sollte abgestillt werden .

Table 2: Complementary nature of two approaches: single-sentence approach learns the preferred translation of "while taking" ("Während der Behandlung"), but mistranslates *Siklos* as *Ivlos*. Dictionary training produces *Siklos* correctly, but makes no other changes. Combined, the overall translation is improved, though it would still require post-editing for correctness.

5.1 Single-Sentence Adaptation Experiments

For hyperparameter optimization, we did a complete grid search over a span of learning rates (0.1, 0.01, 0.001, 0.0001, 0.00001), train epochs (1, 5, 10, 20), and optimizers ($Adam$, SGD) on WMT data and a partial search on EMEA data. We use BLEU (Papineni et al. (2002)) to measure the effect of adaptation. We found the optimum configurations ($optim$, lr, $epochs$) of (SGD, 0.01, 5) for EMEA[9] and (SGD, 0.1, 20) for WMT. The difference in optimum configurations can be partly attributed to the different domains of the two datasets. We note that the best EMEA configuration matched the second-best WMT one.

5.2 Dictionary Training Experiments

For the EMEA dictionary experiments, we completed a grid search over number of epochs (1, 2, 5, 10) and learning rate (0.1, 0.5, 1.0) using SGD as the optimizer.[10] Finding consistent results, we ran a smaller grid search (epochs: 2 and 5 and learning rates 0.1, 0.5, and 1.0) over a development set of the first 20 documents from WMT 2016. Setting the learning rate and/or number of epochs too low resulted in minimal changes, while setting them too high resulted in pathological overfitting (loops of repeated tokens, etc.). Based on these initial experiments, we set a learning rate of 0.5 for both data sets, with 5 epochs for EMEA data and 2 epochs for WMT data. The parameters chosen were those that maximized BLEU score on the development sets.

5.3 Lexically Constrained Decoding Experiments

We compare our dictionary training approach against an approach that uses the same dictionaries

Model	BLEU	Nov. Acc.
EMEA-Adapt. Baseline	51.1	39.9%
Single-Sent. Adapt.	52.8	62.3%
Lex. Const. Decoding	50.4	86.5%
Dictionary Training	53.3	87.9%
Dict. + Single-Sent.	53.8	89.1%

Table 3: Results of baseline and dictionary training across the full set of EMEA test documents. Accuracy is computed for novel words only.

and enforces a lexical constraint: if one of the dictionary entries appears in the source, its translation (acquired as described in Section 3.2) must appear in the translated output. We do this using the grid beam search approach described in Hokamp and Liu (2017). Rather than adapting the underlying machine translation model, this approach constrains the search space to translations containing specified sub-sequences (in this case, the byte-pair encoded representations of the translation of any words from the dictionary which appears in the source sentence). We use the publicly released implementation for Nematus, with a beam size of 12.

5.4 Single Sentence Adaptation with Dictionary Training Experiments

Here we combine the approaches: for every document, we first do dictionary training. Using that as the starting point, we perform single sentence adaptation. We use the best hyperparameters obtained from the grid search for the individual methods.

6 Results & Analysis

We evaluate on two metrics. First, we compute BLEU over the full set of test documents and compare against the baseline translations. Across both domains, single-sentence adaptation provides consistent improvements in BLEU score (1.6 BLEU points on WMT data and 1.7 BLEU points on EMEA data). The dictionary training approach

---

[9]During hyperparameter selection, document lengths were clipped to the first 60 lines.

[10]We also considered lower learning rates (0.01, 0.001, 0.0001), but found that they did not result in much, if any, change to the model.

Model	BLEU	Nov. Acc.
WMT Baseline	25.1	48.9%
Single-Sent. Adapt.	26.7	58.4%
Lex. Const. Decoding	25.0	76.9%
Dictionary Training	25.1	71.7%
Dict. + Single-Sent.	26.9	72.2%

Table 4: Results of baseline and dictionary training across the full set of WMT test documents. Accuracy is computed for novel words only.

has more varied results. We see no clear improvement on the WMT data, but training on these small dictionaries does not *hurt* BLEU score overall. However, for the EMEA data, dictionary training produces a 2.2 BLEU point improvement. This gain can be primarily attributed to producing correct translations of the novel vocabulary, which can make a large difference in n-gram matches.[11] The lexically constrained decoding approach results in a decrease in BLEU score on both domains. Combining both dictionary training and single-sentence adaptation results in modest improvements (0.2 on WMT and 0.5 on EMEA) over the best single approach for each domain. Full results are shown in Tables 3 and 4. The combined approach produces improvements over the baseline for 79.2% of the WMT documents and 83.0% of the EMEA documents.

Figure 1 shows difference in BLEU produced by single-sentence adaptation as compared to the baseline on EMEA data. The overall trend is a net improvement in BLEU which shows up as early as 10 sentences from the start.

We also observe qualitative results that suggest that single-sentence adaptation is performing as expected, learning document- or translator-specific translations. For example, the baseline WMT system initially translates the English bigram "delicate operation" as "delikater Betrieb" while the reference translation prefers "heikle Tätigkeit" as the translation. In the next sentence in which "delicate operation" is observed, the sentence-adapted model successfully translates it as "heikle Tätigkeit" instead. Table 2 shows another example in which the two approaches combine to produce improvements.

We also compute accuracy for the translations of novel words. To compute accuracy, we first run

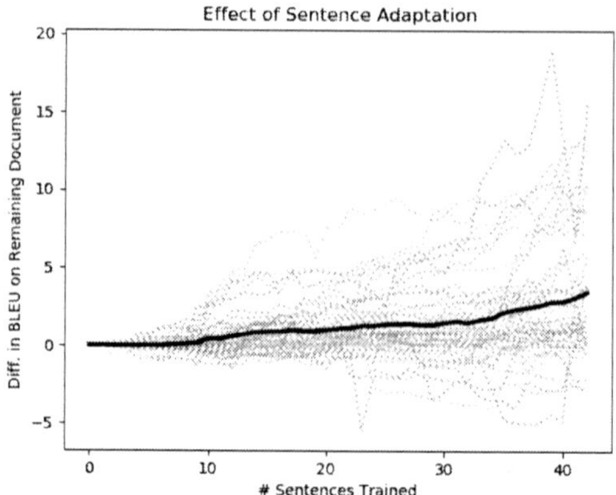

Figure 1: The X-axis shows the number of sentences to which the model has been adapted. The Y-axis shows the difference in BLEU score between this adapted model and the baseline on the document's remaining lines. Dotted lines represent individual documents; the average trend is shown in bold.

a trained fast-align model over the byte-pair encoded source and the byte-pair encoded reference. We use this alignment to map full tokens from the source to full tokens in the reference (as was done for producing the dictionaries). We then align the source sentence and the machine translation output the same way. For each instance of a novel word, we score its aligned machine translated token as correct if it matches the aligned reference token. The dictionary training approach shows, as expected, a major jump in translation accuracy. The single-sentence adaptation approach shows results between the baseline and the dictionary approach. Lexically constrained decoding underperforms dictionary training on EMEA data (in part because it sometimes produces medication names that are concatenated with other subwords, or produces the medication name more times than required), while it outperforms other methods on the WMT data (at a cost to the overall BLEU score, whereas all other methods produce improvements in BLEU). Table 3 shows that EMEA improves from a baseline accuracy of 39.9% to an accuracy of 87.9% after dictionary training, and Table 4 shows a slightly smaller jump from 48.9% to 71.7% for WMT. Both show slight improvements after combining single-sentence adaptation and dictionary training.

With this increase in accuracy comes an increase in consistency of translating the novel

---

[11] Consider the case of the baseline translation *Was ist AFluntis ?* and the (correct) dictionary-adapted version *Was ist Aflunov ?* – the former contains no 4-gram matches.

Model	WMT		EMEA	
	Copy	*Trans.*	*Copy*	*Trans.*
Baseline	80.8%	11.3%	41.9%	28.4%
S.-Sent.	87.9%	23.6%	67.2%	32.7%
Dict.	92.5%	47.3%	92.5%	60.5%
Dict. + S.	94.6%	45.8%	92.9%	66.7%

Table 5: Novel word accuracy divided into tokens to be copied (*Copy*) vs. translated (*Trans.*).

words. In the baseline EMEA-adapted model, the average type-token ratio[12] for translations of novel words that occur at least 3 times (in the source text) is 0.29. With dictionary adaptation, this drops to 0.14 – lower than the reference type-token ration of 0.16 – meaning that the new model produces the exact translation from the dictionary even when a variant (e.g. different case ending) may be appropriate. As we use only one translation per novel source token in the dictionaries used for training, the model overfits slightly. This issue could potentially be alleviated by training on multiple translation options, at the risk of introducing errors from incorrect alignments.

We perform more detailed analysis across two kinds of novel words: those which should simply be copied from source to target (e.g. medication names) and those which must be translated. Table 5 shows results for the baseline and our approaches. WMT data is almost evenly split between these: 46.8% of novel types (54.1% of tokens) must by copied, while EMEA data is skewed towards words that should be copied, with 51.7% of novel types (85.7% of tokens). On WMT data, baseline accuracy of terms to be copied is already quite high, but accuracy of terms to be translated is very low. The EMEA baseline has a much harder time with tokens that should be copied, but does better on non-copied terms. We hypothesize that this may have to do with differences in the morphological attributes of the novel tokens in the different datasets (WMT contains many names of people or places, while EMEA contains many drug names, which tend to contain character sequences not frequent in either source or target language) or with the contexts in which they appear. We observe that for many of the medication names, it takes 10 or more instances of the name being observed for the single-sentence adaptation

approach alone to successfully learn to copy the word (if ever). Though there remains a gap between novel word accuracy on tokens that should be copied and those that should be translated, our approaches demonstrate improvements for *both* types of novel words.

A concern with training on a dictionary as bitext is that the model may overfit to the sentence length; we do not find that to be the case here, as the difference between the full hypothesis lengths is 48,641 tokens for the EMEA-adapted data compared to 48,627 for the dictionary-trained models. However, this is dependent on choosing the correct learning rate and number of epochs. Similarly, there's a potential concern that single-sentence training on the previous sentence may cause some type of overfitting (memorization of the sentence, etc.). We do not observe that to be the case either.

7   Conclusions and Future Work

We propose two approaches to document-level adaptation of NMT systems (single-sentence adaptation, dictionary training) and their combination, which can be effectively used to improve performance, both in terms of BLEU score and in the translation of novel words. Both approaches have minimal training data requirements, can be effective applied with an existing NMT architecture, and show considerable improvements even for short documents.

One area meriting further study is dynamic adaptation of hyper-parameters based on document length or content. During our development and test-runs, we found correlations between hyper-parameter configurations and document lengths with some learning rates and train epochs working better for shorter documents while some working better for longer ones. We could foresee dynamically adapting the hyperparameters based on the overlap between the current sentence being translated and the remainder of the document as a possible area of future study. Additionally, it would be useful to explore these methods in a user-study, to better determine the trade-off between improvement and user input required (such as for dictionary creation).

Acknowledgments

Rebecca Knowles was partially supported by a National Science Foundation Graduate Research Fellowship under Grant No. DGE-1232825.

---

[12]The number of different machine translation outputs for the source type, divided by the number of times that source type appears.

References

Philip Arthur, Graham Neubig, and Satoshi Nakamura. 2016. Incorporating discrete translation lexicons into neural machine translation. In *Proceedings of the 2016 Conference on Empirical Methods in Natural Language Processing*, pages 1557–1567, Austin, Texas. Association for Computational Linguistics.

Marco Baroni and Silvia Bernardini. 2005. A new approach to the study of translationese: Machine-learning the difference between original and translated text. *Literary and Linguistic Computing*, 21(3):259–274.

Marine Carpuat. 2009. One translation per discourse. In *Proceedings of the Workshop on Semantic Evaluations: Recent Achievements and Future Directions, DEW '09*, pages 19–27, Stroudsburg, PA, USA. Association for Computational Linguistics.

Marine Carpuat, Hal Daumé III, Alexander Fraser, Chris Quirk, Fabienne Braune, Ann Clifton, Ann Irvine, Jagadeesh Jagarlamudi, John Morgan, Majid Razmara, Aleš Tamchyna, Katharine Henry, and Rachel Rudinger. 2012. Domain adaptation in machine translation: Final report. In *2012 Johns Hopkins Summer Workshop Final Report*.

Mauro Cettolo, Nicola Bertoldi, Marcello Federico, Holger Schwenk, Loïc Barrault, and Christophe Servan. 2014. Translation project adaptation for mt-enhanced computer assisted translation. *Machine Translation*, 28(2):127–150.

Chenhui Chu, Raj Dabre, and Sadao Kurohashi. 2017. An empirical comparison of domain adaptation methods for neural machine translation. In *Proceedings of the 55th Annual Meeting of the Association for Computational Linguistics (Volume 2: Short Papers)*, pages 385–391, Vancouver, Canada. Association for Computational Linguistics.

Anna Currey, Antonio Valerio Miceli Barone, and Kenneth Heafield. 2017. Copied monolingual data improves low-resource neural machine translation. In *Proceedings of the Second Conference on Machine Translation*, pages 148–156.

Chris Dyer, Victor Chahuneau, and Noah A. Smith. 2013. A simple, fast, and effective reparameterization of ibm model 2. In *Proceedings of the 2013 Conference of the North American Chapter of the Association for Computational Linguistics: Human Language Technologies*, pages 644–648, Atlanta, Georgia. Association for Computational Linguistics.

Marzieh Fadaee, Arianna Bisazza, and Christof Monz. 2017. Data augmentation for low-resource neural machine translation. In *Proceedings of the 55th Annual Meeting of the Association for Computational Linguistics (Volume 2: Short Papers)*, pages 567–573, Vancouver, Canada. Association for Computational Linguistics.

M. Amin Farajian, Marco Turchi, Matteo Negri, and Marcello Federico. 2017. Multi-domain neural machine translation through unsupervised adaptation. In *Proceedings of the Second Conference on Machine Translation, Volume 1: Research Paper*, pages 127–137, Copenhagen, Denmark. Association for Computational Linguistics.

Markus Freitag and Yaser Al-Onaizan. 2016. Fast domain adaptation for neural machine translation. *arXiv preprint arXiv:1612.06897*.

William A. Gale, Kenneth W. Church, and David Yarowsky. 1992. One sense per discourse. In *Proceedings of the Workshop on Speech and Natural Language, HLT '91*, pages 233–237, Stroudsburg, PA, USA. Association for Computational Linguistics.

Jiatao Gu, Zhengdong Lu, Hang Li, and Victor O.K. Li. 2016. Incorporating copying mechanism in sequence-to-sequence learning. In *Proceedings of the 54th Annual Meeting of the Association for Computational Linguistics (Volume 1: Long Papers)*, pages 1631–1640, Berlin, Germany. Association for Computational Linguistics.

Chris Hokamp and Qun Liu. 2017. Lexically constrained decoding for sequence generation using grid beam search. In *Proceedings of the 55th Annual Meeting of the Association for Computational Linguistics (Volume 1: Long Papers)*, pages 1535–1546. Association for Computational Linguistics.

Huda Khayrallah and Philipp Koehn. 2018. On the impact of various types of noise on neural machine translation. In *Proceedings of the Second Workshop on Neural Machine Translation and Generation*, Melbourne. Association for Computational Linguistics.

Diederik P. Kingma and Jimmy Ba. 2014. Adam: A method for stochastic optimization. *CoRR*, abs/1412.6980.

Rebecca Knowles and Philipp Koehn. 2016. Neural interactive translation prediction. In *Proceedings of the Conference of the Association for Machine Translation in the Americas (AMTA)*.

Catherine Kobus, Josep Crego, and Jean Senellart. 2017. Domain control for neural machine translation. In *Proceedings of the International Conference Recent Advances in Natural Language Processing, RANLP 2017*, pages 372–378. INCOMA Ltd.

Xiaoqing Li, Jiajun Zhang, and Chengqing Zong. 2016. One sentence one model for neural machine translation. *CoRR*, abs/1609.06490.

Minh-Thang Luong and Christopher D Manning. 2015. Stanford neural machine translation systems for spoken language domains. In *Proceedings of the International Workshop on Spoken Language Translation*.

Toan Nguyen and David Chiang. 2018. Improving lexical choice in neural machine translation. In *Proc. NAACL HLT*. To appear.

Myle Ott, Michael Auli, David Grangier, and Marc'Aurelio Ranzato. 2018. Analyzing uncertainty in neural machine translation. *CoRR*, abs/1803.00047.

Kishore Papineni, Salim Roukos, Todd Ward, and Wei-Jing Zhu. 2002. Bleu: a method for automatic evaluation of machine translation. In *Proceedings of the 40th annual meeting on association for computational linguistics*, pages 311–318. Association for Computational Linguistics.

Álvaro Peris and Francisco Casacuberta. 2018. Online learning for effort reduction in interactive neural machine translation. *CoRR*, abs/1802.03594.

Rico Sennrich, Orhan Firat, Kyunghyun Cho, Alexandra Birch, Barry Haddow, Julian Hitschler, Marcin Junczys-Dowmunt, Samuel Läubli, Antonio Valerio Miceli Barone, Jozef Mokry, and Maria Nadejde. 2017. Nematus: a toolkit for neural machine translation. In *Proceedings of the Software Demonstrations of the 15th Conference of the European Chapter of the Association for Computational Linguistics*, pages 65–68, Valencia, Spain. Association for Computational Linguistics.

Rico Sennrich, Barry Haddow, and Alexandra Birch. 2016a. Edinburgh neural machine translation systems for WMT 16. In *Proceedings of the First Conference on Machine Translation (WMT)*.

Rico Sennrich, Barry Haddow, and Alexandra Birch. 2016b. Neural machine translation of rare words with subword units. In *Proceedings of the 54th Annual Meeting of the Association for Computational Linguistics (Volume 1: Long Papers)*, pages 1715–1725, Berlin, Germany. Association for Computational Linguistics.

Jörg Tiedemann. 2009. News from OPUS - A collection of multilingual parallel corpora with tools and interfaces. In N. Nicolov, K. Bontcheva, G. Angelova, and R. Mitkov, editors, *Recent Advances in Natural Language Processing*, volume V, pages 237–248. John Benjamins, Amsterdam/Philadelphia, Borovets, Bulgaria.

Rui Wang, Masao Utiyama, Lemao Liu, Kehai Chen, and Eiichiro Sumita. 2017. Instance weighting for neural machine translation domain adaptation. In *Proceedings of the 2017 Conference on Empirical Methods in Natural Language Processing*, pages 1482–1488.

Joern Wuebker, Spence Green, John DeNero, Sasa Hasan, and Minh-Thang Luong. 2016. Models and inference for prefix-constrained machine translation. In *Proceedings of the 54th Annual Meeting of the Association for Computational Linguistics (Volume 1: Long Papers)*, pages 66–75, Berlin, Germany. Association for Computational Linguistics.

On the Impact of Various Types of Noise on Neural Machine Translation

Huda Khayrallah
Center for Language & Speech Processing
Computer Science Department
Johns Hopkins University
huda@jhu.edu

Philipp Koehn
Center for Language & Speech Processing
Computer Science Department
Johns Hopkins University
phi@jhu.edu

Abstract

We examine how various types of noise in the parallel training data impact the quality of neural machine translation systems. We create five types of artificial noise and analyze how they degrade performance in neural and statistical machine translation. We find that neural models are generally more harmed by noise than statistical models. For one especially egregious type of noise they learn to just copy the input sentence.

1 Introduction

While neural machine translation (NMT) has shown large gains in quality over statistical machine translation (SMT) (Bojar et al., 2017), there are significant exceptions to this, such as low resource and domain mismatch data conditions (Koehn and Knowles, 2017).

In this work, we consider another challenge to neural machine translation: noisy parallel data. As a motivating example, consider the numbers in Table 1. Here, we add an equally sized noisy web crawled corpus to high quality training data provided by the shared task of the Conference on Machine Translation (WMT). This addition leads to a 1.2 BLEU point increase for the statistical machine translation system, but degrades the neural machine translation system by 9.9 BLEU.

The maxim *more data is better* that holds true for statistical machine translation does seem to come with some caveats for neural machine translation. The added data cannot be too noisy. But what kind of noise harms neural machine translation models?

In this paper, we explore several types of noise and assess their impact by adding synthetic noise

	NMT	SMT
WMT17	27.2	24.0
+ noisy corpus	17.3 (–9.9)	25.2 (+1.2)

Table 1: Adding noisy web crawled data (raw data from paracrawl.eu) to a WMT 2017 German–English statistical system obtains small gains (+1.2 BLEU), a neural system falls apart (–9.9 BLEU).

to an existing parallel corpus. We find that for almost all types of noise, neural machine translation systems are harmed more than statistical machine translation systems. We discovered that one type of noise, copied source language segments, has a catastrophic impact on neural machine translation quality, leading it to learn a copying behavior that it then exceedingly applies.

2 Related Work

There is a robust body of work on filtering out noise in parallel data. For example: Taghipour et al. (2011) use an outlier detection algorithm to filter a parallel corpus; Xu and Koehn (2017) generate synthetic noisy data (inadequate and non-fluent translations) and use this data to train a classifier to identify good sentence pairs from a noisy corpus; and Cui et al. (2013) use a graph-based random walk algorithm and extract phrase pair scores to weight the phrase translation probabilities to bias towards more trustworthy ones.

Most of this work was done in the context of statistical machine translation, but more recent work (Carpuat et al., 2017) targets neural models. That work focuses on identifying semantic differences in translation pairs using cross-lingual textual entailment and additional length-based features, and demonstrates that removing such sentences improves neural machine translation performance.

Proceedings of the 2nd Workshop on Neural Machine Translation and Generation, pages 74–83
Melbourne, Australia, July 20, 2018. ©2018 Association for Computational Linguistics

As Rarrick et al. (2011) point out, one problem of parallel corpora extracted from the web is translations that have been created by machine translation. Venugopal et al. (2011) propose a method to watermark the output of machine translation systems to aid this distinction. Antonova and Misyurev (2011) report that rule-based machine translation output can be detected due to certain word choices, and statistical machine translation output due to lack of reordering.

In 2016, a shared task on sentence pair filtering was organized[1] (Barbu et al., 2016), albeit in the context of cleaning translation memories which tend to be cleaner than web crawled data. This year, a shared task is planned for the type of noise that we examine in this paper.[2]

Belinkov and Bisk (2017) investigate noise in neural machine translation, but they focus on creating systems that can *translate* the kinds of orthographic errors (typos, misspellings, etc.) that humans can comprehend. In contrast, we address noisy *training* data and focus on types of noise occurring in web-crawled corpora.

There is a rich literature on data selection which aims at sub-sampling parallel data relevant for a task-specific machine translation system (Axelrod et al., 2011). van der Wees et al. (2017) find that the existing data selection methods developed for statistical machine translation are less effective for neural machine translation. This is different from our goals of handling noise since those methods tend to discard perfectly fine sentence pairs (say, about cooking recipes) that are just not relevant for the targeted domain (say, software manuals). Our work is focused on noise that is harmful for all domains.

Since we begin with a clean parallel corpus and potentially noisy data to it, this work can be seen as a type of data augmentation. Sennrich et al. (2016a) incorporate monolingual corpora into NMT by first translating it using an NMT system trained in the opposite direction. While such a corpus has the potential to be noisy, the method is very effective. Currey et al. (2017) create additional parallel corpora by copying monolingual corpora in the target language into the source, and find it improves over back-translation for some language pairs. Fadaee et al. (2017) improve NMT performance in low-resource settings by altering

Type of Noise	Count
Okay	23%
Misaligned sentences	41%
Third language	3%
Both English	10%
Both German	10%
Untranslated sentences	4%
Short segments ($\leq$2 tokens)	1%
Short segments (3–5 tokens)	5%
Non-linguistic characters	2%

Table 2: Noise in the raw Paracrawl corpus.

existing sentences to create training data that includes rare words in different contexts.

3 Real-World Noise

What types of noise are prevalent in crawled web data? We manually examined 200 sentence pairs of the above-mentioned Paracrawl corpus and classified them into several error categories. Obviously, the results of such a study depend very much on how crawling and extraction is executed, but the results (see Table 2) give some indication of what noise to expect.

We classified any pairs of German and English sentences that are not translations of each other as misaligned sentences. These may be caused by any problem in alignment processes (at the document level or the sentence level), or by forcing the alignment of content that is not indeed parallel. Such misaligned sentences are the biggest source of error (41%).

There are three types of wrong language content (totaling 23%): one or both sentences may be in a language different from German and English (3%), both sentences may be German (10%), or both languages may be English (10%).

4% of sentence pairs are untranslated, i.e., source and target are identical. 2% sentence pairs consist of random byte sequences, only HTML markup, or Javascript. A number of sentence pairs have very short German or English sentences, containing at most 2 tokens (1%) or 5 tokens (5%).

Since it is a very subjective value judgment what constitutes disfluent language, we do not classify these as errors. However, consider the following sentence pairs that we did count as okay, although they contain mostly untranslated names and numbers.

---

[1]NLP4TM 2016: rgcl.wlv.ac.uk/nlp4tm2016/shared-task
[2]statmt.org/wmt18/parallel-corpus-filtering.html

At first sight, some types of noise seem to be easier to automatically identify than others. However, consider, for instance, content in a wrong language. While there are established methods for language identification (typically based on character n-grams), these do not work well on a sentence-level basis, especially for short sentences. Or, take the apparently obvious problem of untranslated sentences. If they are completely identical, that is easy to spot — although even those may have value, such as the list of country names which are often spelled identical in different languages. However, there are many degrees of near-identical content of unclear utility.

4   Types of Noise

The goal of this paper is not to develop methods to detect noise but to ascertain the impact of different types of noise on translation quality when present in parallel data. We hope that our findings inform future work on parallel corpus cleaning.

We now formally define five types of naturally occurring noise and describe how we simulate them. By creating artificial noisy data, we avoid the hard problem of detecting specific types of noise but are still able to study their impact.

MISALIGNED SENTENCES   As shown above, a common source of noise in parallel corpora is faulty document or sentence alignment. This results in sentences that are not matched to their translation. Such noise is rare in corpora such as Europarl where strong clues about debate topics and speaker turns reduce the scale of the task of alignment to paragraphs, but more common in the alignment of less structured web sites. We artificially create misaligned sentence data by randomly shuffling the order of sentences on one side of the original clean parallel training corpus.

MISORDERED WORDS   Language may be disfluent in many ways. This may be the product of machine translation, poor human translation, or heavily specialized language use, such as bul-

let points in product descriptions (recall also the examples above). We consider one extreme case of disfluent language: sentences from the original corpus where the words are reordered randomly. We do this on the source or target side.

WRONG LANGUAGE   A parallel corpus may be polluted by text in a third language, say French in a German–English corpus. This may occur on the source or target side of the parallel corpus. To simulate this, we add French–English (bad source) or German–French (bad target) data to a German–English corpus.

UNTRANSLATED SENTENCES   Especially in parallel corpora crawled from the web, there are often sentences that are untranslated from the source in the target. Examples are navigational elements or copyright notices in the footer. Purportedly multi-lingual web sites may be only partially translated, while some original text is copied. Again, this may show up on the source or the target side. We take sentences from either the source or target side of the original parallel corpus and simply copy them to the other side.

SHORT SEGMENTS   Sometimes additional data comes in the form of bilingual dictionaries. Can we simply add them as additional sentence pairs, even if they consist of single words or short phrases? We simulate this kind of data by sub-subsampling a parallel corpus to include only sentences of maximum length 2 or 5.

5   Experimental Setup

5.1   Neural Machine Translation

Our neural machine translation systems are trained using Marian (Junczys-Dowmunt et al., 2018).[3] We build shallow RNN-based encoder-decoder models with attention (Bahdanau et al., 2015). We train Byte-Pair Encoding segmentation models (BPE) (Sennrich et al., 2016b) with a vocab size of $50,000$ on both sides of the parallel corpus for each experiment. We apply drop-out with 20% probability on the RNNs, and with 10% probability on the source and target words. We stop training after convergence of cross-entropy on the development set, and we average the 4 highest performing models (as determined by development set BLEU performance) to use as an ensemble for decoding (checkpoint assembling). Training of

---

[3]marian-nmt.github.io

each system takes 2–4 days on a single GPU (GTX 1080ti).

While we focus on RNN-based models with attention as our NMT architecture, we note that different architectures have been proposed, including based on convolutional neural networks (Kalchbrenner and Blunsom, 2013; Gehring et al., 2017) and the self-attention based Transformer model (Vaswani et al., 2017).

5.2 Statistical Machine Translation

Our statistical machine translation systems are trained using Moses (Koehn et al., 2007).[4] We build phrase-based systems using standard features commonly used in recent system submissions to WMT (Haddow et al., 2015; Ding et al., 2016, 2017). We trained our systems with the following settings: a maximum sentence length of 80, grow-diag-final-and symmetrization of GIZA++ alignments, an interpolated Kneser-Ney smoothed 5-gram language model with KenLM (Heafield, 2011), hierarchical lexicalized reordering (Galley and Manning, 2008), a lexically-driven 5-gram operation sequence model (OSM) (Durrani et al., 2013), sparse domain indicator, phrase length, and count bin features (Blunsom and Osborne, 2008; Chiang et al., 2009), a maximum phrase-length of 5, compact phrase table (Junczys-Dowmunt, 2012) minimum Bayes risk decoding (Kumar and Byrne, 2004), cube pruning (Huang and Chiang, 2007), with a stack-size of 1000 during tuning. We optimize feature function weights with k-best MIRA (Cherry and Foster, 2012).

While we focus on phrase based systems as our SMT paradigm, we note that there are other statistical machine translation approaches such as hierarchical phrase-based models (Chiang, 2007) and syntax-based models (Galley et al., 2004, 2006) that may have better performance in certain language pairs and in low resource conditions.

5.3 Clean Corpus

In our experiments, we translate from German to English. We use datasets from the shared translation task organized alongside the Conference on Machine Translation (WMT)[5] as clean training data. For our baseline we use: Europarl (Koehn, 2005),[6] News Commentary,[7] and the Rapid EU Press Release parallel corpus. The corpus size is about 83 million tokens per language. We use newstest2015 for tuning SMT systems, newstest2016 as a development set for NMT systems, and report results on newstest2017.

Note that we do not add monolingual data to our systems since this would make our study more complex. So, we always train our language model on the target side of the parallel corpus for that experiment. While using monolingual data for language modelling is standard practice in statistical machine translation, how to use such data for neural models is less obvious.

5.4 Noisy Corpora

For MISALIGNED SENTENCE and MISORDERED WORD noise, we use the clean corpus (above) and perturb the data. To create UNTRANSLATED SENTENCE noise, we also use the clean corpus and create pairs of identical sentences.

For WRONG LANGUAGE noise, we do not have French–English and German–French data of the same size. Hence, we use the EU Bookstore corpus (Skadiņš et al., 2014).[8]

The SHORT SEGMENTS are extracted from OPUS corpora (Tiedemann, 2009, 2012; Lison and Tiedemann, 2016):[9] EMEA (descriptions of medicines),[10] Tanzil (religious text),[11] Open Subtitles 2016,[12] Acquis (legislative text),[13] GNOME (software localization files),[14] KDE (localization files), PHP (technical manual),[15] Ubuntu (localization files),[16] and Open Office.[17] We use only pairs where both the English and German segments are at most 2 or 5 words long. Since this results in small data sets (2 million and 15 tokens per language, respectively), they are duplicated multiple times.

We also show the results for naturally occurring noisy web data from the raw 2016 ParaCrawl corpus (deduplicated raw set).[18]

---

[4]statmt.org/moses
[5]statmt.org/wmt17/

[6]statmt.org/europarl
[7]casmacat.eu/corpus/news-commentary.html
[8]opus.nlpl.eu/EUbookshop.php
[9]opus.nlpl.eu
[10]emea.europa.eu
[11]tanzil.net/trans
[12]opensubtitles.org
[13]ec.europa.eu/jrc/en/language-technologies/jrc-acquis
[14]l10n.gnome.org
[15]se.php.net/download-docs
[16]translations.launchpad.net
[17]openoffice.org
[18]paracrawl.eu

We sample the noisy corpus in an amount equal to 5%, 10%, 20%, 50%, and 100% of the clean corpus. This reflects the realistic situation where there is a clean corpus, and one would like to add additional data that has the potential to be noisy. For each experiment, we use the target side of the parallel corpus to train the SMT language model, including the noisy text.

6 Impact on Translation Quality

Table 3 shows the effect of adding each type of noise to the clean corpus.[19] For some types of noise NMT is harmed more than SMT: MIS-MATCHED SENTENCES (up to -1.9 for NMT, -0.6 for SMT), MISORDERED WORDS (source) (-1.7 vs. -0.3), WRONG LANGUAGE (target) (-2.2 vs. -0.6).

SHORT SEGMENTS, UNTRANSLATED SOURCE SENTENCES and WRONG SOURCE LANGUAGE have little impact on either (at most a degradation of -0.7). MISORDERED TARGET WORDS decreases BLEU scores for both SMT and NMT by just over 1 point (100% noise).

The most dramatic difference is UNTRANS-LATED TARGET SENTENCE noise. When added at 5% of the original data, it degrades NMT performance by 9.6 BLEU, from 27.2 to 17.6. Adding this noise at 100% of the original data degrades performance by 24.0 BLEU, dropping the score from 27.2 to 3.2. In contrast, the SMT system only drops 2.9 BLEU, from 24.0 to 21.1.

6.1 Copied output

Since the noise type where the target side is a copy of the source has such a big impact, we examine the system output in more detail.

We report the percent of sentences in the evaluation set that are identical to the source for the UNTRANSLATED TARGET SENTENCE and RAW CRAWL data in Figures 1 and 2 (solid bars). The SMT systems output 0 or 1 sentences that are exact copies. However, with just 20% of the UN-TRANSLATED TARGET SENTENCE noise, 60% of the NMT output sentences are identical to the source.

This suggests that the NMT systems learn to copy, which may be useful for named entities. However, with even a small amount of this data it is doing far more harm than good.

---

[19]We report case-sensitive detokenized BLEU (Papineni et al., 2002) calculated using mteval-v13a.pl.

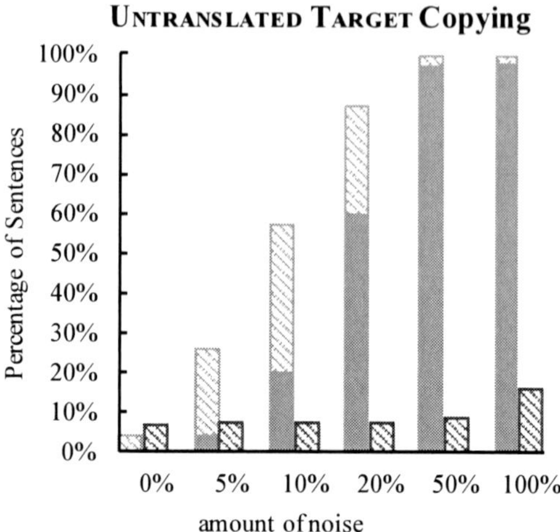

Figure 1: Copied sentences in the UNTRANS-LATED (TARGET) experiments. NMT is the left green bars, SMT is the right blue bars. Sentences that are exact matches to the source are the solid bars, sentences that are more similar to the source than the target are the shaded bars.

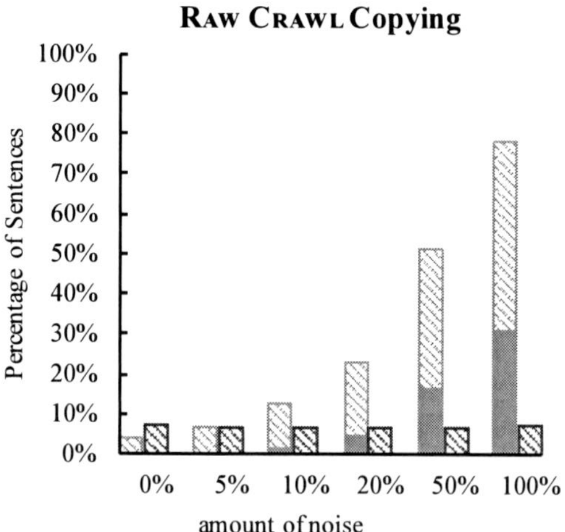

Figure 2: Copied sentences in the RAW CRAWL experiments. NMT is the left green bars, SMT is the right blue bars. Sentences that are exact matches to the source are the solid bars, sentences that are more similar to the source than the target are the shaded bars.

	5%		10%		20%		50%		100%	
MISALIGNED SENTENCES	26.5	24.0	26.5	24.0	26.3	23.9	26.1	23.9	25.3	23.4
	-0.7	-0.0	-0.7	-0.0	-0.9	-0.1	-1.1	-0.1	-1.9	-0.6
MISORDERED WORDS (SOURCE)	26.9	24.0	26.6	23.6	26.4	23.9	26.6	23.6	25.5	23.7
	-0.3	-0.0	-0.6	-0.4	-0.8	-0.1	-0.6	-0.4	-1.7	-0.3
MISORDERED WORDS (TARGET)	27.0	24.0	26.8	24.0	26.4	23.4	26.7	23.2	26.1	22.9
	-0.2	-0.0	-0.4	-0.0	-0.8	-0.6	-0.5	-0.8	-1.1	-1.1
WRONG LANGUAGE (FRENCH SOURCE)	26.9	24.0	26.8	23.9	26.8	23.9	26.8	23.9	26.8	23.8
	-0.3	-0.0	-0.4	-0.1	-0.4	-0.1	-0.4	-0.1	-0.4	-0.2
WRONG LANGUAGE (FRENCH TARGET)	26.7	24.0	26.6	23.9	26.7	23.8	26.2	23.5	25.0	23.4
	-0.5	-0.0	-0.6	-0.1	-0.5	-0.2	-1.0	-0.5	-2.2	-0.6
UNTRANSLATED (ENGLISH SOURCE)	27.2	23.9	27.0	23.9	26.7	23.6	26.8	23.7	26.9	23.5
	-0.0	-0.1	-0.2	-0.1	-0.5	-0.4	-0.4	-0.3	-0.3	-0.5
UNTRANSLATED (GERMAN TARGET)	17.6	23.8	11.2	23.9	5.6	23.8	3.2	23.4	3.2	21.1
	-9.8	-0.2	-16.0	-0.1	-21.6	-0.2	-24.0	-0.6	-24.0	-2.9
SHORT SEGMENTS (max 2)	27.1	24.1	26.5	23.9	26.7	23.8				
	-0.1	+0.1	-0.7	-0.1	-0.5	-0.2				
SHORT SEGMENTS (max 5)	27.8	24.2	27.6	24.5	28.0	24.5	26.6	24.2		
	+0.6	+0.2	+0.4	+0.5	+0.8	+0.5	-0.6	+0.2		
RAW CRAWL DATA	27.4	24.2	26.6	24.2	24.7	24.4	20.9	24.8	17.3	25.2
	+0.2	+0.2	-0.6	+0.2	-2.5	+0.4	-6.3	+0.8	-9.9	+1.2

Table 3: Results from adding different amounts of noise (ratio of original clean corpus) for various types of noise in German-English Translation. Generally neural machine translation (left green bars) is harmed more than statistical machine translation (right blue bars). The worst type of noise are segments in the source language copied untranslated into the target.

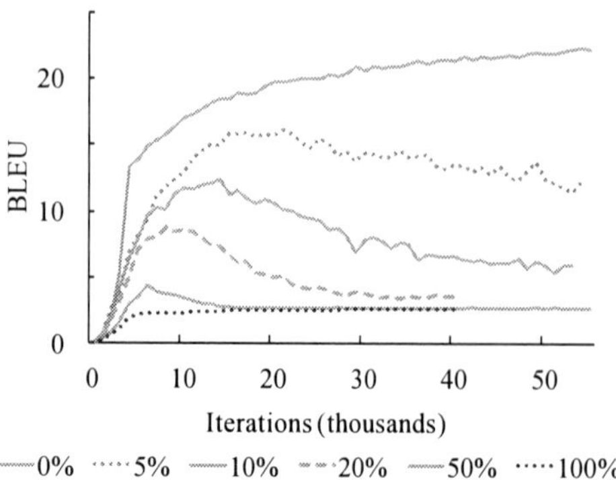

Figure 3: Learning curves for the NMT UN-TRANSLATED TARGET SENTENCE experiments.

Figures 1 and 2 show the percent of sentences that have a worse TER score against the reference than against the source (shaded bars). This means that it would take fewer edits to transform the sentence into the source than it would to transform it into the target. When just 10% UNTRANSLATED TARGET SENTENCE data is added, 57% of the sentences are more similar to the source than to the reference, indicating partial copying.

This suggests that the NMT system is overfitting the copied portion of the training corpus. This is supported by Figure 3, which shows the learning curve on the development set for the UNTRANSLATED TARGET SENTENCE noise setup. The performance for the systems trained on noisy corpora begin to improve, before over-fitting to the copy portion of the training set. Note that we plot the BLEU performance on the development set with beam search, while the system is optimizing cross-entropy given a perfect prefix.

Other work has also considered copying in NMT. Currey et al. (2017) add copied data and back-translated data to a clean parallel corpus. They report improvements on EN $\leftrightarrow$ RO when adding as much back-translated and copied data as they have parallel (1:1:1 ratio). For EN$\leftrightarrow$TR and EN$\leftrightarrow$DE, they add twice as much back translated and copied data as parallel data (1:2:2 ratio), and report improvements on EN$\leftrightarrow$TR but not on EN$\leftrightarrow$DE. However, their EN$\leftrightarrow$DE systems trained with the copied corpus did not perform worse than baseline systems. Ott et al. (2018) found that while copied training sentences represent less than 2.0% of their training data

(WMT 14 EN$\leftrightarrow$DE and EN$\leftrightarrow$FR), copies are over-represented in the output of beam search. Using a subset of training data from WMT 17, they replace a subset of the true translations with a copy of the input. They analyze varying amounts of copied noise, and a variety of beam sizes. Larger beams are more effected by this kind of noise; however, for all beam sizes performance degrades completely with 50% copied sentences.[20]

6.2 Incorrect Language output

Another interesting case is when a German–French corpus is added to a German–English corpus (WRONG TARGET LANGUAGE). Both neural and statistical machine translation are surprisingly robust, even when these corpora are provided in equal amounts.

We performed a manual analysis of the neural machine translation experiments. For the each of the noise levels, we report the percentage of NMT output sentences in French (out of of 3004: 5%: 0.20%, 10%: 0.60%, 20%: 1.7%, 50%: 3.3%, 100%: 6.7%. Most NMT output sentences were either entirely French or English, with the exception of a few mis-translated cognates (e.g.: 'façade', 'accessibilité').

In the SMT experiment with 100% noisy data added, there are a couple of French words in mostly English sentences. These are much less frequent than unknown German words passed through. Only 1 sentence is mostly French.

It is surprising that such a small percentage of the output sentences were French, since up to half of the target data in training was in French. We attribute this to the domain of the added data differing from the test data. Source sentences in the test set are more similar to the domain-relevant clean parallel training corpus than the domain-divergent noise corpus.

7   Conclusion

We defined five types of noise in parallel data, motivated by a study of raw web crawl data. We found that neural machine translation is less robust to many types of noise than statistical machine translation. In the most extreme case, when the reference is an untranslated copy of the source data, neural machine translation may learn to excessively copy the input. These findings should inform future work on corpus cleaning.

---

[20]See Figure 3 in Ott et al. (2018).

Acknowledgements

This work has been partially supported by the DARPA LORELEI and the IARPA MATERIAL programs. It also benefited from the Paracrawl web crawling project which is funded by a Google faculty grant and the European Union (CEF).

References

Alexandra Antonova and Alexey Misyurev. 2011. Building a web-based parallel corpus and filtering out machine-translated text. In *Proceedings of the 4th Workshop on Building and Using Comparable Corpora: Comparable Corpora and the Web*. Association for Computational Linguistics, Portland, Oregon, pages 136–144. http://www.aclweb.org/anthology/W11-1218.

Amittai Axelrod, Xiaodong He, and Jianfeng Gao. 2011. Domain adaptation via pseudo in-domain data selection. In *Proceedings of the 2011 Conference on Empirical Methods in Natural Language Processing*. Association for Computational Linguistics, Edinburgh, Scotland, UK., pages 355–362. http://www.aclweb.org/anthology/D11-1033.

Dzmitry Bahdanau, Kyunghyun Cho, and Yoshua Bengio. 2015. Neural machine translation by jointly learning to align and translate. In *ICLR*. http://arxiv.org/pdf/1409.0473v6.pdf.

Eduard Barbu, Carla Parra Escartín, Luisa Bentivogli, Matteo Negri, Marco Turchi, Constantin Orasan, and Marcello Federico. 2016. The first automatic translation memory cleaning shared task. *Machine Translation* 30(3):145–166. https://doi.org/10.1007/s10590-016-9183-x.

Yonatan Belinkov and Yonatan Bisk. 2017. Synthetic and natural noise both break neural machine translation. *CoRR* abs/1711.02173. http://arxiv.org/abs/1711.02173.

Phil Blunsom and Miles Osborne. 2008. Probabilistic inference for machine translation. In *Proceedings of the 2008 Conference on Empirical Methods in Natural Language Processing*. Association for Computational Linguistics, Honolulu, Hawaii, pages 215–223. http://www.aclweb.org/anthology/D08-1023.

Ondrej Bojar, Rajen Chatterjee, Christian Federmann, Yvette Graham, Barry Haddow, Shujian Huang, Matthias Huck, Philipp Koehn, Qun Liu, Varvara Logacheva, Christof Monz, Matteo Negri, Matt Post, Raphael Rubino, Lucia Specia, and Marco Turchi. 2017. Findings of the 2017 conference on machine translation (WMT17). In *Proceedings of the Second Conference on Machine Translation*. Association for Computational Linguistics, Copenhagen, Denmark, pages 169–214.

Marine Carpuat, Yogarshi Vyas, and Xing Niu. 2017. Detecting cross-lingual semantic divergence for neural machine translation. In *Proceedings of the First Workshop on Neural Machine Translation*. Association for Computational Linguistics, Vancouver, pages 69–79. http://www.aclweb.org/anthology/W17-3209.

Colin Cherry and George Foster. 2012. Batch tuning strategies for statistical machine translation. In *Proceedings of the 2012 Conference of the North American Chapter of the Association for Computational Linguistics: Human Language Technologies*. Association for Computational Linguistics, Montréal, Canada, pages 427–436. http://www.aclweb.org/anthology/N12-1047.

David Chiang. 2007. Hierarchical phrase-based translation. *Computational Linguistics* 33(2). http://www.aclweb.org/anthology-new/J/J07/J07-2003.pdf.

David Chiang, Kevin Knight, and Wei Wang. 2009. 11,001 new features for statistical machine translation. In *Proceedings of Human Language Technologies: The 2009 Annual Conference of the North American Chapter of the Association for Computational Linguistics*. Association for Computational Linguistics, Boulder, Colorado, pages 218–226. http://www.aclweb.org/anthology/N/N09/N09-1025.

Lei Cui, Dongdong Zhang, Shujie Liu, Mu Li, and Ming Zhou. 2013. Bilingual data cleaning for smt using graph-based random walk. In *Proceedings of the 51st Annual Meeting of the Association for Computational Linguistics (Volume 2: Short Papers)*. Association for Computational Linguistics, Sofia, Bulgaria, pages 340–345. http://www.aclweb.org/anthology/P13-2061.

Anna Currey, Antonio Valerio Miceli Barone, and Kenneth Heafield. 2017. Copied monolingual data improves low-resource neural machine translation. In *Proceedings of the Second Conference on Machine Translation, Volume 1: Research Paper*. Association for Computational Linguistics, Copenhagen, Denmark, pages 148–156. http://www.aclweb.org/anthology/W17-4715.

Shuoyang Ding, Kevin Duh, Huda Khayrallah, Philipp Koehn, and Matt Post. 2016. The jhu machine translation systems for wmt 2016. In *Proceedings of the First Conference on Machine Translation*. Association for Computational Linguistics, Berlin, Germany, pages 272–280. http://www.aclweb.org/anthology/W/W16/W16-2310.

Shuoyang Ding, Huda Khayrallah, Philipp Koehn, Matt Post, Gaurav Kumar, and Kevin Duh. 2017. The jhu machine translation systems for wmt 2017. In *Proceedings of the Second Conference on Machine Translation, Volume 2: Shared*

Task Papers. Association for Computational Linguistics, Copenhagen, Denmark, pages 276–282. http://www.aclweb.org/anthology/W17-4724.

Nadir Durrani, Alexander Fraser, Helmut Schmid, Hieu Hoang, and Philipp Koehn. 2013. Can Markov Models Over Minimal Translation Units Help Phrase-Based SMT? In *Proceedings of the 51st Annual Meeting of the Association for Computational Linguistics*. Association for Computational Linguistics, Sofia, Bulgaria.

Marzieh Fadaee, Arianna Bisazza, and Christof Monz. 2017. Data augmentation for low-resource neural machine translation. In *Proceedings of the 55th Annual Meeting of the Association for Computational Linguistics (Volume 2: Short Papers)*. Association for Computational Linguistics, Vancouver, Canada, pages 567–573. http://aclweb.org/anthology/P17-2090.

Michel Galley, Jonathan Graehl, Kevin Knight, Daniel Marcu, Steve DeNeefe, Wei Wang, and Ignacio Thayer. 2006. Scalable inference and training of context-rich syntactic translation models. In *Proceedings of the 21st International Conference on Computational Linguistics and 44th Annual Meeting of the Association for Computational Linguistics*. Association for Computational Linguistics, Sydney, Australia, pages 961–968. http://www.aclweb.org/anthology/P/P06/P06-1121.

Michel Galley, Mark Hopkins, Kevin Knight, and Daniel Marcu. 2004. What's in a translation rule? In *Proceedings of the Joint Conference on Human Language Technologies and the Annual Meeting of the North American Chapter of the Association of Computational Linguistics (HLT-NAACL)*. http://www.aclweb.org/anthology/N04-1035.pdf.

Michel Galley and Christopher D. Manning. 2008. A simple and effective hierarchical phrase reordering model. In *Proceedings of the 2008 Conference on Empirical Methods in Natural Language Processing*. Association for Computational Linguistics, Honolulu, Hawaii, pages 848–856. http://www.aclweb.org/anthology/D08-1089.

Jonas Gehring, Michael Auli, David Grangier, and Yann Dauphin. 2017. A convolutional encoder model for neural machine translation. In *Proceedings of the 55th Annual Meeting of the Association for Computational Linguistics (Volume 1: Long Papers)*. Association for Computational Linguistics, Vancouver, Canada, pages 123–135. http://aclweb.org/anthology/P17-1012.

Barry Haddow, Matthias Huck, Alexandra Birch, Nikolay Bogoychev, and Philipp Koehn. 2015. The edinburgh/jhu phrase-based machine translation systems for wmt 2015. In *Proceedings of the Tenth Workshop on Statistical Machine Translation*. Association for Computational Linguistics, Lisbon, Portugal, pages 126–133. http://aclweb.org/anthology/W15-3013.

Kenneth Heafield. 2011. Kenlm: Faster and smaller language model queries. In *Proceedings of the Sixth Workshop on Statistical Machine Translation*. Association for Computational Linguistics, Edinburgh, Scotland, pages 187–197. http://www.aclweb.org/anthology/W11-2123.

Liang Huang and David Chiang. 2007. Forest rescoring: Faster decoding with integrated language models. In *Proceedings of the 45th Annual Meeting of the Association of Computational Linguistics*. Association for Computational Linguistics, Prague, Czech Republic, pages 144–151. http://www.aclweb.org/anthology/P/P07/P07-1019.

M. Junczys-Dowmunt. 2012. A phrase table without phrases: Rank encoding for better phrase table compression. In Mauro Cettolo, Marcello Federico, Lucia Specia, and Andy Way, editors, *Proceedings of th 16th International Conference of the European Association for Machine Translation (EAMT)*. pages 245–252. http://www.mt-archive.info/EAMT-2012-Junczys-Dowmunt.

Marcin Junczys-Dowmunt, Roman Grundkiewicz, Tomasz Dwojak, Hieu Hoang, Kenneth Heafield, Tom Neckermann, Frank Seide, Ulrich Germann, Alham Fikri Aji, Nikolay Bogoychev, André F. T. Martins, and Alexandra Birch. 2018. Marian: Fast neural machine translation in C++. *arXiv preprint arXiv:1804.00344* https://arxiv.org/abs/1804.00344.

Nal Kalchbrenner and Phil Blunsom. 2013. Recurrent continuous translation models. In *Proceedings of the 2013 Conference on Empirical Methods in Natural Language Processing*. Association for Computational Linguistics, Seattle, Washington, USA, pages 1700–1709. http://www.aclweb.org/anthology/D13-1176.

Philipp Koehn. 2005. Europarl: A parallel corpus for statistical machine translation. In *Proceedings of the Tenth Machine Translation Summit (MT Summit X)*. Phuket, Thailand. http://mt-archive.info/MTS-2005-Koehn.pdf.

Philipp Koehn, Hieu Hoang, Alexandra Birch, Chris Callison-Burch, Marcello Federico, Nicola Bertoldi, Brooke Cowan, Wade Shen, Christine Moran, Richard Zens, Christopher J. Dyer, Ondřej Bojar, Alexandra Constantin, and Evan Herbst. 2007. Moses: Open source toolkit for statistical machine translation. In *Proceedings of the 45th Annual Meeting of the Association for Computational Linguistics Companion Volume Proceedings of the Demo and Poster Sessions*. Association for Computational Linguistics, Prague, Czech Republic, pages 177–180. http://www.aclweb.org/anthology/P/P07/P07-2045.

Philipp Koehn and Rebecca Knowles. 2017. Six challenges for neural machine translation. In *Proceedings of the First Workshop on Neural Machine Translation*. Association for Computational Linguistics, Vancouver, pages 28–39. http://www.aclweb.org/anthology/W17-3204.

Shankar Kumar and William J. Byrne. 2004. Minimum Bayes-Risk Decoding for Statistical Machine Translation. In *HLT-NAACL*. pages 169–176.

Pierre Lison and Jörg Tiedemann. 2016. Opensubtitles2016: Extracting large parallel corpora from movie and tv subtitles. In *Proceedings of the 10th International Conference on Language Resources and Evaluation (LREC 2016)*.

Myle Ott, Michael Auli, David Grangier, and Marc'Aurelio Ranzato. 2018. Analyzing uncertainty in neural machine translation. *CoRR* abs/1803.00047. http://arxiv.org/abs/1803.00047.

Kishore Papineni, Salim Roukos, Todd Ward, and Wei-Jing Zhu. 2002. Bleu: a method for automatic evaluation of machine translation. In *Proceedings of 40th Annual Meeting of the Association for Computational Linguistics*. Association for Computational Linguistics, Philadelphia, Pennsylvania, USA, pages 311–318. https://doi.org/10.3115/1073083.1073135.

Spencer Rarrick, Chris Quirk, and Will Lewis. 2011. MT detection in web-scraped parallel corpora. In *Proceedings of the 13th Machine Translation Summit (MT Summit XIII)*. International Association for Machine Translation, pages 422–430. http://www.mt-archive.info/MTS-2011-Rarrick.pdf.

Rico Sennrich, Barry Haddow, and Alexandra Birch. 2016a. Improving neural machine translation models with monolingual data. In *Proceedings of the 54th Annual Meeting of the Association for Computational Linguistics (Volume 1: Long Papers)*. Association for Computational Linguistics, Berlin, Germany, pages 86–96. http://www.aclweb.org/anthology/P16-1009.

Rico Sennrich, Barry Haddow, and Alexandra Birch. 2016b. Neural Machine Translation of Rare Words with Subword Units. In *Proceedings of the 54th Annual Meeting of the Association for Computational Linguistics*. Association for Computational Linguistics, Berlin, Germany. http://www.aclweb.org/anthology/P16-1162.

Raivis Skadiņš, Jörg Tiedemann, Roberts Rozis, and Daiga Deksne. 2014. Billions of parallel words for free: Building and using the eu bookshop corpus. In *Proceedings of the 9th International Conference on Language Resources and Evaluation (LREC-2014)*. European Language Resources Association (ELRA), Reykjavik, Iceland.

Kaveh Taghipour, Shahram Khadivi, and Jia Xu. 2011. Parallel corpus refinement as an outlier detection algorithm. In *Proceedings of the 13th Machine Translation Summit (MT Summit XIII)*. International Association for Machine Translation, pages 414–421. http://www.mt-archive.info/MTS-2011-Taghipour.pdf.

Jörg Tiedemann. 2009. News from OPUS - A collection of multilingual parallel corpora with tools and interfaces. In N. Nicolov, K. Bontcheva, G. Angelova, and R. Mitkov, editors, *Recent Advances in Natural Language Processing*, John Benjamins, Amsterdam/Philadelphia, Borovets, Bulgaria, volume V.

Jörg Tiedemann. 2012. Parallel Data, Tools and Interfaces in OPUS. In *Proceedings of the 8th International Conference on Language Resources and Evaluation*.

Marlies van der Wees, Arianna Bisazza, and Christof Monz. 2017. Dynamic data selection for neural machine translation. In *Proceedings of the 2017 Conference on Empirical Methods in Natural Language Processing*. Association for Computational Linguistics, pages 1411–1421. http://aclweb.org/anthology/D17-1148.

Ashish Vaswani, Noam Shazeer, Niki Parmar, Jakob Uszkoreit, Llion Jones, Aidan N. Gomez, Lukasz Kaiser, and Illia Polosukhin. 2017. Attention is all you need. *CoRR* abs/1706.03762. http://arxiv.org/abs/1706.03762.

Ashish Venugopal, Jakob Uszkoreit, David Talbot, Franz Och, and Juri Ganitkevitch. 2011. Watermarking the outputs of structured prediction with an application in statistical machine translation. In *Proceedings of the 2011 Conference on Empirical Methods in Natural Language Processing*. Association for Computational Linguistics, Edinburgh, Scotland, UK., pages 1363–1372. http://www.aclweb.org/anthology/D11-1126.

Hainan Xu and Philipp Koehn. 2017. Zipporah: a fast and scalable data cleaning system for noisy web-crawled parallel corpora. In *Proceedings of the 2017 Conference on Empirical Methods in Natural Language Processing*. Association for Computational Linguistics, pages 2935–2940. http://aclweb.org/anthology/D17-1318.

Bi-Directional Neural Machine Translation with Synthetic Parallel Data

Xing Niu
University of Maryland
xingniu@cs.umd.edu

Michael Denkowski
Amazon.com, Inc.
mdenkows@amazon.com

Marine Carpuat
University of Maryland
marine@cs.umd.edu

Abstract

Despite impressive progress in high-resource settings, Neural Machine Translation (NMT) still struggles in low-resource and out-of-domain scenarios, often failing to match the quality of phrase-based translation. We propose a novel technique that combines back-translation and multilingual NMT to improve performance in these difficult cases. Our technique trains a single model for both directions of a language pair, allowing us to back-translate source or target monolingual data without requiring an auxiliary model. We then continue training on the augmented parallel data, enabling a cycle of improvement for a single model that can incorporate any source, target, or parallel data to improve both translation directions. As a byproduct, these models can reduce training and deployment costs significantly compared to uni-directional models. Extensive experiments show that our technique outperforms standard back-translation in low-resource scenarios, improves quality on cross-domain tasks, and effectively reduces costs across the board.

1 Introduction

Neural Machine Translation (NMT) has been rapidly adopted in industry as it consistently outperforms previous methods across domains and language pairs (Bojar et al., 2017; Cettolo et al., 2017). However, NMT systems still struggle compared to Phrase-based Statistical Machine Translation (SMT) in low-resource or out-of-domain scenarios (Koehn and Knowles, 2017). This performance gap is a significant roadblock to full adoption of NMT.

In many low-resource scenarios, parallel data is prohibitively expensive or otherwise impractical to collect, whereas monolingual data may be more abundant. SMT systems have the advantage of a dedicated language model that can incorporate all available target-side monolingual data to significantly improve translation quality (Koehn et al., 2003; Koehn and Schroeder, 2007). By contrast, NMT systems consist of one large neural network that performs full sequence-to-sequence translation (Sutskever et al., 2014; Cho et al., 2014). Trained end-to-end on parallel data, these models lack a direct avenue for incorporating monolingual data. Sennrich et al. (2016a) overcome this challenge by back-translating target monolingual data to produce *synthetic* parallel data that can be added to the training pool. While effective, back-translation introduces the significant cost of first building a reverse system.

Another technique for overcoming a lack of data is multitask learning, in which domain knowledge can be transferred between related tasks (Caruana, 1997). Johnson et al. (2017) apply the idea to multilingual NMT by concatenating parallel data of various language pairs and marking the source with the desired output language. The authors report promising results for translation between languages that have zero parallel data. This approach also dramatically reduces the complexity of deployment by packing multiple language pairs into a single model.

We propose a novel combination of back-translation and multilingual NMT that trains both directions of a language pair jointly in a single model. Specifically, we initialize a bi-directional model on parallel data and then use it to translate select source and target monolingual data. Training is then continued on the augmented parallel data, leading to a cycle of improvement. This approach has several advantages:

Proceedings of the 2nd Workshop on Neural Machine Translation and Generation, pages 84–91
Melbourne, Australia, July 20, 2018. ©2018 Association for Computational Linguistics

- A single NMT model with standard architecture that performs all forward and backward translation during training.

- Training costs reduced significantly compared to uni-directional systems.

- Improvements in translating quality for low-resource languages, even over uni-directional systems with back-translation.

- Effectiveness in domain adaptation.

Via comprehensive experiments, we also contribute to best practices in selecting most suitable combinations of synthetic parallel data and choosing appropriate amount of monolingual data.

2 Approach

In this section, we introduce an efficient method for improving bi-directional neural machine translation with synthetic parallel data. We also present a strategy for selecting suitable monolingual data for back-translation.

2.1 Bi-Directional NMT with Synthetic Parallel Data

We use the techniques described by Johnson et al. (2017) to build a multilingual model that combines forward and backward directions of a single language pair. To begin, we construct training data by swapping the source and target sentences of a parallel corpus and appending the swapped version to the original. We then add an artificial token to the beginning of each source sentence to mark the desired target language, such as <2en> for English. A standard NMT system can then be trained on the augmented dataset, which is naturally balanced between language directions.[1] A shared Byte-Pair Encoding (BPE) model is built on source and target data, alleviating the issue of unknown words and reducing the vocabulary to a smaller set of items shared across languages (Sennrich et al., 2016b; Johnson et al., 2017). We further reduce model complexity by tying source and target word embeddings. The full training process significantly saves the total computing resources compared to training an individual model for each language direction.

Generating synthetic parallel data is straightforward with a bi-directional model: sentences from both source and target monolingual data can be translated to produce synthetic sentence pairs. Synthetic parallel data of the form `synthetic → monolingual` can then be used in the forward direction, the backward direction, or both. Crucially, this approach leverages both source and target monolingual data while always placing the real data on the target side, eliminating the need for work-arounds such as freezing certain model parameters to avoid degradation from training on MT output (Zhang and Zong, 2016).

2.2 Monolingual Data Selection

Given the goal of improving a base bi-directional model, selecting ideal monolingual data for back-translation presents a significant challenge. Data too close to the original training data may not provide sufficient new information for the model. Conversely, data too far from the original data may be translated too poorly by the base model to be useful. We manage these risks by leveraging a standard pseudo in-domain data selection technique, cross-entropy difference (Moore and Lewis, 2010; Axelrod et al., 2011), to rank sentences from a general domain. Smaller cross-entropy difference indicates a sentence that is simultaneously more similar to the in-domain corpus (e.g. real parallel data) and less similar to the average of the general-domain monolingual corpus. This allows us to begin with "safe" monolingual data and incrementally expand to higher risk but potentially more informative data.

3 Experiments

In this section, we describe data, settings, and experimental methodology. We then present the results of comprehensive experiments designed to answer the following questions: (1) How can synthetic data be most effectively used to improve translation quality? (2) Does the reduction in training time for bi-directional NMT come at the cost of lower translation quality? (3) Can we further improve training speed and translation quality training with incremental training and re-decoding? (4) How can we effectively choose monolingual training data? (5) How well does bi-directional NMT perform on domain adaptation?

3.1 Data

Diverse Language Pairs: We evaluate our approach on both high and low-resource data sets:

---

[1] Johnson et al. (2017) report the need to oversample when data is significantly unbalanced between language pairs.

Type	Dataset	# Sentences
High-resource: German↔English		
Training	Common Crawl +	
	Europarl v7 +	
	News Comm. v12	4,356,324
Dev	Newstest 2015+2016	5,168
Test	Newstest 2017	3,004
Mono-DE	News Crawl 2016	26,982,051
Mono-EN	News Crawl 2016	18,238,848
Low-resource: Tagalog↔English		
Training	News/Blog	50,705
Dev/Test	News/Blog	491/508
Dev/Test*	Bible	500/500
Sample*	Bible	61,195
Mono-TL	Common Crawl	26,788,048
Mono-EN	ICWSM 2009 blog	48,219,743
Low-resource: Swahili↔English		
Training	News/Blog	23,900
Dev/Test	News/Blog	491/509
Dev/Test*	Bible-NT	500/500
Sample*	Bible-NT	14,699
Mono-SW	Common Crawl	12,158,524
Mono-EN	ICWSM 2009 blog	48,219,743

Table 1: Data sizes of training, development, test, sample and monolingual sets. Sample data serves as the in-domain seed for data selection.

German↔English (DE↔EN), Tagalog↔English TL↔EN, and Swahili↔English (SW↔EN). Parallel and monolingual DE↔EN data are provided by the WMT17 news translation task (Bojar et al., 2017). Parallel data for TL↔EN and SW↔EN contains a mixture of domains such as news and weblogs, and is provided as part of the IARPA MATERIAL program.[2] We split the original corpora into training, dev, and test sets, therefore they share a homogeneous n-gram distribution. For these low-resource pairs, TL and SW monolingual data are provided by the Common Crawl (Buck et al., 2014) while EN monolingual data is provided by the ICWSM 2009 Spinn3r blog dataset (tier-1) (Burton et al., 2009).

Diverse Domain Settings: For WMT17 DE↔EN, we choose news articles from 2016 (the closest year to the test set) as in-domain data for back-translation. For TL↔EN and SW↔EN, we identify in-domain and out-of-domain mono-

[2]https://www.iarpa.gov/index.php/research-programs/material

lingual data and apply data selection to choose pseudo in-domain data (see Section 2.2). We use the training data as in-domain and either Common Crawl or ICWSM as out-of-domain. We also include a low-resource, long-distance domain adaptation task for these languages: training on News/Blog data and testing on Bible data. We split a parallel Bible corpus (Christodoulopoulos and Steedman, 2015) into sample, dev, and test sets, using the sample data as the in-domain seed for data selection.

Preprocessing: Following Hieber et al. (2017), we apply four pre-processing steps to parallel data: normalization, tokenization, sentence-filtering (length 80 cutoff), and joint source-target BPE with 50,000 operations (Sennrich et al., 2016b). Low-resource language pairs are also true-cased to reduce sparsity. BPE and true-casing models are rebuilt whenever the training data changes. Monolingual data for low-resource settings is filtered by retaining sentences longer than nine tokens. Itemized data statistics after pre-processing can be found in Table 1.

3.2 NMT Configuration

We use the attentional RNN encoder-decoder architecture implemented in the Sockeye toolkit (Hieber et al., 2017). Our translation model uses a bi-directional encoder with a single LSTM layer of size 512, multilayer perceptron attention with a layer size of 512, and word representations of size 512 (Bahdanau et al., 2015). We apply layer normalization (Ba et al., 2016) and tie source and target embedding parameters. We train using the Adam optimizer with a batch size of 64 sentences and checkpoint the model every 1000 updates (10,000 for DE↔EN) (Kingma and Ba, 2015). Training stops after 8 checkpoints without improvement of perplexity on the development set. We decode with a beam size of 5.

For TL↔EN and SW↔EN, we add dropout to embeddings and RNNs of the encoder and decoder with probability 0.2. We also tie the output layer's weight matrix with the source and target embeddings to reduce model size (Press and Wolf, 2017). The effectiveness of tying input/output target embeddings has been verified on several low-resource language pairs (Nguyen and Chiang, 2018).

For TL↔EN and SW↔EN, we train four randomly seeded models for each experiment and combine them in a linear ensemble for decod-

ID	Training Data	TL→EN	EN→TL	SW→EN	EN→SW	DE→EN	EN→DE
U-1	L1→L2	31.99	31.28	32.60	39.98	29.51	23.01
U-2	L1→L2 + L1*→L2	**24.21**	**29.68**	**25.84**	**38.29**	**33.20**	**25.41**
U-3	L1→L2 + L1→L2*	22.13	27.14	24.89	36.53	30.89	23.72
U-4	L1→L2 + L1*→L2 + L1→L2*	23.38	29.31	25.33	37.46	33.01	25.05
	L1=EN	L2=TL		L2=SW		L2=DE	
B-1	L1↔L2	32.72	31.66	33.59	39.12	28.84	22.45
B-2	L1↔L2 + L1*↔L2	32.90	**32.33**	33.70	**39.68**	29.17	**24.45**
B-3	L1↔L2 + L2*↔L1	32.71	31.10	33.70	39.17	**31.71**	21.71
B-4	L1↔L2 + L1*↔L2 + L2*↔L1	**33.25**	**32.46**	**34.23**	38.97	30.43	22.54
B-5	L1↔L2 + L1*→L2 + L2*→L1	**33.41**	**33.21**	**34.11**	**40.24**	**31.83**	**24.61**
B-5*	L1↔L2 + L1*→L2 + L2*→L1	33.79	32.97	34.15	40.61	31.94	24.45
B-6*	L1↔L2 + <u>L1*</u>→L2 + <u>L2*</u>→L1	**34.50**	**33.73**	**34.88**	**41.53**	**32.49**	**25.20**

Table 2: BLEU scores for uni-directional models (U-*) and bi-directional NMT models (B-*) trained on different combinations of real and synthetic parallel data. Models in B-5* are fine-tuned from base models in B-1. Best models in B-6* are fine-tuned from precedent models in B-5* and underscored synthetic data is re-decoded using precedent models. Scores with largest improvement within each zone are highlighted.

ing. For DE↔EN experiments, we train a single model and average the parameters of the best four checkpoints for decoding (Junczys-Dowmunt et al., 2016). We report case-insensitive BLEU with standard WMT tokenization.[3]

3.3 Uni-Directional NMT

We first evaluate the impact of synthetic parallel data on standard uni-directional NMT. Baseline systems trained on real parallel data are shown in row U-1 of Table 2.[4] In all tables, we use L1→L2 to indicate real parallel data where the source language is L1 and the target language is L2. Synthetic data is annotated by asterisks, such as L1*→L2 indicating that L1* is the synthetic back-translation of real monolingual data L2.

We always select monolingual data as an integer multiple of the amount of real parallel data n, i.e. $|L1→L2*| = |L1*→L2| = kn$. For DE↔EN models, we simply choose the top-n sentences from shuffled News Crawl corpus. For all models of low-resource languages, we select the top-$3n$ sentences ranked by cross-entropy difference as described in Section 2.2. The choice of k is discussed in Section 3.4.2.

Shown in rows U-2 through U-4 of Table 2, we compare the results of incorporating differ-

ent combinations of real and synthetic parallel data. Models trained on **only real data of target language** (i.e. in U-2) achieve better performance in BLEU than using other combinations. This is an expected result since translation quality is highly correlated with target language models. By contrast, standard back-translation is not effective for our low-resource scenarios. A significant drop (∼7 BLEU comparing U-1 and U-2 for TL/SW→EN) is observed when back-translating English. One possible reason is that the quality of the selected monolingual data, especially English, is not ideal. We will encounter this issue again when using bi-directional models with the same data in Section 3.4.

3.4 Bi-Directional NMT

We map the same synthetic data combinations to bi-directional NMT, comparing against uni-directional models with respect to both translation quality and training time. Training bi-directional models requires doubling the training data by adding a second copy of the parallel corpus where the source and target are swapped. We use the notation L1↔L2 to represent the concatenation of L1→L2 and its swapped copy L2→L1 in Table 2.

Compared to independent models (i.e. U-1), the bi-directional DE↔EN model in B-1 is slightly worse (by ∼0.6 BLEU). These losses match observations by Johnson et al. (2017) on many-to-many multilingual NMT models. By contrast, bi-directional low-resource models slightly outper-

---

Model		TL→EN	EN→TL	SW→EN	EN→SW	DE→EN	EN→DE
	Baseline	76	78	63	66	41	48
Uni-directional	Synthetic	177	176	137	104	88	75
	TOTAL		507		371		252
	Baseline		125		93		61
Bi-directional	Synthetic		285		218		113
	TOTAL	↓ 19%	410	↓ 14%	311	↓ 31%	174
(fine-tuning)	Synthetic	↓ 23%	219	↓ 44%	122	↓ 24%	86

Table 3: Number of checkpoints (= |updates|/1000 for TL/SW↔EN or |updates|/10,000 for DE↔EN) used by various NMT models. Bi-directional models reduce the training time by 15-30% (comparing 'TOTAL' rows). Fine-tuning bi-directional baseline models on synthetic parallel data reduces the training time by 20-40% (comparing 'Synthetic' rows).

form independent models. We hypothesize that in low-resource scenarios the neural model's capacity is far from exhausted due to the redundancy in neural network parameters (Denil et al., 2013), and the benefit of training on twice as much data surpasses the detriment of confusing the model by mixing two languages.

We generate synthetic parallel data from the same monolingual data as in the uni-directional experiments. If we build training data symmetrically (i.e. B-2,3,4), back-translated sentences are distributed equally on the source and target sides, forcing the model to train on some amount of synthetic target data (MT output). For DE↔EN models, the best BLEU scores are achieved when synthetic training data is only present on the source side while for low-resource models, the results are mixed. We see a particularly counter-intuitive result when using monolingual English data — no significant improvement (see B-3 for TL/SW→EN). As bi-directional models are able to leverage monolingual data of both languages, better results are achieved when combining all synthetic parallel data (see B-4 for TL/SW→EN). By further excluding potentially harmful target-side synthetic data (i.e. B-4 → B-5), the most unified and slim models achieve best overall performance.

While the best bi-directional NMT models thus far (B-5) outperform the best uni-directional models (U-1,2) for low-resource language pairs, they struggle to match performance in the high-resource DE↔EN scenario.

In terms of efficiency, bi-directional models consistently reduce the training time by 15-30% as shown in Table 3. Note that checkpoints are summed over all independent runs when ensemble decoding is used.

3.4.1 Fine-Tuning and Re-Decoding

Training new NMT models from scratch after generating synthetic data is incredibly expensive, working against our goal of reducing the overall cost of deploying strong translation systems. Following the practice of mixed fine-tuning proposed by Chu et al. (2017), we continue training baseline models on augmented data as shown in B-5* of Table 2. These models achieve comparable translation quality to those trained from scratch (B-5) at a significantly reduced cost, up to 20-40% computing time in the experiments illustrated in Table 3.

We also explore re-decoding the same monolingual data using improved models (Sennrich et al., 2016a). Underscored synthetic data in B-6* is re-decoded by models in B-5*, leading to the best results for all low-resource scenarios and competitive results for our high-resource scenario.

3.4.2 Size of Selected Monolingual Data

In our experiments, the optimal amount of monolingual data for constructing synthetic parallel data is task-dependent. Factors such as size and linguistic distribution of data and overlap between real parallel data, monolingual data, and test data can influence the effectiveness curve of synthetic data. We illustrate the impact of varying the size of selected monolingual data in our low-resource scenario. Shown in Figure 1, all language pairs have an increasing momentum and tend to converge with more synthetic parallel data. The optimal point is a hyper-parameter that can be empirically determined.

3.4.3 Domain Adaptation

We evaluate the performance of using the same bi-directional NMT framework on a long-distance

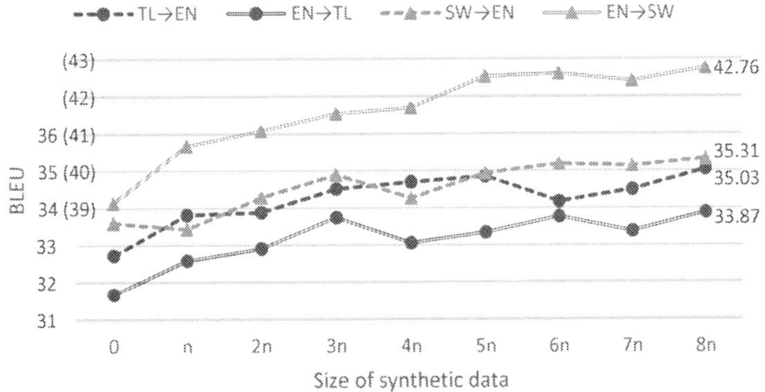

Figure 1: BLEU scores for four translation directions vs. the size of selected monolingual data. n in x-axis equals to the size of real parallel data. EN→SW models use BLEU in parentheses in y-axis. All language pairs have an increasing momentum and tend to converge with more synthetic parallel data.

		L2=TL		L2=SW	
ID	Training Data (L1=EN)	TL→EN	EN→TL	SW→EN	EN→SW
A-1	L1↔L2	11.03	10.17	6.56	3.80
A-2	L1↔L2 + L1⋆→L2 + L2⋆→L1	16.49	22.33	8.70	7.47
A-3	L1↔L2 + <u>L1⋆</u>→L2 + <u>L2⋆</u>→L1	**18.91**	**23.41**	**11.01**	**8.06**

Table 4: BLEU scores for bi-directional NMT models on Bible data. Models in A-2 are fine-tuned from baseline models in A-1. Highlighted best models in A-3 are fine-tuned from precedent models in A-2 and underscored synthetic data is re-decoded using precedent models. Baseline models are significantly improved in terms of BLEU.

domain adaptation task: News/Blog to Bible. This task is particularly challenging because out-of-vocabulary rates of Bible test sets are as high as 30-45% when training on News/Blog. Significant linguistic differences also exist between modern and Biblical language use. The impact of this domain mismatch is demonstrated by the incredibly low BLEU scores of baseline News/Blog systems (Table 4, A-1). After fine-tuning baseline models on augmented parallel data (A-2) and re-decoding (A-3),[5] we see BLEU scores increase by 70-130%. Despite being based on extremely weak baseline performance, they still show the promise of our approach for domain adaptation.

4 Related Work

Leveraging monolingual data in NMT is challenging. For example, integrating language models in the decoder (Gülçehre et al., 2015) or initializing the encoder and decoder with pre-trained language models (Ramachandran et al., 2017) would require

significant changes to system architecture.

In this work, we build on the elegant and effective approach of turning incomplete (monolingual) data into complete (parallel) data by back-translation. Sennrich et al. (2016a) used an auxiliary reverse-directional NMT system to generate synthetic source data from real monolingual target data, with promising results (+3 BLEU on strong baselines). Symmetrically, Zhang and Zong (2016) used an auxiliary same-directional translation system to generate synthetic target data from the real source language. However, parameters of the decoder have to be frozen while training on synthetic data, otherwise the decoder would fit to noisy MT output. By contrast, our approach effectively leverages synthetic data from both translation directions, with consistent gains in translation quality. A similar idea is used by Zhang et al. (2018) with a focus on re-decoding iteratively. However, their NMT models of both directions are still trained independently.

Another technique for using monolingual data in NMT is round-trip machine translation. Sup-

---

[5]The concatenation of development sets from both News/Blog and Bible serves for validation.

pose sentence f from a monolingual dataset is translated forward to e and then translated back to f', then f' and f should be identical (Brislin, 1970). Cheng et al. (2016) optimize $\arg\max_\theta P(f'|f;\theta)$ as an autoencoder; Wang et al. (2018) minimize the difference between $P(f)$ and $P(f'|\theta)$ based on the law of total probability, while He et al. (2016) set the quality of both e and f' as rewards for reinforcement learning. They all achieve promising improvement but rely on non-standard training frameworks.

Multitask learning has been used in past work to combine models trained on different parallel corpora by sharing certain components. These components, such as the attention mechanism (Firat et al., 2016), benefit from being trained on an effectively larger dataset. In addition, the more parameters are shared, the faster a joint model can be trained — this is particularity beneficial in industry settings. Baidu built one-to-many translation systems by sharing both encoder and attention (Dong et al., 2015). Google enabled a standard NMT framework to support many-to-many translation directions by simply attaching a language specifier to each source sentence (Johnson et al., 2017). We adopted Google's approach to build bidirectional systems that successfully combine actual and synthetic parallel data.

5 Conclusion

We propose a novel technique for bi-directional neural machine translation. A single model with a standard NMT architecture performs both forward and backward translation, allowing it to back-translate and incorporate any source or target monolingual data. By continuing training on augmented parallel data, bi-directional NMT models consistently achieve improved translation quality, particularly in low-resource scenarios and cross-domain tasks. These models also reduce training and deployment costs significantly compared to standard uni-directional models.

Acknowledgments

Part of this research was conducted while the first author was an intern at Amazon. At Maryland, this research is based upon work supported in part by the Clare Boothe Luce Foundation, and by the Office of the Director of National Intelligence (ODNI), Intelligence Advanced Research Projects Activity (IARPA), via contract #FA8650-17-C-9117. The views and conclusions contained herein are those of the authors and should not be interpreted as necessarily representing the official policies, either expressed or implied, of ODNI, IARPA, or the U.S. Government. The U.S. Government is authorized to reproduce and distribute reprints for governmental purposes notwithstanding any copyright annotation therein.

References

Amittai Axelrod, Xiaodong He, and Jianfeng Gao. 2011. Domain adaptation via pseudo in-domain data selection. In *EMNLP*, pages 355–362. ACL.

Lei Jimmy Ba, Ryan Kiros, and Geoffrey E. Hinton. 2016. Layer normalization. *CoRR*, abs/1607.06450.

Dzmitry Bahdanau, Kyunghyun Cho, and Yoshua Bengio. 2015. Neural machine translation by jointly learning to align and translate. In *ICLR*.

Ondrej Bojar, Rajen Chatterjee, Christian Federmann, Yvette Graham, Barry Haddow, Shujian Huang, Matthias Huck, Philipp Koehn, Qun Liu, Varvara Logacheva, Christof Monz, Matteo Negri, Matt Post, Raphael Rubino, Lucia Specia, and Marco Turchi. 2017. Findings of the 2017 conference on machine translation (WMT17). In *WMT*, pages 169–214. Association for Computational Linguistics.

Richard W Brislin. 1970. Back-translation for cross-cultural research. *Journal of cross-cultural psychology*, 1(3):185–216.

Christian Buck, Kenneth Heafield, and Bas van Ooyen. 2014. N-gram counts and language models from the common crawl. In *LREC*, pages 3579–3584. European Language Resources Association (ELRA).

Kevin Burton, Akshay Java, and Ian Soboroff. 2009. The ICWSM 2009 Spinn3r dataset. In *Proceedings of the Third Annual Conference on Weblogs and Social Media (ICWSM 2009), San Jose, CA*.

Rich Caruana. 1997. Multitask learning. *Machine Learning*, 28(1):41–75.

Mauro Cettolo, Marcello Federico, Luisa Bentivogli, Jan Niehues, Sebastian Stüker, Katsuitho Sudoh, Koichiro Yoshino, and Christian Federmann. 2017. Overview of the IWSLT 2017 evaluation campaign. In *International Workshop on Spoken Language Translation*, pages 2–14.

Yong Cheng, Wei Xu, Zhongjun He, Wei He, Hua Wu, Maosong Sun, and Yang Liu. 2016. Semi-supervised learning for neural machine translation. In *ACL (1)*. The Association for Computer Linguistics.

Kyunghyun Cho, Bart van Merrienboer, Çaglar Gülçehre, Dzmitry Bahdanau, Fethi Bougares, Holger Schwenk, and Yoshua Bengio. 2014. Learning phrase representations using RNN encoder-decoder for statistical machine translation. In *EMNLP*, pages 1724–1734. ACL.

Christos Christodoulopoulos and Mark Steedman. 2015. A massively parallel corpus: the bible in 100 languages. *Language Resources and Evaluation*, 49(2):375–395.

Chenhui Chu, Raj Dabre, and Sadao Kurohashi. 2017. An empirical comparison of domain adaptation methods for neural machine translation. In *ACL (2)*, pages 385–391. Association for Computational Linguistics.

Misha Denil, Babak Shakibi, Laurent Dinh, Marc'Aurelio Ranzato, and Nando de Freitas. 2013. Predicting parameters in deep learning. In *NIPS*, pages 2148–2156.

Daxiang Dong, Hua Wu, Wei He, Dianhai Yu, and Haifeng Wang. 2015. Multi-task learning for multiple language translation. In *ACL (1)*, pages 1723–1732. The Association for Computer Linguistics.

Orhan Firat, Kyunghyun Cho, and Yoshua Bengio. 2016. Multi-way, multilingual neural machine translation with a shared attention mechanism. In *HLT-NAACL*, pages 866–875. The Association for Computational Linguistics.

Çaglar Gülçehre, Orhan Firat, Kelvin Xu, Kyunghyun Cho, Loïc Barrault, Huei-Chi Lin, Fethi Bougares, Holger Schwenk, and Yoshua Bengio. 2015. On using monolingual corpora in neural machine translation. *CoRR*, abs/1503.03535.

Di He, Yingce Xia, Tao Qin, Liwei Wang, Nenghai Yu, Tie-Yan Liu, and Wei-Ying Ma. 2016. Dual learning for machine translation. In *NIPS*, pages 820–828.

Felix Hieber, Tobias Domhan, Michael Denkowski, David Vilar, Artem Sokolov, Ann Clifton, and Matt Post. 2017. Sockeye: A toolkit for neural machine translation. *CoRR*, abs/1712.05690.

Melvin Johnson, Mike Schuster, Quoc V. Le, Maxim Krikun, Yonghui Wu, Zhifeng Chen, Nikhil Thorat, Fernanda B. Viégas, Martin Wattenberg, Greg Corrado, Macduff Hughes, and Jeffrey Dean. 2017. Google's multilingual neural machine translation system: Enabling zero-shot translation. *TACL*, 5:339–351.

Marcin Junczys-Dowmunt, Tomasz Dwojak, and Rico Sennrich. 2016. The AMU-UEDIN submission to the WMT16 news translation task: Attention-based NMT models as feature functions in phrase-based SMT. In *WMT*, pages 319–325. The Association for Computer Linguistics.

Diederik P. Kingma and Jimmy Ba. 2015. Adam: A method for stochastic optimization. In *ICLR*.

Philipp Koehn and Rebecca Knowles. 2017. Six challenges for neural machine translation. In *NMT@ACL*, pages 28–39. Association for Computational Linguistics.

Philipp Koehn, Franz Josef Och, and Daniel Marcu. 2003. Statistical phrase-based translation. In *HLT-NAACL*. The Association for Computational Linguistics.

Philipp Koehn and Josh Schroeder. 2007. Experiments in domain adaptation for statistical machine translation. In *WMT@ACL*, pages 224–227. Association for Computational Linguistics.

Robert C. Moore and William D. Lewis. 2010. Intelligent selection of language model training data. In *ACL (Short Papers)*, pages 220–224. The Association for Computer Linguistics.

Toan Q. Nguyen and David Chiang. 2018. Improving lexical choice in neural machine translation. In *HLT-NAACL*. The Association for Computational Linguistics.

Ofir Press and Lior Wolf. 2017. Using the output embedding to improve language models. In *EACL (2)*, pages 157–163. Association for Computational Linguistics.

Prajit Ramachandran, Peter J. Liu, and Quoc V. Le. 2017. Unsupervised pretraining for sequence to sequence learning. In *EMNLP*, pages 383–391. Association for Computational Linguistics.

Rico Sennrich, Barry Haddow, and Alexandra Birch. 2016a. Improving neural machine translation models with monolingual data. In *ACL (1)*. The Association for Computer Linguistics.

Rico Sennrich, Barry Haddow, and Alexandra Birch. 2016b. Neural machine translation of rare words with subword units. In *ACL (1)*. The Association for Computer Linguistics.

Ilya Sutskever, Oriol Vinyals, and Quoc V. Le. 2014. Sequence to sequence learning with neural networks. In *NIPS*, pages 3104–3112.

Yijun Wang, Yingce Xia, Li Zhao, Jiang Bian, Tao Qin, Guiquan Liu, and Tie-Yan Liu. 2018. Dual transfer learning for neural machine translation with marginal distribution regularization. In *AAAI*. AAAI Press.

Jiajun Zhang and Chengqing Zong. 2016. Exploiting source-side monolingual data in neural machine translation. In *EMNLP*, pages 1535–1545. The Association for Computational Linguistics.

Zhirui Zhang, Shujie Liu, Mu Li, Ming Zhou, and Enhong Chen. 2018. Joint training for neural machine translation models with monolingual data. In *AAAI*. AAAI Press.

Multi-Source Neural Machine Translation with Missing Data

Yuta Nishimura[1] , **Katsuhito Sudoh**[1] , **Graham Neubig**[2,1] , **Satoshi Nakamura**[1]
[1]Nara Institute of Science and Technology, 8916-5 Takayama-cho, Ikoma, Nara 630-0192, Japan
[2]Carnegie Mellon University, 5000 Forbes Avenue, Pittsburgh, PA 15213, USA
{nishimura.yuta.nn9, sudoh, s-nakamura}@is.naist.jp
gneubig@cs.cmu.edu

Abstract

Multi-source translation is an approach to exploit multiple inputs (e.g. in two different languages) to increase translation accuracy. In this paper, we examine approaches for multi-source neural machine translation (NMT) using an *incomplete* multilingual corpus in which some translations are missing. In practice, many multilingual corpora are not complete due to the difficulty to provide translations in *all* of the relevant languages (for example, in TED talks, most English talks only have subtitles for a small portion of the languages that TED supports). Existing studies on multi-source translation did not explicitly handle such situations. This study focuses on the use of incomplete multilingual corpora in multi-encoder NMT and mixture of NMT experts and examines a very simple implementation where missing source translations are replaced by a special symbol <NULL>. These methods allow us to use incomplete corpora both at training time and test time. In experiments with real incomplete multilingual corpora of TED Talks, the multi-source NMT with the <NULL> tokens achieved higher translation accuracies measured by BLEU than those by any one-to-one NMT systems.

1 Introduction

In general, machine translation systems translate from one source language to a target language. For example, we may translate a document or speech that was written in English to a new language such as French. However, in many real translation scenarios, there are cases where there are multiple

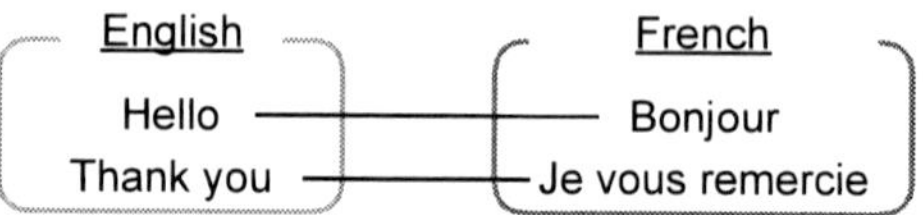

(a) A standard bilingual corpus

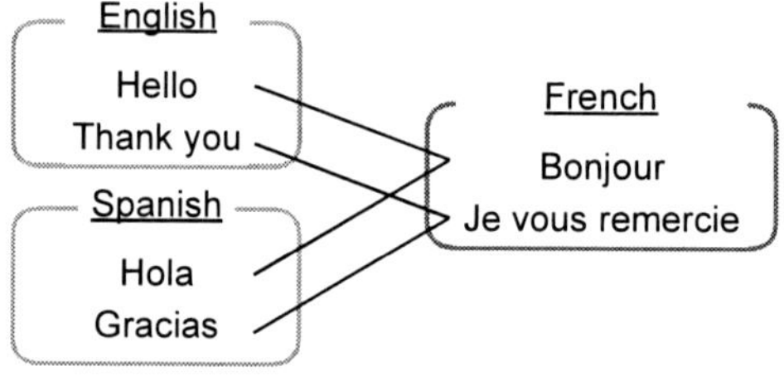

(b) A complete multi-source corpus

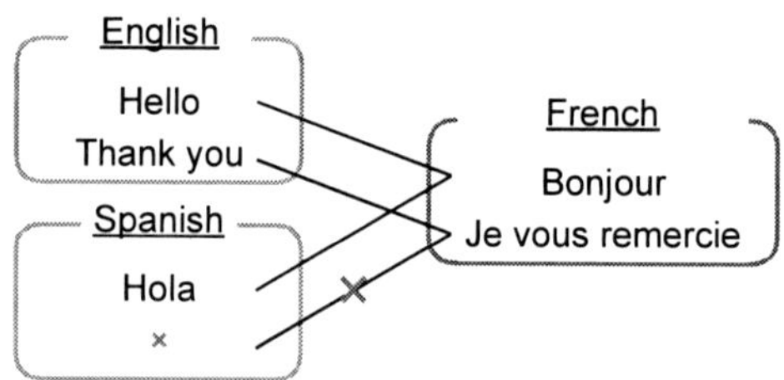

(c) An incomplete multi-source corpus with missing data

Figure 1: Example of type of corpora.

languages involved in the translation process. For example, we may have an original document in English, that we want to translate into several languages such as French, Spanish, and Portuguese. Some examples of these scenarios are the creation of video captions for talks (Cettolo et al., 2012) or Movies (Tiedemann, 2009), or translation of official documents into all the languages of a governing body, such as the European parliament (Koehn, 2005) or UN (Ziemski et al., 2016). In these cases, we are very often faced with a situation where we *already* have good, manually cu-

Proceedings of the 2nd Workshop on Neural Machine Translation and Generation, pages 92–99
Melbourne, Australia, July 20, 2018. ©2018 Association for Computational Linguistics

rated translations in a number of languages, and we'd like to generate translations in the remaining languages for which we do not yet have translations.

In this work, we focus on this sort of multilingual scenario using multi-source translation (Och and Ney, 2001; Zoph and Knight, 2016; Garmash and Monz, 2016). Multi-source translation takes in multiple inputs, and references all of them when deciding which sentence to output. Specifically, in the context of neural machine translation (NMT), there are several methods proposed to do so. For example, Zoph and Knight (2016) propose a method where multiple sentences are each encoded separately, then all referenced during the decoding process (the "multi-encoder" method). In addition, Garmash and Monz (2016) propose a method where NMT systems over multiple inputs are ensembled together to make a final prediction (the "mixture-of-NMT-experts" method).

However, this paradigm assumes that we have data in *all* of the languages that go into our multi-source system. For example, if we decide that English and Spanish are our input languages and that we would like to translate into French, we are limited to training and testing only on data that contains all of the source languages. However, it is unusual that translations in all of these languages are provided– there will be many sentences where we have only one of the sources. In this work, we consider methods for multi-source NMT with missing data, such situations using an *incomplete* multilingual corpus in which some translations are missing, as shown in Figure 1. This incomplete multilingual scenario is useful in practice, such as when creating translations for incomplete multilingual corpora such as subtitles for TED Talks.

In this paper, we examine a simple implementation of multi-source NMT using such an incomplete multilingual corpus that uses a special symbol <NULL> to represent the missing sentences. This can be used with any existing multi-source NMT implementations without no special modifications. Experimental results with real incomplete multilingual corpora of TED Talks show that it is effective in allowing for multi-source NMT in situations where full multilingual corpora are not available, resulting in BLEU score gains of up to 2 points compared to standard bi-lingual NMT.

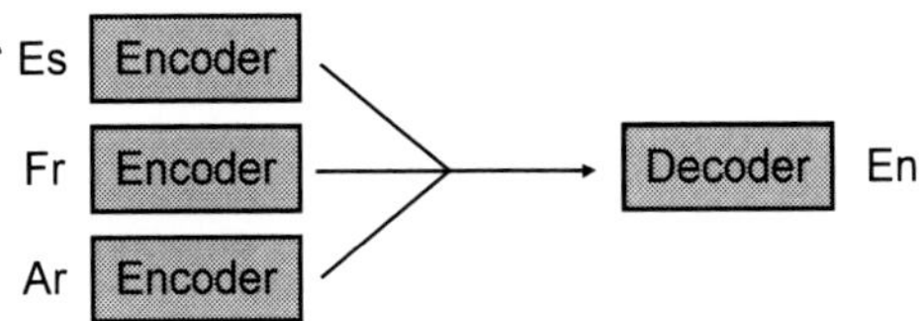

Figure 2: Multi-encoder NMT

2 Multi-Source NMT

At the present, there are two major approaches to multi-source NMT: multi-encoder NMT (Zoph and Knight, 2016) and mixture of NMT experts (Garmash and Monz, 2016). We first review them in this section.

2.1 Multi-Encoder NMT

Multi-encoder NMT (Zoph and Knight, 2016) is similar to the standard attentional NMT framework (Bahdanau et al., 2015) but uses multiple encoders corresponding to the source languages and a single decoder, as shown in Figure 2.

Suppose we have two LSTM-based encoders and their hidden states and cell states at the end of the inputs are h_1, h_2 and c_1, c_2, respectively. The multi-encoder NMT method initializes its decoder hidden states h and cell state c as follows:

$$h = \tanh(W_c[h_1; h_2]) \qquad (1)$$

$$c = c_1 + c_2 \qquad (2)$$

Attention is then defined over each encoder at each time step t and resulting context vectors c_t^1 and c_t^2, which are concatenated together with the corresponding decoder hidden state h_t to calculate the final context vector $\tilde{h}_t$.

$$\tilde{h}_t = \tanh(W_c[h_t; c_t^1; c_t^2]) \qquad (3)$$

The method we base our work upon is largely similar to Zoph and Knight (2016), with the exception of a few details. Most notably, they used *local-p* attention, which focuses only on a small subset of the source positions for each target word (Luong et al., 2015). In this work, we used *global* attention, which attends to all words on the source side for each target word, as this is the standard method used in the great majority of recent NMT work.

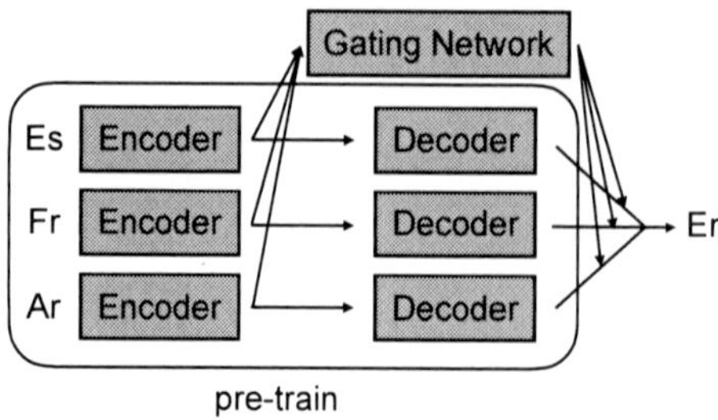

Figure 3: Mixture of NMT Experts

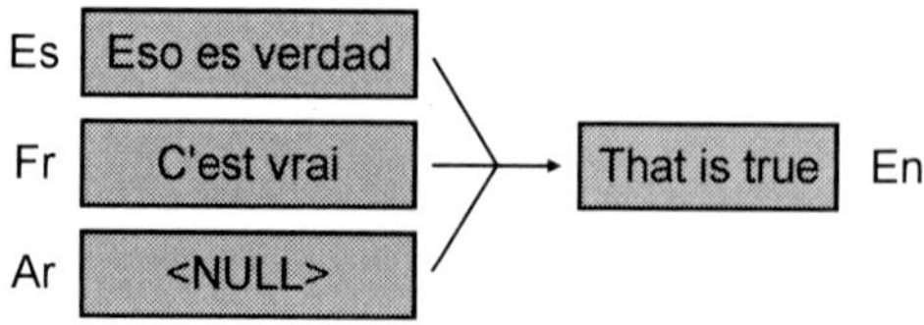

Figure 4: Multi-encoder NMT with a missing input sentence

2.2 Mixture of NMT Experts

Garmash and Monz (2016) proposed another approach to multi-source NMT called *mixture of NMT experts*. This method ensembles together independently-trained encoder-decoder networks. Each NMT model is trained using a bilingual corpus with one source language and the target language, and the outputs from the one-to-one models are summed together, weighted according to a gating network to control contributions of the probabilities from each model, as shown in Figure 3.

The mixture of NMT experts determines an output symbol at each time step t from the final output vector p_t^ϵ, which is the weighted sum of the probability vectors from one-to-one models denoted as follows:

$$p_t^\epsilon = \sum_{j=1}^{m} g_t^j p_t^j \qquad (4)$$

where p_t^j and g_t^j are the probability vector from j-th model and the corresponding weight at time step t, respectively. m is the number of one-to-one models. g_t is calculated by the gating network as follows:

$$g_t = \mathrm{softmax}(W_{gate} \tanh(W_{hid}[f_t^{1}(x); ...f_t^{m}(x)])) \qquad (5)$$

where $f_t^j(x)$ is the input vector to the decoder of the j-th model, typically the embedding vector for the output symbol at the previous time step t-1.

3 Multi-Source NMT with Missing Data

In this work, we examine methods to use incomplete multilingual corpora to improve NMT in a specific language pair. This allows multi-source techniques to be applied, reaping the benefits of other additional languages even if some translations in these additional languages are missing.

Specifically, we attempt to extend the methods in the previous section to use an incomplete multilingual corpus in this work.

3.1 Multi-encoder NMT

In multi-encoder NMT, each encoder must be provide with an input sentence, so incomplete multilingual corpora cannot be used as-is.

In this work, we employ a very simple modification that helps resolve this issue: replacing each missing input sentence with a special symbol <NULL>. The special symbol <NULL> can be expected to be basically ignored in multi-encoder NMT, with the decoder choosing word hypotheses using other input sentences. Note that this method can be applied easily to any existing implementation of the multi-encoder NMT with no modification of the codes.

Figure 4 illustrates the modified multi-encoder NMT method. Here the source languages are Spanish, French, and Arabic and the target language is English, and the Arabic input sentence is missing. Here, the Spanish and French input sentences are passed into the corresponding encoders and <NULL> is input to the Arabic encoder.

3.2 Mixture of NMT Experts

In the mixture of NMT experts method, each one-to-one NMT model can be trained independently using incomplete multilingual corpora. However, we still need a complete multilingual corpus to train the gating network.

We also employ a special symbol <NULL> in the mixture of NMT experts to deal with missing input sentences in the same way as the multi-encoder NMT described above. The gating network can also be expected to learn to ignore the outputs from the missing inputs.

4   Experiments

We conducted two experiments with different incomplete multilingual corpora. One is an experiment with a pseudo-incomplete multilingual corpus, the other is an experiment with an actual incomplete multilingual corpus.

4.1   NMT settings

We describe the settings of common parts for all NMT models: multi-encoder NMT, mixture of NMT experts, and one-to-one NMT. We used global attention and attention feeding (Luong et al., 2015) for the NMT models and used a bidirectional encoder (Bahdanau et al., 2015) in their encoders. The number of units was 512 for the hidden and embedding layers. Vocabulary size was the most frequent 30,000 words in the training data for each source and target languages. The parameter optimization algorithm was Adam (Kingma and Ba, 2015) and gradient clipping was set to 5. The number of hidden state units in the gating network for the mixture of NMT experts experiments was 256. We used BLEU (Papineni et al., 2002) as the evaluation metric. We performed early stopping, saving parameter values that had the smallest log perplexities on the validation data and used them when decoding test data.

4.2   Pseudo-incomplete multilingual corpus (UN6WAY)

First, we conducted experiments using a *complete* multilingual corpus and a *pseudo-incomplete* corpus derived by excluding some sentences from the complete corpus, to compare the performance in complete and incomplete situations.

4.2.1   Data

We used UN6WAY (Ziemski et al., 2016) as the complete multilingual corpus. We chose Spanish (Es), French (Fr), and Arabic (Ar) as source languages and English (En) as a target language The training data in the experiments were the one million sentences from the UN6WAY corpus whose sentence lengths were less than or equal to 40 words. We excluded 200,000 sentences for each language for the pseudo-incomplete multilingual corpus as shown in Table 1. "Sentence number" in Table 1 represents the line number in the corpus, and the *x* means the part removed for the incomplete multilingual corpus. We also chose 1,000 and 4,000 sentences for validation and test from

Sentence No.	Es	Fr	Ar	En
1-200,000	x			
200,001-400,000			x	
400,001-600,000		x		
600,001-800,000				

Table 1: Settings of the pseudo-incomplete UN multilingual corpus (x means that this part was deleted)

the UN6WAY corpus, apart from the training data. Note that the validation and test data here had no missing translations.

4.2.2   Setup

We compared multi-encoder NMT and the mixture of NMT experts in the complete and incomplete situations. The three one-to-one NMT systems, Es-En, Fr-En, and Ar-En, which were used as submodels in the mixture of NMT experts, were also compared for reference.

First, we conducted experiments using all of the one million sentences in the complete multilingual corpus, *Complete (0.8M)*. In case of the mixture of NMT experts, the gating network was trained using the one million sentences.

Then, we tested in the incomplete data situation. Here there were just 200,000 complete multilingual sentences (sentence No. 600,001-800,000), *Complete (0.2M)*. Here, a standard multi-encoder NMT and mixture of NMT experts could be trained using this complete data. On the other hand, the multi-source NMT with <NULL> could be trained using 800,000 sentences (sentence No. 1-800,000), *Pseudo-incomplete (0.8M)*. Each one-to-one NMT could be trained using these 800,000 sentences, but the missing sentences replaced with the <NULL> tokens were excluded so resulting 600,000 sentences were actually used.

4.2.3   Results

Table 2 shows the results in BLEU. The multi-source approaches achieved consistent improvements over the one-to-one NMTs in the all conditions, as demonstrated in previous multi-source NMT studies. Our main focus here is Pseudo-incomplete (0.8M), in which the multi-source results were slightly worse than those in Complete (0.8M) but better than those in Complete (0.2M). This suggests the additional use of incomplete corpora is beneficial in multi-source NMT compared to the use of only the complete parts of the cor-

Condition	One-to-one			Multi-encoder	Mix. NMT Experts
	Es-En	Fr-En	Ar-En		
Complete (0.8M)	31.87	25.78	23.08	37.55 (+5.68)*	33.28 (+1.41)
Complete (0.2M)	27.62	22.01	17.88	31.24 (+3.62)	32.16 (+4.54)
Pseudo-incomplete (0.8M)	30.98	25.62	22.02	**36.43** (+5.45)*	32.44 (+1.47)

Table 2: Results in BLEU for one-to-one and multi-source ({Es, Fr, Ar}-to-En) translation on UN6WAY data (parentheses are BLEU gains against the best one-to-one results). * indicates the difference from mixture of NMT experts is statistically significant ($p < 0.01$).

Source	Training	Valid.	Test
{En, Fr, Pt (br)}-to-Es			
English	189,062	4,076	5,451
French	170,607	3,719	4,686
Portuguese (br)	166,205	3,623	4,647
{En, Es, Pt (br)}-to-Fr			
English	185,405	4,164	4,753
Spanish	170,607	3,719	4,686
Portuguese (br)	164,630	3,668	4,289
{En, Es, Fr}-to-Pt (br)			
English	177,895	3,880	4,742
Spanish	166,205	3,623	4,647
French	164,630	3,668	4,289

Table 3: Data statistics in the tasks on TED data (in the number of sentences). Note that the number of target sentences is equal to that of English for each task.

Target	Training	Valid.	Test
Spanish	83.4	85.0	78.2
French	85.0	83.2	89.7
Portuguese (br)	88.6	89.3	90.0

Table 4: The percentage of data without missing sentences on TED data.

pus, even if just through the simple modification of replacing missing sentences with <NULL>.

With respect to the difference between the multi-encoder NMT and mixture of NMT experts, the multi-encoder achieved much higher BLEU in Pseudo-incomplete (0.8M) and Complete (1M), but this was not the case in Complete (0.2M). One possible reason here is the model complexity; the multi-encoder NMT uses a large single model while one-to-one sub-models in the mixture of NMT experts can be trained independently.

4.3 An actual incomplete multilingual corpus (TED Talks)

4.3.1 Data

We used a collection of transcriptions of TED Talks and their multilingual translations. Because these translations are created by volunteers, and the number of translations for each language is dependent on the number of volunteers who created them, this collection is an actual incomplete multilingual corpus. The great majority of the talks are basically in English, so we chose English as a source language. We used three translations in other languages for our multi-source scenario: Spanish, French, Brazilian Portuguese. We prepared three tasks choosing one of each of these three languages as the target language and the others as the additional source languages. Table 3 shows the number of available sentences in these tasks, chosen so that their lengths are less than or equal to 40 words.

4.3.2 Setup

We compared multi-encoder NMT, mixture of NMT experts and one-to-one NMT with English as the source language. The validation and test data for these experiments were also incomplete. This is in contrast to the experiments on UN6WAY where the test and validation data were complete, and thus this setting is arguable of more practical use.

4.3.3 Results

Table 5 shows the results in BLEU and BLEU gains with respect to the one-to-one results. All the differences are statistically significant ($p < 0.01$) by significance tests with bootstrap resampling (Koehn, 2004). The multi-source NMTs achieved consistent improvements over the one-to-one baseline as expected, but the BLEU gains were smaller than those in the previous experiments using the UN6WAY data. This is possibly because the baseline performance was relatively low compared with the previous experiments and the size of available resources was also smaller.

In comparison between the multi-source NMT and the mixture of NMT experts, results were mixed; the mixture of NMT experts was better in the task to French.

4.3.4 Discussion

We analyzed the results using the TED data in detail to investigate the mixed results above. Figure 5 (in the last page) shows the breakdown of BLEU in the test data, separating the results for complete and incomplete multilingual inputs. When all source sentences are present in the test data, multi-encoder NMT has better performance than mixture of NMT experts except for {En, Es, Pt (br)}-to-Fr. However, when the input is incomplete, mixture of NMT experts achieves performance better than or equal to multi-encoder NMT. From this result, we can assume that mixture of NMT experts, with its explicit gating network, is better at ignoring the irrelevant missing sentences. It's possible that if we designed a better attention strategy for multi-encoder NMT we may be able to resolve this problem. These analyses would support the results using the pseudo incomplete data shown in Table 2, where the validation and test data were complete.

4.3.5 Translation examples

Table 6 shows a couple of translation examples in the {English, French, Brazilian Portuguese}-to-Spanish experiment. In Example(1), BLEU+1 of mixture of NMT Experts is larger than one-to-one (English-to-Spanish) because of the French sentence, although the source sentence of Brazilian Portuguese is missing. BLEU+1 of multi-encoder is same as one-to-one, but the generation word is different. The word of "minar" is generated from multi-encoder, and "estudiar" is generated from one-to-one. "minar" means "look" in English, and "estudiar" means "study", so the meaning of sentence which was generated from multi-encoder is close to the reference one than that from one-to-one. Besides the word of "ver" which is generated from mixture of NMT experts meas "see" in English, so the sentence of multi-encoder is more appropriate than the reference sentence.

In Example(2), there is only the English sentence in the source sentences. We can see that sentences which are generated from all models are

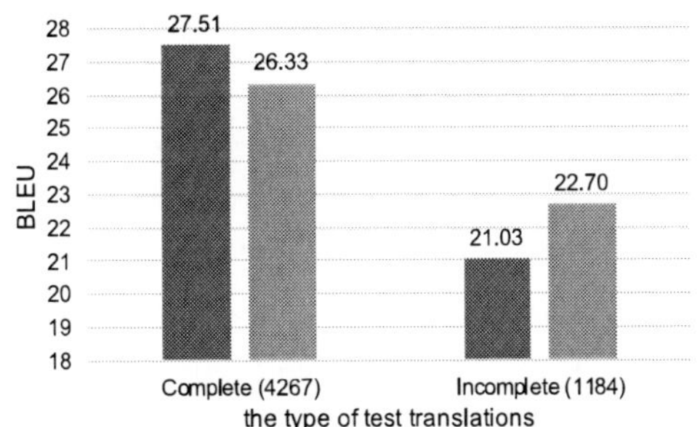

(a) TED: {En,Fr,Pt (br)}-to-Es

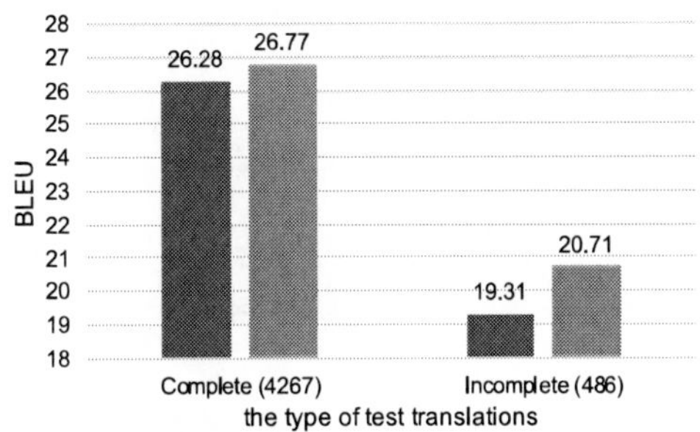

(b) TED: {En,Es,Pt (br)}-to-Fr

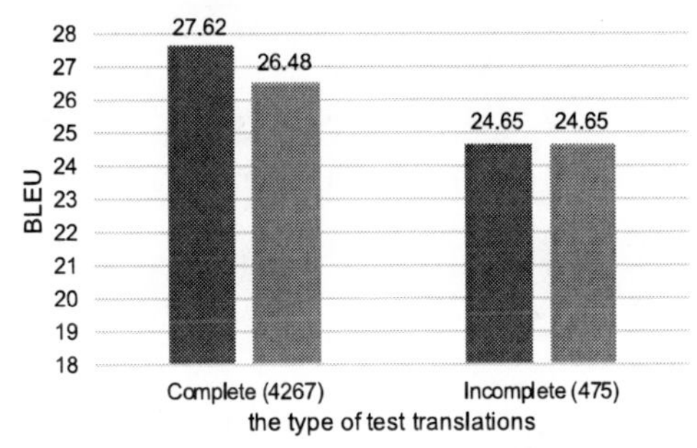

(c) TED: {En,Es,Fr}-to-Pt (br)

Figure 5: Detailed comparison of BLEU in TED test data. *Complete* means the part of test data, in which there is no missing translation, and *incomplete* means that, in which there are some missing translation. The number in a parenthesis is the number of translations.

same as the reference sentences, although French and Brazilian Portuguese sentences are missing. Therefore multi-source NMT models work properly even if there are missing sentences.

Task	One-to-one (En-to-target)	Multi-encoder	Mix. NMT Experts
{En, Fr, Pt (br)}-to-Es	24.32	**26.01** (+1.69)	25.51 (+1.19)
{En, Es, Pt (br)}-to-Fr	24.54	25.62 (+1.08)	**26.23** (+1.69)
{En, Es, Fr}-to-Pt (br)	25.14	**27.36** (+2.22)	26.39 (+1.25)

Table 5: Results in BLEU (and BLEU gains) by one-to-one and multi-source NMT on TED data. Note that the target language in each row differs so the results in different rows cannot be compared directly. All the differences are statistically significant ($p < 0.01$).

Type	Sentence	BLEU+1
Example (1)		
Source (En)	Then I started looking at the business model.	
Source (Fr)	Puis j'ai regard le modle conomique.	
Source (Pt (br))	<NULL>	
Reference	Despus empec a ver el modelo de negocio.	
En-to-Es	Luego empec a estudiar el modelo empresarial.	0.266
Multi-encoder	Luego empec a mirar el modelo empresarial.	0.266
Mix. NMT experts	Luego empec a ver el modelo de negocios.	0.726
Example (2)		
Source (En)	Sometimes they agree.	
Source (Fr)	<NULL>	
Source (Pt (br))	<NULL>	
Reference	A veces estn de acuerdo.	
En-to-Es	A veces estn de acuerdo.	1.000
Multi-encoder	A veces estn de acuerdo.	1.000
Mix. NMT experts	A veces estn de acuerdo.	1.000

Table 6: Translation examples in {English, French, Brazilian Portuguese}-to-Spanish translation.

5 Related Work

In this paper, we examined strategies for multi-source NMT. On the other hand, there are there are other strategies for multilingual NMT that do not use multiple source sentences as their input. Dong et al. (2015) proposed a method for multi-target NMT. Their method is using one sharing encoder and decoders corresponding to the number of target languages. Firat et al. (2016) proposed a method for multi-source multi-target NMT using multiple encoders and decoders with a shared attention mechanism. Johonson et al. (2017) and Ha et al. (2016) proposed multi-source and multi-target NMT using one encoder and one decoder, and sharing all parameters with all languages. Notably, these methods use multilingual data to better train one-to-one NMT systems. However, our motivation of this study is to improve NMT further by the help of other translations that are available on the source side at test time, and thus their approaches are different from ours.

6 Conclusion

In this paper, we examined approaches for multi-source NMT using *incomplete* multilingual corpus in which each missing input sentences is replaced by a special symbol <NULL>. The experimental results with simulated and actual incomplete multilingual corpora show that this simple modification allows us to effectively use all available translations at both training and test time.

The performance of multi-source NMT depends on source and target languages, and the size of missing data. As future work, we will investigate the relation of the languages included in the multiple sources and the number of missing inputs to the translation accuracy in multi-source scenarios.

7 Acknowledgement

Part of this work was supported by JSPS KAKENHI Grant Numbers and JP16H05873 and JP17H06101.

References

Dzmitry Bahdanau, Kyunghyun Cho, and Yoshua Bengio. 2015. Neural Machine Translation by Jointly Learning to Align and Translate. In *Proceedings of the 3rd International Conference on Learning Representations.*

Mauro Cettolo, Christian Girardi, and Marcello Federico. 2012. WIT^3: Web Inventory of Transcribed and Translated Talks. In *Proceedings of the 16th EAMT Conference*, pages 261–268.

Daxiang Dong, Hua Wu, Wei He, Dianhai Yu, and Haifeng Wang. 2015. Multi-Task Learning for Multiple Language Translation. In *Proceedings of the 53rd Annual Meeting of the Association for Computational Linguistics*, pages 1723–1732, Beijing, China. Association for Computational Linguistics.

Orhan Firat, Kyunghyun Cho, and Yoshua Bengio. 2016. Multi-Way, Multilingual Neural Machine Translation with a Shared Attention Mechanism. In *Proceedings of the 2016 Conference of the North American Chapter of the Association for Computational Linguistics: Human Language Technologies*, pages 866–875, San Diego, California. Association for Computational Linguistics.

Ekaterina Garmash and Christof Monz. 2016. Ensemble Learning for Multi-Source Neural Machine Translation. In *Proceedings of COLING 2016, the 26th International Conference on Computational Linguistics: Technical Papers*, pages 1409–1418, Osaka, Japan. The COLING 2016 Organizing Committee.

Thanh-Le Ha, Jan Niehues, and Alexander Waibel. 2016. Toward Multilingual Neural Machine Translation with Universal Encoder and Decoder. In *Proceedings of the 13th International Workshop on Spoken Language Translation*, Seattle, Washington.

Melvin Johonson, Mike Schuster, Quoc V. Le, Maxim Krikun, Yonghui Wu, Zhifeng Chen, Nikhil Thorat, Fernanda Vigas, Martin Wattenberg, Greg Corrado, Macduff Hughes, and Jeffrey Dean. 2017. Google's Multilingual Neural Machine Translation System: Enabling Zero-Shot Translation. *Transactions of the Association for Computational Linguistics, vol. 5*, pages 339–351.

Diederik P. Kingma Kingma and Jimmy Ba. 2015. Adam: A Method for Stochastic Optimization. In *Proceedings of the 3rd International Conference on Learning Representations.*

Philipp Koehn. 2004. Statistical Significance Tests for Machine Translation Evaluation. In *Proceedings of EMNLP 2004*, pages 388–395, Barcelona, Spain. Association for Computational Linguistics.

Philipp Koehn. 2005. Europarl: A Parallel Corpus for Statistical Machine Translation. In *Conference Proceedings: the tenth Machine Translation Summit*, pages 79–86, Phuket, Thailand. AAMT, AAMT.

Thang Luong, Hieu Pham, and Christopher D. Manning. 2015. Effective Approaches to Attention-based Neural Machine Translation. In *Proceedings of the 2015 Conference on Empirical Methods in Natural Language Processing*, pages 1412–1421, Lisbon, Portugal. Association for Computational Linguistics.

Franz Josef Och and Hermann Ney. 2001. Statistical Multi-Source Translation. In *Proceedings of the eighth Machine Translation Summit (MT Summit VIII)*, pages 253–258.

Kishore Papineni, Salim Roukos, Todd Ward, and Wei-Jing Zhu. 2002. BLEU: a Method for Automatic Evaluation of Machine Translation. In *Proceedings of the 40th Annual Meeting of the Association for Computational Linguistics (ACL)*, pages 311–318, Philadelphia.

Jörg Tiedemann. 2009. News from OPUS - A Collection of Multilingual Parallel Corpora with Tools and Interfaces. In N. Nicolov, K. Bontcheva, G. Angelova, and R. Mitkov, editors, *Recent Advances in Natural Language Processing*, volume V, pages 237–248. John Benjamins, Amsterdam/Philadelphia, Borovets, Bulgaria.

Micha Ziemski, Marcin Junczys-Dowmunt, and Bruno Pouliquen. 2016. The United Nations Parallel Corpus v1.0. In *Proceedings of the Tenth International Conference on Language Resources and Evaluation (LREC 2016)*, Paris, France. European Language Resources Association (ELRA).

Barret Zoph and Kevin Knight. 2016. Multi-Source Neural Translation. In *Proceedings of the 2016 Conference of the North American Chapter of the Association for Computational Linguistics: Human Language Technologies*, pages 30–34, San Diego, California. Association for Computational Linguistics.

Towards one-shot learning for rare-word translation with external experts

Ngoc-Quan Pham and **Jan Niehues** and **Alex Waibel**
Karlsruhe Institute of Technology
`ngoc.pham@kit.edu jan.niehues@kit.edu alex.waibel@kit.edu`

Abstract

Neural machine translation (NMT) has significantly improved the quality of automatic translation models. One of the main challenges in current systems is the translation of rare words. We present a generic approach to address this weakness by having external models annotate the training data as **Experts**, and control the model-expert interaction with a pointer network and reinforcement learning. Our experiments using phrase-based models to simulate Experts to complement neural machine translation models show that the model can be trained to copy the annotations into the output consistently. We demonstrate the benefit of our proposed framework in out-of-domain translation scenarios with only lexical resources, improving more than 1.0 BLEU point in both translation directions English→Spanish and German→English.

1 Introduction

Sequence to sequence models have recently become the state-of-the-art approach for machine translation (Luong et al., 2015; Vaswani et al., 2017). This model architecture can directly approximate the conditional probability of the target sequence given a source sequence using neural networks (Kalchbrenner and Blunsom, 2013). As a result, not only do they model a smoother probability distribution (Bengio et al., 2003) than the sparse phrase tables in statistical machine translation (Koehn et al., 2003), but they can also jointly learn translation models, language models and even alignments in a single model (Bahdanau et al., 2014).

One of the main weaknesses of neural machine translation models is poor handling of low frequency events. Neural models tend to prioritize output fluency over translation adequacy, and faced with rare words either silently ignore input (Koehn and Knowles, 2017) or fall into under- or over-translation (Tu et al., 2016). Examples of these situations include named entities, dates, and rare morphological forms. Improper handling of rare events can be harmful to industrial systems (Wu et al., 2016), where translation mistakes can have serious ramifications. Similarly, translating in specific domains such as information technology or biology, a slight change in vocabulary can drastically alter meaning. It is important, then, to address translation of rare words.

While domain-specific parallel corpora can be used to adapt translation models efficiently (Luong and Manning, 2015), parallel corpora for many domains can be difficult to collect, and this requires continued training. Translation lexicons, however, are much more commonly available. In this work, we introduce a strategy to incorporate external lexical knowledge, dubbed "Expert annotation," into neural machine translation models. First, we annotate the lexical translations directly into the source side of the parallel data, so that the information is exposed during both training and inference. Second, inspired by CopyNet (Gu et al., 2016), we utilize a pointer network (Vinyals et al., 2015) to introduce a copy distribution over the source sentence, to increase the generation probability of rare words. Given that the expert annotation can differ from the reference, in order to encourage the model to copy the annotation we use reinforcement learning to guide the search, giving rewards when the annotation is used. Our work is motivated to be able to achieve One-Shot learning, which can help the model to accurately translate the events that are annotated during inference. Such ability can be transferred from an Expert

100

Proceedings of the 2nd Workshop on Neural Machine Translation and Generation, pages 100–109
Melbourne, Australia, July 20, 2018. ©2018 Association for Computational Linguistics

which is capable of learning to translate lexically with one or few examples, such as dictionaries, or phrase-tables, or even human annotators.

We realize our proposed framework with experiments on English→Spanish and German→English translation tasks. We focus on translation of rare events using translation suggestions from an Expert, here simulated by an additional phrase table. Specifically, we annotate rare words in our parallel data with best candidates from a phrase table before training, so that rare events are provided with suggested translations. Our model can be explicitly trained to copy the annotation approximately 90% of the time, and it outperformed the baselines on translation accuracy of rare words, reaching up to 97% accuracy. Also importantly, this performance is maintained when translating data in a different domain. Further analysis was done to verify the potential of our proposed framework.

2 Background - Neural Machine Translation

Neural machine translation (NMT) consists of an encoder and a decoder (Sutskever et al., 2014; Vaswani et al., 2017) that directly approximate the conditional probability of a target sequence $Y = y_1, y_2, \cdots, y_T$ given a source sequence $X = x_1, x_2, \cdots, x_M$. The model is normally trained to maximize the log-likelihood of each target token given the previous words as well as the source sequence with respect to model parameters θ as in Equation 1:

$$\log P(Y|X; \theta) = \Sigma_{t=1}^{T} (\log P(y_t|X, y_1, y_2, \cdots, y_t - 1)) \tag{1}$$

The advantages of NMT compared to phrased-based machine translation come from the neural architecture components:

- The embedding layers, which are shared between samples, allow the model to continuously represent discrete words and effectively capture word relationship (Bengio et al., 2003; Mikolov et al., 2013). Notably we refer to two different embedding layers being used in most models, one for the first input layer of the encoder/decoder, and another one at the decoder output layer that is used to compute the probability distribution (Equation 1).

Figure 1: A generic illustration of our framework. The source sentence is annotated with experts before learning. The model learns to utilize the annotation by using them directly in the translation)

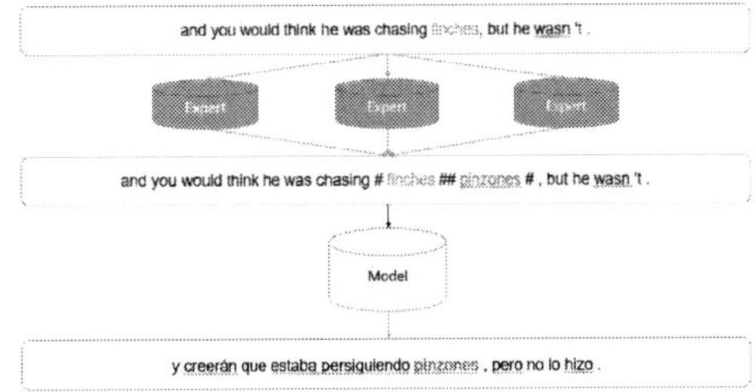

- Complex neural architectures like LSTMs (Hochreiter and Schmidhuber, 1997) or Transformers (Vaswani et al., 2017) can represent structural sequences (sentences, phrases) effectively.

- Attention models (Bahdanau et al., 2014; Luong et al., 2015) are capable of hierarchically modeling the translation mapping between sentence pairs.

The challenges of NMT These models are often attacked over their inability to learn to translate rare events, which are often named entities and rare morphological variants (Arthur et al., 2016; Koehn and Knowles, 2017; Nguyen and Chiang, 2017). Learning from rare events is difficult due to the fact that the model parameters are not adequately updated. For example, the embeddings of the rare words are only updated a few times during training, and similarly for the patterns learned by the recurrent structures in the encoders / decoders and attention models.

3 Expert framework description

Human translators can benefit from external knowledge such as dictionaries, particularly in specific domains. Similarly, the idea behind our framework is to rely on external models to annotate extra input into the source side of the training data, which we refer as **Experts**. Such expert models would not necessarily outperform NMT models themselves, but rather complement them and compensate for their weaknesses.

The illustration of the proposed framework is given in Figure 1. Before the learning process, the source sentence is annotated by one or several expert models, which we abstract as any model that can show additional data perspectives. For example, these experts could be a terminology list or a statistical phrase-based system to generate translations for specific phrases, but it can also be used in various other situations. For example, we might use it to integrate a model that can do metric conversion or handling of links to web addresses, which can be useful for certain applications. Then NMT model then learns to translate to the target sentence using the annotated source.

3.1 Annotation

The aforementioned idea of Experts in our work is inspired by the fact that human translators can benefit from domain experts when translating domain-specific content. Accordingly, we design the annotation and training process as follows:

- Words are identified as candidates for annotation using a frequency threshold.

- Look up possible translations of the candidates from the Expert and annotate them directly next to the candidates. We use special bounding symbols to help guide the model to copy the annotation during translation.

- Train a neural machine translation model using these annotated sentences.

- During inference, we annotate the source sentence in the same fashion as in training.

Byte-Pair encoding We consider BPE (Sennrich et al., 2016) one of the crucial factors for annotation in order to efficiently represent words that do not appear in the training data. The rare words (and their translation suggestions, which can be rare as well) are split into smaller segments, alleviating the problem of dealing with UNK tokens (Luong et al., 2014).

Embedding sharing Our annotation method includes target language tokens directly in the source sentence. In order to make the model perceive these words the same way in the source and the target, we create a joint vocabulary of the source and target language and simply tie the embedding projection matrices of the source encoder, target encoder and target decoder. This practice has been explored in various language modeling works (Press and Wolf, 2016; Inan et al., 2016) to improve regularisation.

3.2 Copy-Generator

Hypothetically, the model could learn to simply ignore the annotation during optimization because it contains strange symbols (the target language) in source language sentences. If this were the case, adding annotations would not help translate rare events.

Therefore, inspired by the CopyNet (Gu et al., 2016; Gulcehre et al., 2016), which originates from pointer networks (Vinyals et al., 2015) that learn to pick the tokens that appeared in the memory of the models, we incorporate the copy-mechanism into the neural translation model so that the annotations can be simply pasted into the translation. Explicitly, the conditional probability is now presented as a mixture of two distributions: copy and generated.

$$P(Y|X;\theta) =$$
$$\Sigma_{t=1}^{T}[\gamma P_G(y_t|X, y_1, y_2, \cdots, y_t - 1) \quad (2)$$
$$+(1 - \gamma)P_C(y_t|X, y_1, y_2, \cdots, y_t - 1)]$$

The distribution over the whole vocabulary P_G is estimated from the softmax layer using equation 1, and the copy distribution P_C is used from the attention layer from the decoder state over the context (dubbed 'alignment' in previous works (Bahdanau et al., 2014)). The mixture coefficient γ controls the bias between the mixtures and is estimated using a feed-forward neural network layer with a sigmoid function, which is placed on top of the decoder hidden state (before the final output softmax layer [1]). Ideally, the model learns to adjust between copying the input annotation or generating a translation.

It is important to note that, in previous works the authors had to build dynamic vocabulary for each sample due to the vocabulary mismatch between the source and target (Gu et al., 2016). Since we tied the embeddings of source and target languages, it becomes trivial to combine the two distributions. The use of byte-pair encodings also helps to eliminate unknown words on both sides, alleviating the task of excluding copying unknown tokens.

3.3 Reinforcement Learning

Why reinforcement learning While our annotation provides target language tokens that can be

---

[1]Using an additional attention layer yields similar result.

directly copied to the generated output, and the copy generator allows a direct gradient path from the output to the annotation, the annotation is not guaranteed to be in the reference. When this is the case, the model does not receive the learning signal to copy the annotation.

In order to remedy this, we propose to cast the problem as a reinforcement learning task (Ranzato et al., 2015) in which we have the model sample and provide a learning signal by rewarding the model if it copies the annotation into the target, as seen in the loss function in Equation 3:

$$L(\theta) = -\mathbb{E}_{W \sim p_\theta}(r(W, REF)) \quad (3)$$

Reward function For this purpose, we designed a reward function that can encourage the model to prioritize copying the annotation into the target, but still maintain a reasonable translation quality. For suggestion utilization, we denote HIT as the score function that gives rewards for every overlap of the output and the suggestion. If all annotated words are used then $HIT(W, REF) = 1.0$, otherwise the percentage of the copied words. For the translation score, we use the GLEU function (Wu et al., 2016) - the minimum of recall and precision of the n-grams up to 4-gram between the sample and the reference, which has been reported to correspond well with corpus-level translation metrics such as BLEU (Papineni et al., 2002). The reward function is defined as in Equation 4:

$$r(W, REF) = \alpha HIT(W, REF) + (1 - \alpha)GLEU(W, REF) \quad (4)$$

Variance reduction The use of reinforcement learning with translation models has been explored in various works (Ranzato et al., 2015; Bahdanau et al., 2016; Rennie et al., 2016; Nguyen et al., 2017), in which the models are difficult to train due to the high variance of the gradients (Schulman et al., 2017). To tackle this problem, we follow the Self-Critical model proposed by (Rennie et al., 2016) for variance reduction:

- Pre-training the model using cross-entropy loss (Eq. 1) to obtain a solid initialization presearch, which allows the model to achieve reasonable rewards to learn faster.

- During the reinforcement phase, for each sample/mini-batch, the decoder explores the search space with Markov chain Monte Carlo sampling, and at the same time performs a greedy search for a 'baseline' performance. We encourage the model to perform better than baseline, which is used to decide the sign of the gradients (Williams, 1992).

Notably, there is no gradient flowing in the baseline subgraph since the argmax operators used in the greedy search are not differentiable.

4 Experiment setup

In the experiments, we realise the generic framework described in Section 3 with the tasks of translating from English→Spanish and German→English.

For both language pairs, we used data from Europarl (version 7) (Koehn, 2005) and IWSLT17 (Cettolo et al., 2012) to train our neural networks. For validation, we use the IWSLT validation set (dev2010) to select the best models based on perplexity (for cross-entropy loss) and BLEU score (for reinforcement learning). For evaluation, we use IWSLT tst2010 as the in-domain test set. We also evaluate our models on out-of-domain corpora. For English→Spanish an additional Business dataset is used. The corpus statistics can be seen on Table 1. The out-of-domain experiments for the German→English are carried out on the medical domain, in which we use the UFAL Medical Corpus v1.0 corpus (2.2 million sentences) to train the Expert and the Oracle system. The test data for this task is the HIML2017 dataset with 1517 sentences. We preprocess all the data using standard tokenization, true-casing and BPE splitting with 40K joined operations.

4.1 Implementation details

Our base neural machine translation follows the neural machine translation with global attention model described in (Luong et al., 2015) [2]. The encoder is a bidirectional LSTM network, while the decoder is an LSTM with attention, which is a 2-layer feed-forward neural network (Bahdanau et al., 2014). We also use the input-feeding method (Luong et al., 2015) and context-gate (Tu et al., 2016) to improve model coverage. All networks in our experiments have layer size (embedding and hidden) of 512 (English→Spanish)

---

[2]The framework is implemented in PyTorch, which will be made public with the final version of the paper

and 1024 (German→English) with 2 LSTM layers. Dropout is put vertically between LSTM layers to improve regularization (Pham et al., 2014). We create mini-batches with maximum 128 sentence pairs of the same source size. For cross-entropy training, the parameters are optimized using Adam (Kingma and Ba, 2014) with a learning rate annealing schedule suggested in (Denkowski and Neubig, 2017), starting from 0.001 until 0.00025. After reaching convergence on the training data, we fine-tune the models on the IWSLT training set with learning rate of 0.0002. Finally, we use our best models on the validation data as the initialization for reinforcement learning using a learning rate of 0.0001, which is done on the IWSLT set for 50 epochs. Beam search is used for decoding.

4.2 Phrase-based Experts

We selected phrase tables for the Experts in our experiments. While other resources like terminology lists can also be used for the translation annotations, our motivation here is that the phrase-tables can additionally capture multi-word phrase pairs, and additionally can better capture the distribution tail of rare phrases as compared to neural models (Koehn and Knowles, 2017). We selected the translation with the highest average probabilities in the 4 phrase table scores for annotation.

On the English→Spanish task, the phrase tables are trained on the same data as the NMT model, while on the German→English direction, we simulate the situation when the expert is not in the same domain as the test data to observe the potentials. Therefore, we train an additional table on the UFAL Medical Corpus v.1.0 corpus (which is not observed by the NMT model) to for the out-of-domain annotation.

5 Evaluation

5.1 Research questions

We aim to find the answers to the following research questions:

- Given the annotation quality being imperfect, how much does it affect the overall translation quality?

- How much does annotation participate in translating rare words, and how consistently can the model learn to copy the annotation?

- How will the model perform in a new domain? The copy mechanism does not depend on the domain of the training or adaptation data, which is optimal.

5.2 Evaluation Metrics

To serve the research questions above, we use the following evaluation metrics:

- BLEU: score for general translation quality.

- SUGGESTION (SUG): The overlap between the hypothesis and the phrase-table (on word level), showing how much the expert content is used by the model.

- SUGGESTION ACCURACY (SAC): The intersection between the hypothesis, the phrase-table suggestions and the reference. This metrics shows us the accuracy of the system on the rare-words which are suggested by the phrase-table.

Discussion The SUG metric shows the consistency of the model on the copy mechanism. Models with lower SUG are not necessarily worse, and models with high SUG can potentially have very low recall on rare-word translation by systematically copying bad suggestions and failing to translate rare-words where the annotator is incorrect. However, we argue that a high SUG system can be used reliably with a high quality expert. For example, in censorship management or name translation which is strictly sensitive, this quality can help reducing output inconsistency. On the other hand, the SAC metrics show improvement on rare-word translation, but only on the intersection of the phrase table and the reference. This subset is our main focus. General rare-word translation quality requires additional effort to find the reference aligned to the rare words in the source sentences, which we consider for future work.

5.3 Experimental results

English→Spanish Results for this task are presented on table 2. First, the main difference between the settings is the SUG and SAC figures for all test sets. Both of them increase dramatically from baseline to annotation, and also increase according to the level of supervision in our model proposals. While the copy mechanism can help us to copy more from the annotation, the REINFORCE models are successfully trained to

| | English→Spanish | | German→English | |
Portion	N. Sentences	Rare words coverage	N. Sentences	Rare words coverage
All	2.2M	82% (68K)	1.9M	82% (68K)
IWSLT Dev2010	1435	48% (135)	505	51% (196)
IWSLT Test2010	1701	46% (124)	1460	50% (136)
Out-of-domain	749	80% (384)	1511	66.64% (1334)

Table 1: Phrase-table coverage statistics. The out-of-domain section in English-Spanish is Business and Biomedical in German-English. We show the total number of rare words detected by frequency (in parentheses) and the percentage covered by the Experts (intersecting with the reference).

| System—Data | dev2010 | | | tst2010 | | | BusinessTest | | |
	BLEU	SAC	SUG	BLEU	SAC	SUG	BLEU	SAC	SUG
1. Baseline	37.0	78.8	48.1	31.1	73.7	46.0	32.1	69.6	58.1
2. + AN	37.0	97.0	71.9	31.1	93.0	74.2	32.0	91.5	79.1
3. + AN-RF	**37.97**	92.42	82.2	31.3	**94.73**	**89.5**	**33.82**	**96.1**	**93.0**
4. + AN-CP	37.3	90.9	77.8	30.7	96.5	85.5	33.2	89.8	84.9
5. + AN-CP-RF	**38.1**	**100**	99.2	31.13	**100**	99.2	33.34	98.3	97.6

Table 2: The results of English - Spanish on various domains: TEDTalks and Business. We use AN for using annotations from the phrase table, RF for using REINFORCE (α= 0.5) and CP for using the Copy mechanism.

| System—Data | dev2010 | | | tst2010 | | | HIML | | |
	BLEU	SAC	SUG	BLEU	SAC	SUG	BLEU	SAC	SUG
1. Baseline	**37.5**	66	45	**36.14**	66.9	45.1	32.4	46.3	37.2
2. + AN	37.1	93	84.1	35.6	91.9	84.4	33.99	87.1	85.1
3. + AN-CP	37.2	96	88.2	35.89	94.1	90.7	34.1	**96.5**	**95.0**
4. + AN-CP-RF	36.6	**97**	**92.9**	35.89	**98.5**	**95.5**	33.1	**98.0**	**97.6**
Biomedical-Oracle	-	-	-	-	-	-	**37.82**	81.77	65.44

Table 3: The results of German→English on various domains: TEDTalks and Biomedical. We use AN for using annotations from the phrase table, RF for using REINFORCE (α= 0.5) and CP for using the Copy mechanism.

make the model copy more consistently. Their combination helps us achieve the desired behavior, in which almost all of the annotations given are copied, and we achieve 100% accuracy on the rare-words section that the phrase table covers. As mentioned in the discussion above, the SAC and SUG figures, while being not enough to quantitatively prove that the total number of rare words translated, show that the phrase table is complementary to the neural machine translation, and the more coverage the expert has, the more benefit this method can bring.

We notice an improvement of 1 BLEU point on dev2010 but only slight changes compared to the baseline on tst2010. On the out-of-domain set, however, the improved rare-word performance

leads to an increase of 1.7 BLEU points over the baseline without annotation. Our models, despite training on a noisier dataset, are able to improve translation quality.

German→English Results are shown in Table 3. On the dev2010 and tst2010 in-domain datasets, we observe similar phenomena to the En-Es direction. Rare-word performance increases with the number of words copied, and the combination of the copy mechanism and REINFORCE help us copy consistently. Surprisingly, however, the BLEU score drops with annotations. This may be because of the relative morphologically complexity of the German words compared to the English, making it harder to generate the correct word form.

In the experiments with an out-of-domain test set (HIML), we use annotations from that domain to simulate a domain-expert. For comparison, we also trained an NMT model adapted to the UFAL corpus, which we call the Oracle model. In this domain, our models show the same behavior, in which almost every word annotated is copied to the output. The annotation efficiently improves translation quality by 1.7 BLEU points over the baseline without annotation. The adapted model has a higher BLEU score, but here performs worse than our annotated model in terms of phrase-table overlap and rare-word translation accuracy for words in this set. Our model shows significantly better rare word handling than the baseline. Though the best obtainable system is adapted to the in-domain data, this requires parallel text: this experiment shows the high potential to improve NMT on out-of-domain scenarios using only lexical-level materials. We notice a surprising drop of 1.0 BLEU points for the REINFORCE model. Possible reasons include inefficient beam search on REINFORCE models, or the GLEU signal was out-weighted by the HIT one during training, which is known for the difficulty (Zaremba and Sutskever, 2015).

5.4 Further Analysis

Name translation Names can often be translated by BPE, but it is noticeable about examples of the inconsistency, which can be alleviated using annotations, as illustrated in Figure 2-Top.

Copying long phrases We find that with very high supervision, the model can learn to copy even phrases completely into the output, as in Figure 2-Bottom. Though this is potentially dangerous, as the output may the lose the additional fluency which comes from NMT, it is controllable by combining RL and cross entropy loss (Paulus et al., 2017).

Attention Plotting the attention map for the decoded sequences we notice that, while we marked the beginning and end of annotated sections and the separation between the source and the suggestion with # and ## tokens, those positions received very little weight from the decoder. One possible explanation is that these tokens do not contribute to the translation when decoding, and the annotations may useful without bounding tags. For the annotations used in the translation, we identified

two prominent cases; for the rare words whose annotation need only be identically copied to the target, the attention map focuses evenly on both source and annotation, while the heat map typically heavily emphasizes only the annotation otherwise. An example is illustrated in figure 3.

Effect of α The full results with respect to different α values which are used in Equation 3 for reward weighting can be seen in Table 4. Higher α values emphasize the signal to copy the source annotation, as can be seen from the increase in terms of Accuracy and Suggestion utilization across the values. As expected, as α goes toward 1.0, the model gradually loses the signal needed to maintain translation quality and finally diverges.

α	tst2010			BusinessTest		
	BL	**AC**	**SUG**	**BL**	**AC**	**SUG**
0.0	31.3	91.2	78.2	33.7	76.5	71.9
0.2	31.0	94.7	88.2	33.9	78.1	76.8
0.5	31.3	94.7	89.5	33.8	96.1	93.0
1.0	did not converge					

Table 4: Performances w.r.t to different alpha values. Metrics shown are BLEU (BL), ACCURACY (AC) and SUGGESTION (SUG)

6 Related Work

Translating rare words in neural machine translation is a rich and active topic, particularly when translating morphologically rich languages or translating named entities. Sub-word unit decomposition or BPE (Sennrich et al., 2016) has become the de-facto standard in most neural translation systems (Wu et al., 2016). Using phrase tables to handle rare words was previously explored in (Luong et al., 2014), but was not compatible with BPE. (Gulcehre et al., 2016) explored using pointer networks to copy source words to the translation output, which could benefit from our design but would require significant changes to the architecture and likely be limited to copying only. Additionally, models that can learn to remember rare events were explored in (Kaiser et al., 2017).

Our work builds on the idea of using a phrase-based neural machine translation to augment source data, (Niehues et al., 2016; Denkowski and Neubig, 2017), but can be extended to any annotation type without complicated hybrid phrase-based neural machine translation systems. We were additionally inspired by the use of feature functions with lexical-based features from dictio-

Figure 2: **Top**: Examples of name annotations with our framework from tst2010. The name Kean is originally split by BPE into 'K' and 'ean'. This is incorrectly translated without annotation (in blue) and corrected with the annotation (in red). **Bottom**: An example of phrase copying, in which the German word is translated into a long English phrase.

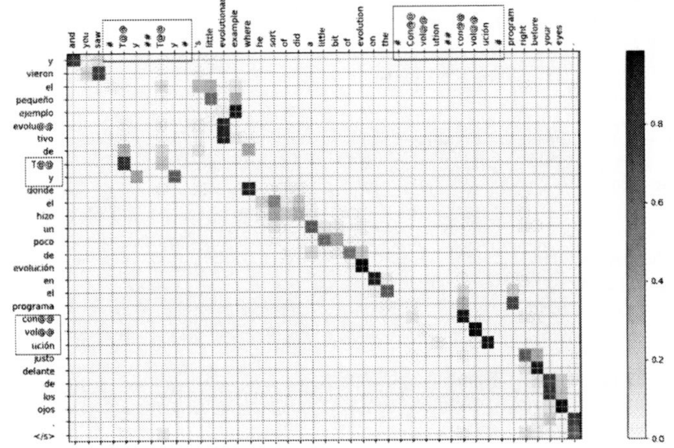

Figure 3: An attention heat map of an English-Spanish sentence pair (source on X-axis, target on Y-axis) with annotated sections in red rectangles. Annotations and their source are bounded by # characters.

naries and phrase-tables in (Zhang et al., 2017). They also rely on sample-based techniques, (Shen et al., 2015), to train their networks, but their computation is more expensive than the self-critical network in our work. We focus here on rare events, with the possibility to construct interactive models for fast updating without retraining. We also use the ideas of using REINFORCE to train sequence generators for arbitrary rewards (Ranzato et al., 2015; Nguyen et al., 2017; Bahdanau et al., 2016). While this method remains difficult to train, it is promising to use to achieve non-probabilistic features for neural models: for example enforcing formality in outputs in German, or censoring undesired outputs.

7 Conclusion

In this work, we presented a framework to alleviate the weaknesses of neural machine translation models by incorporating external knowledge as **Experts** and training the models to use their annotations using reinforcement learning and a pointer network. We show improvements over the unannotated model on both in- and out-of-domain datasets. When only lexical resources are available and in-domain fine-tuning cannot be performed, our framework can improve performance. The annotator might potentially be trained together with the main model to balance translation quality with copying annotations, which our current framework seems to be biased to.

Acknowledgments

This work was supported by the Carl-Zeiss-Stiftung. We thank Elizabeth Salesky for the constructive comments.

References

Philip Arthur, Graham Neubig, and Satoshi Nakamura. 2016. Incorporating discrete translation lexicons into neural machine translation. *arXiv preprint arXiv:1606.02006* .

D. Bahdanau, K. Cho, and Y. Bengio. 2014. Neural machine translation by jointly learning to align and translate. *CoRR* abs/1409.0473.

Dzmitry Bahdanau, Philemon Brakel, Kelvin Xu, Anirudh Goyal, Ryan Lowe, Joelle Pineau, Aaron Courville, and Yoshua Bengio. 2016. An actor-critic algorithm for sequence prediction. *arXiv preprint arXiv:1607.07086* .

Yoshua Bengio, Réjean Ducharme, Pascal Vincent, and Christian Jauvin. 2003. A neural probabilistic language model. *Journal of machine learning research* 3(Feb):1137–1155.

M. Cettolo, C. Girardi, and M. Federico. 2012. Wit: Web inventory of transcribed and translated talks. In *Proceedings of the 16th Conference of the European Association for Machine Translation (EAMT)*. Trento, Italy, pages 261–268.

Michael Denkowski and Graham Neubig. 2017. Stronger baselines for trustable results in neural machine translation. *arXiv preprint arXiv:1706.09733* .

Jiatao Gu, Zhengdong Lu, Hang Li, and Victor OK Li. 2016. Incorporating copying mechanism in sequence-to-sequence learning. *arXiv preprint arXiv:1603.06393* .

Caglar Gulcehre, Sungjin Ahn, Ramesh Nallapati, Bowen Zhou, and Yoshua Bengio. 2016. Pointing the unknown words. *arXiv preprint arXiv:1603.08148* .

S. Hochreiter and J. Schmidhuber. 1997. Long short-term memory. *Neural Comput.* 9(8):1735–1780. https://doi.org/10.1162/neco.1997.9.8.1735.

Hakan Inan, Khashayar Khosravi, and Richard Socher. 2016. Tying word vectors and word classifiers: A loss framework for language modeling. *arXiv preprint arXiv:1611.01462* .

Lukasz Kaiser, Ofir Nachum, Aurko Roy, and Samy Bengio. 2017. Learning to remember rare events. *CoRR* abs/1703.03129. http://arxiv.org/abs/1703.03129.

Nal Kalchbrenner and Phil Blunsom. 2013. Recurrent continuous translation models. In *EMNLP*. volume 3, page 413.

Diederik Kingma and Jimmy Ba. 2014. Adam: A method for stochastic optimization. *arXiv preprint arXiv:1412.6980* .

Philipp Koehn. 2005. Europarl: A parallel corpus for statistical machine translation. In *MT summit*. volume 5, pages 79–86.

Philipp Koehn and Rebecca Knowles. 2017. Six challenges for neural machine translation. *arXiv preprint arXiv:1706.03872* .

Philipp Koehn, Franz Josef Och, and Daniel Marcu. 2003. Statistical phrase-based translation. In *Proceedings of the 2003 Conference of the North American Chapter of the Association for Computational Linguistics on Human Language Technology-Volume 1*. Association for Computational Linguistics, pages 48–54.

Minh-Thang Luong and Christopher D Manning. 2015. Stanford neural machine translation systems for spoken language domains. In *Proceedings of the International Workshop on Spoken Language Translation*. pages 76–79.

Minh-Thang Luong, Hieu Pham, and Christopher D Manning. 2015. Effective approaches to attention-based neural machine translation. *arXiv preprint arXiv:1508.04025* .

Minh-Thang Luong, Ilya Sutskever, Quoc V Le, Oriol Vinyals, and Wojciech Zaremba. 2014. Addressing the rare word problem in neural machine translation. *arXiv preprint arXiv:1410.8206* .

Tomas Mikolov, Ilya Sutskever, Kai Chen, Greg S Corrado, and Jeff Dean. 2013. Distributed representations of words and phrases and their compositionality. In *Advances in neural information processing systems*. pages 3111–3119.

Khanh Nguyen, Hal Daumé III, and Jordan Boyd-Graber. 2017. Reinforcement learning for bandit neural machine translation with simulated human feedback. In *Proceedings of the 2017 Conference on Empirical Methods in Natural Language Processing*. pages 1465–1475.

Toan Q Nguyen and David Chiang. 2017. Improving lexical choice in neural machine translation. *arXiv preprint arXiv:1710.01329* .

Jan Niehues, Eunah Cho, Thanh-Le Ha, and Alex Waibel. 2016. Pre-translation for neural machine translation. *arXiv preprint arXiv:1610.05243* .

Kishore Papineni, Salim Roukos, Todd Ward, and Wei-Jing Zhu. 2002. Bleu: a method for automatic evaluation of machine translation. In *Proceedings of the 40th annual meeting on association for computational linguistics*. Association for Computational Linguistics, pages 311–318.

Romain Paulus, Caiming Xiong, and Richard Socher. 2017. A deep reinforced model for abstractive summarization. *arXiv preprint arXiv:1705.04304* .

Vu Pham, Théodore Bluche, Christopher Kermorvant, and Jérôme Louradour. 2014. Dropout improves recurrent neural networks for handwriting recognition. In *Frontiers in Handwriting Recognition (ICFHR), 2014 14th International Conference on*. IEEE, pages 285–290.

Ofir Press and Lior Wolf. 2016. Using the output embedding to improve language models. *arXiv preprint arXiv:1608.05859* .

Marc'Aurelio Ranzato, Sumit Chopra, Michael Auli, and Wojciech Zaremba. 2015. Sequence level training with recurrent neural networks. *arXiv preprint arXiv:1511.06732* .

Steven J Rennie, Etienne Marcheret, Youssef Mroueh, Jarret Ross, and Vaibhava Goel. 2016. Self-critical sequence training for image captioning. *arXiv preprint arXiv:1612.00563* .

John Schulman, Filip Wolski, Prafulla Dhariwal, Alec Radford, and Oleg Klimov. 2017. Proximal policy optimization algorithms. *arXiv preprint arXiv:1707.06347* .

R. Sennrich, B. Haddow, and A. Birch. 2016. Neural machine translation of rare words with subword units. In *Proceedings of the 54st Annual Meeting of the Association for Computational Linguistics (ACL 2016)*. Berlin, Germany.

Shiqi Shen, Yong Cheng, Zhongjun He, Wei He, Hua Wu, Maosong Sun, and Yang Liu. 2015. Minimum risk training for neural machine translation. *arXiv preprint arXiv:1512.02433* .

I. Sutskever, O. Vinyals, and Q. V. Le. 2014. Sequence to sequence learning with neural networks. In *Advances in Neural Information Processing Systems 27: Annual Conference on Neural Information Processing Systems 2014*. Quebec, Canada, pages 3104–3112.

Zhaopeng Tu, Zhengdong Lu, Yang Liu, Xiaohua Liu, and Hang Li. 2016. Modeling coverage for neural machine translation. *arXiv preprint arXiv:1601.04811* .

Ashish Vaswani, Noam Shazeer, Niki Parmar, Jakob Uszkoreit, Llion Jones, Aidan N Gomez, Lukasz Kaiser, and Illia Polosukhin. 2017. Attention is all you need. *arXiv preprint arXiv:1706.03762* .

Oriol Vinyals, Meire Fortunato, and Navdeep Jaitly. 2015. Pointer networks. In *Advances in Neural Information Processing Systems*. pages 2692–2700.

Ronald J Williams. 1992. Simple statistical gradient-following algorithms for connectionist reinforcement learning. *Machine learning* 8(3-4):229–256.

Yonghui Wu, Mike Schuster, Zhifeng Chen, Quoc V Le, Mohammad Norouzi, Wolfgang Macherey, Maxim Krikun, Yuan Cao, Qin Gao, Klaus Macherey, et al. 2016. Google's neural machine translation system: Bridging the gap between human and machine translation. *arXiv preprint arXiv:1609.08144* .

Wojciech Zaremba and Ilya Sutskever. 2015. Reinforcement learning neural turing machines-revised. *arXiv preprint arXiv:1505.00521* .

Jiacheng Zhang, Yang Liu, Huanbo Luan, Jingfang Xu, and Maosong Sun. 2017. Prior knowledge integration for neural machine translation using posterior regularization pages 1514–1523.

NICT Self-Training Approach to Neural Machine Translation at NMT-2018

Kenji Imamura and **Eiichiro Sumita**

National Institute of Information and Communications Technology
3-5 Hikaridai, Seika-cho, Soraku-gun, Kyoto 619-0289, Japan
`{kenji.imamura,eiichiro.sumita}@nict.go.jp`

Abstract

This paper describes the NICT neural machine translation system submitted at the NMT-2018 shared task. A characteristic of our approach is the introduction of self-training. Since our self-training does not change the model structure, it does not influence the efficiency of translation, such as the translation speed.

The experimental results showed that the translation quality improved not only in the sequence-to-sequence (seq-to-seq) models but also in the transformer models.

1 Introduction

In this study, we introduce the NICT neural translation system at the Second Workshop on Neural Machine Translation and Generation (NMT-2018) (Birch et al., 2018). A characteristic of the system is that translation qualities are improved by introducing self-training, using open-source neural translation systems and defined training data.

The self-training method discussed herein is based on the methods proposed by Sennrich et al. (2016a) and Imamura et al. (2018), and they are applied to a self training strategy. It extends only the source side of the training data to increase variety. The merit of the proposed self-training strategy is that it does not influence the efficiency of the translation, such as the translation speed, because it does not change the model structure. (However, the training time increases due to an increase in the training data size.)

The proposed approach can be applied to any translation method. However, we want to confirm on which model our approach is practically effective. This paper verifies the effect of our self-training method in the following two translation models:

- Sequence-to-sequence (seq-to-seq) models (Sutskever et al., 2014; Bahdanau et al., 2014) based on recurrent neural networks (RNNs). Herein, we use OpenNMT (Klein et al., 2017) as an implementation of the seq-to-seq model.

- The transformer model proposed by Vaswani et al. (2017). We used Marian NMT (Junczys-Dowmunt et al., 2018) as an implementation of the transformer model.

The remainder of this paper is organized as follows. Section 2 describes the proposed approach. Section 3 describes the details of our system. Section 4 explains the results of experiments, and Section 5 concludes the paper.

2 Self-training Approach

2.1 Basic Flow

The self-training approach in this study is based on a method proposed by Imamura et al. (2018). Their method extends the method proposed by Sennrich et al. (2016a) that a target monolingual corpus is translated back into source sentences and generates a synthetic parallel corpus. Then, the forward translation model is trained using the original and synthetic parallel corpora. The synthetic parallel corpus contains multiple source sentences of a target sentence to enhance the encoder and attention. The diversity of the synthetic source sentences is important in this study. Imamura et al. (2018) confirmed that the translation quality improved when synthetic source sentences were generated by sampling, rather than when they were generated by n-best translation.

Although Imamura et al. (2018) assumed the usage of monolingual corpora, it can be modified to a self-training form by assuming the target side of parallel corpora as monolingual corpora. In fact,

Proceedings of the 2nd Workshop on Neural Machine Translation and Generation, pages 110–115
Melbourne, Australia, July 20, 2018. ©2018 Association for Computational Linguistics

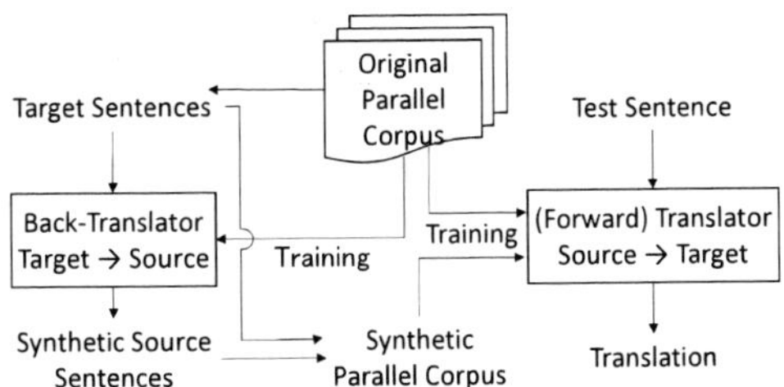

Figure 1: Flow of Self-training

they proposed such self-training strategy and confirmed the effect on their own corpus.

Figure 1 shows the flow of self-training. The procedure is summarized as follows.

1. First, train the back-translator that translates the target language into the source using original parallel corpus.

2. Extract the target side of the original parallel corpus, and translate it into the source language (synthetic source sentences) using the above back-translator. During back-translation, it not only generates one sentence but also generates multiple source sentences per target sentence using a sampling method.

3. Construct the synthetic parallel corpus making pairs of the synthetic source sentences and their original target sentences. If we define the number of synthetic source sentences per target sentence as N, the size of the synthetic parallel corpus becomes N-times larger than the original parallel corpus.

4. Train the forward translator, which translates the source to the target, using a mixture of the original and synthetic parallel corpora.

In this study, we modify the method proposed by Imamura et al. (2018) to improve the efficiency of the training while maintaining the diversity of the source sentences.

2.2 Diversity Control

Imamura et al. (2018) generates synthetic source sentences by sampling. The sampling is based on the posterior probability of an output word as follows.

$$y_t \sim \Pr(y|\boldsymbol{y}_{<t}, \boldsymbol{x}), \tag{1}$$

where y_t, $\boldsymbol{y}_{<t}$, and $\boldsymbol{x}$ denote the output word sequence at time t, history of the output words, and input word sequence, respectively.

To control the diversity of generated sentences, the synthetic source generation in this paper introduces an inverse temperature parameter $1/\tau$ into the softmax function.

$$y_t \sim \frac{\Pr(y|\boldsymbol{y}_{<t}, \boldsymbol{x})^{1/\tau}}{\sum_{y'} \Pr(y'|\boldsymbol{y}_{<t}, \boldsymbol{x})^{1/\tau}} \tag{2}$$

If we set the inverse temperature parameter $1/\tau$ greater than 1.0, high probability words become preferable, and if we set it to infinity, the sampling becomes identical to the argmax operation. On the contrary, if we set it less than 1.0, diverse words will be selected, and the distribution becomes uniform if we set it zero.

2.3 Dynamic Generation

A problem in the research proposed by Imamura et al. (2018) is that the training time increases $(N+1)$-times with an increase in the training data size. To alleviate this problem, we introduce dynamic generation that uses different synthetic parallel sets for each epoch (Kudo, 2018). Specifically, a synthetic parallel sentence set, which contains one synthetic source sentence per target sentence, is used for an epoch of the training. By changing the synthetic parallel sentence set for each epoch, we expect a similar effect to using multiple source sentences in the training.

For implementation, we do not embed the dynamic generation in the training program but perform it offline. Multiple synthetic source sentences were generated in advance, whose number N is 20 this time, and N synthetic parallel sets are constructed. During training, a synthetic set is selected for each epoch using round-robin scheduling, and learns the model using the synthetic set and the original corpus. We can use the same learning rates because the sizes of the original and synthetic sets are the same. Using the dynamic generation, the size of the training data is restricted to double of the original parallel corpus. [1]

The training procedure is summarized as follows.

1. First, train the back-translator using the original parallel corpus.

2. Translate the target side of the original corpus into N synthetic source sentences per target sentence using the above back-translator.

---

[1] Although the size is restricted double, the training time takes more than double because of late convergence.

Note that the sampling method described in Section 2.2 is used for the generation.

3. Make N sets of the synthetic parallel sentences by pairing the synthetic source sentences generated in Step 2 and the target side of the original parallel corpus.

4. Train the forward translator. In each epoch, select one synthetic parallel set, and train the model using the mixture of the synthetic and original parallel sets.

3 Applied Systems

In this paper, we apply the proposed self-training approach to two translator types; the seq-to-seq model (Sutskever et al., 2014; Bahdanau et al., 2014) implemented by OpenNMT (LUA version) (Klein et al., 2017) and the transformer model (Vaswani et al., 2017) implemented by Marian NMT (Junczys-Dowmunt et al., 2018). Table 1 summarizes the system description.

3.1 Back-Translator

The back-translator used herein is OpenNMT, which employs an RNN-based seq-to-seq model.

The training corpus for the back-translation is preprocessed using the byte-pair encoding (BPE) (Sennrich et al., 2016b). For each language, 16K subword types were independently computed. The model was optimized using the stochastic gradient descent (SGD) whose learning rate was 1.0.

For the back-translation, we modified OpenNMT to generate synthetic source sentences by sampling. This time, we generated three types of synthetic source sentences changing the inverse temperature parameter $1/\tau$ to 1.0, 1.2, and 1.5.

3.2 Forward Translator 1: Transformer Model

The first forward translator is Marian NMT, which is based on the transformer model. We used this system for the submission. The settings were almost identical to the base model of Vaswani et al. (2017). [2] The vocabulary sets were equal to those of the back-translator for the original parallel corpus. For the synthetic source sentences, we directly used subword sequences output from the back-translator.

---

[2] We referred the settings described at https://github.com/marian-nmt/marian-examples/tree/master/transformer.

Marian NMT performs the length normalization using the following equation.

$$ll_{\mathrm{norm}}(\boldsymbol{y}|\boldsymbol{x}) = \frac{\sum_t \log \Pr(y_t|\boldsymbol{y}_{<t}, \boldsymbol{x})}{T^{WP}}, \quad (3)$$

where $ll_{\mathrm{norm}}(\boldsymbol{y}|\boldsymbol{x})$, WP, and T denote the log-likelihood normalized by the output length, word penalty, and number of output words, respectively. If we set the word penalty greater than 0.0, long hypotheses are preferred. The setting of the word penalty will be further discussed in Section 4.1.

3.3 Forward Translator 2: Seq-to-Seq Model

The other forward translator used herein is OpenNMT based on the seq-to-seq model. The settings were almost the same as the back-translator. SGD was used for the optimization, but the learning rate was set to 0.5 because all target sentences appear twice in an epoch.

At the translation, we translated the source sentence into 10-best, and the best hypothesis was selected using the length reranking based on the following equation (Oda et al., 2017).

$$ll_{\mathrm{bias}}(\boldsymbol{y}|\boldsymbol{x}) = \sum_t \log \Pr(y_t|\boldsymbol{y}_{<t}, \boldsymbol{x}) + WP \cdot T,$$
$$(4)$$

where $ll_{\mathrm{bias}}(\boldsymbol{y}|\boldsymbol{x})$ denotes the log-likelihood biased by output length. Although this formula differs from Equation 3, there is an equivalent effect that long hypotheses are preferred if the word penalty WP is set to a positive value.

4 Experiments

In this section, we describe our results for the NMT-2018 shared task in English-German translation. Note that the shared task uses the WMT-2014 data set preprocessed by Stanford NLP Group.

In our experiments, we add two baselines. One is the model trained from the original parallel corpus only. Another is the model trained using the synthetic corpus, which contains 1-best generation and did not use the dynamic generation, with the original corpus. For the inverse temperature parameter $1/\tau$, we tested 1.0, 1.2, and 1.5. This is because the translation quality was better when the diversity was slightly inhibited in our preliminary experiments. Note that the submitted system was Marian NMT (the transformer model) trained using $1/\tau = 1.0$ synthetic corpus.

	Marian NMT	OpenNMT
Preprocessing	BPE 16K (independent)	BPE 16K (independent)
Model	Transformer	Seq-to-Seq
Word Embedding	512 units	500 units
Encoder	6-layer ($d_{model} = 512$, $d_{ff} = 2048$)	2-layer Bi-LSTM (500 + 500 units)
Decoder	6-layer ($d_{model} = 512$, $d_{ff} = 2048$)	2-layer LSTM (1,000 units)
Training	Adam (early stopping by cross-entropy)	SGD (14 + 6 epochs)
Learning Rate	0.0003	Back-translator: 1.0
		Forward Translator: 0.5
Dropout	$d_{drop} = 0.1$	$d_{drop} = 0.3$
Maximum Length	100	80
Mini-batch Size	64	64
Translation	Beam Width: 6	Beam Width: 10
Program Arguments (for Training)	(see below)	(see below)

Program Arguments (for Training):

Marian NMT:
```
--type transformer
--max-length 100
--mini-batch-fit --maxi-batch 1000
--early-stopping 10
--valid-freq 5000
--valid-metrics cross-entropy
         perplexity translation
--beam-size 6
--enc-depth 6 --dec-depth 6
--transformer-heads 8
--transformer-postprocess-emb d
--transformer-postprocess dan
--transformer-dropout 0.1
--label-smoothing 0.1
--learn-rate 0.0003 --lr-warmup 16000
--lr-decay-inv-sqrt 16000 --lr-report
--optimizer-params 0.9 0.98 1e-09
--clip-norm 5
--sync-sgd --seed 1111
--exponential-smoothing
```

OpenNMT:
```
-brnn -brnn_merge concat
-rnn_size 1000
-end_epoch 20
-start_decay_at 14
-param_init 0.06
-learning_rate 0.5
```

Table 1: Summary of our Systems

4.1 Word Penalty / Length Ratio

The BLEU score significantly changes due to the translation length (Morishita et al., 2017). For instance, Figure 2 shows BLEU scores of our submitted system (a) when the word penalty was changed from 0.0 to 2.0 and (b) on various length ratios (LRs), which indicate the ratios of the number of words of the system outputs to the reference translations (sys/ref).

As shown in Figure 2 (a), the BLEU scores change over 0.5 when we change the word penalty. The penalties of the peaks are different among the development/test sets. The BLEU score peaks were at $WP = 1.2$, 0.2, and 0.5 in the newstest2013, newstest2014, and newstest2015 sets, respectively. Therefore, the BLEU scores significantly depend on the word penalty. However, as shown in Figure 2 (b), we can see that the peaks of the BLEU scores were at $LR = 1.0$ in all development/test sets. This setting supports no brevity penalty and high n-gram precision. [3]

These results reveal that the length ratio should be constant for fair comparison when we compare different systems because they generate translations of different lengths. Therefore, we compare different models and settings by tuning the word penalty to maintain the stable length ratio on the development set (newstest2013). In this experiment, we show results of the two length ratios based on the "original parallel corpus only" of the transformer model. Note that the submitted system employs the first setting.

1. $LR \simeq 0.988$, which is the length ratio when $WP = 1.0$.

2. $LR \simeq 0.973$, which is the length ratio when $WP = 0.5$.

4.2 Results

Tables 2 and 3 show the results of Marian NMT (the transformer model) and OpenNMT (the seq-

---

[3]If we tune the word penalty to make the BLEU score maximum on the newstest2013, the length ratios of newstest2014 and 2015 become greater than 1.0.

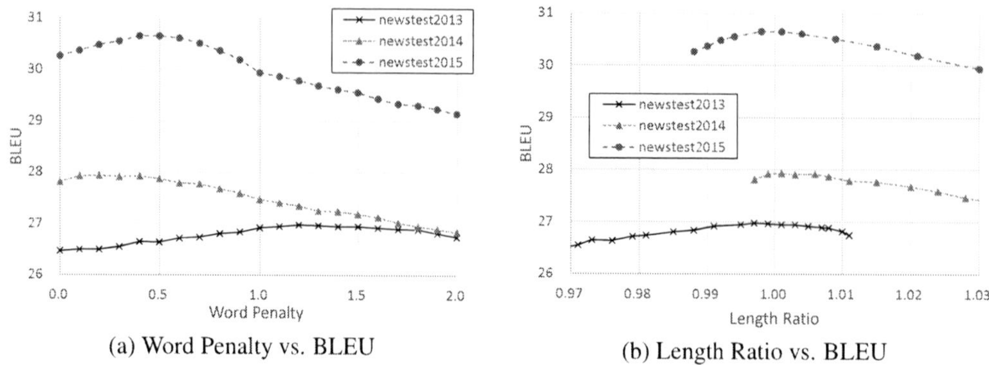

(a) Word Penalty vs. BLEU   (b) Length Ratio vs. BLEU

Figure 2: Word Penalty, Length Ratio and BLEU Scores (Marian NMT; $1/\tau = 1.0$)

to-seq model), respectively. These tables consist of three information groups. The first group shows training results; the number of training epochs and perplexity of the development set. The second and third groups show the BLEU scores when the length ratio in the development set become 0.988 and 0.973, respectively. The results of Marian NMT were better than those of OpenNMT in all cases. The following discussion mainly focuses on the results of Marian NMT (Table 2), but there was similarity in Table 3.

First, in comparison with the "original parallel corpus only" and the "one-best without dynamic generation," the perplexity of the one-best case increased from 4.37 to 4.43. Along with increasing the perplexity, the BLEU scores of the test sets (`newstest2014` and `newstest2015`) degraded to 26.19 and 28.49 when $LR \simeq 0.988$. This result indicates that the self-training, which simply uses one-best translation result, is not effective.

On the contrary, using our self-training method, the perplexities were decreased and the BLEU scores improved significantly regardless of the inverse temperature parameters in most cases. [4] For example, when $1/\tau = 1.0$, the perplexity were decreased to 4.20, and the BLEU scores improved to 27.59 and 30.19 on the `newstest2014` and 2015, respectively, when $LR \simeq 0.988$. When $LR \simeq 0.973$, the BLEU scores further improved, but the improvements come from the length ratio. The same tendency was observed in OpenNMT. We can conclude that the proposed self-training method is effective for the transformer and seq-

to-seq models.

The effectiveness of the inverse temperature parameter is still unclear because the BLEU scores were depend on the parameters.

5 Conclusions

The self-training method in this paper improves the accuracy without changing the model structure. The experimental results show that the proposed method is effective for both the transformer and seq-to-seq models. Although our self-training method increases training time by more than double, we believe that it is effective for the tasks that emphasize on translation speed because it does not change the translation efficiency.

In this paper, only restricted settings were tested. We require further experiments such as another back-translation methodology and settings of the inverse temperature parameters.

Acknowledgments

This work was supported by "Promotion of Global Communications Plan — Research and Development and Social Demonstration of Multilingual Speech Translation Technology," a program of the Ministry of Internal Affairs and Communications, Japan.

References

Dzmitry Bahdanau, Kyunghyun Cho, and Yoshua Bengio. 2014. Neural machine translation by jointly learning to align and translate. *CoRR*, abs/1409.0473.

Alexandra Birch, Andrew Finch, Minh-Thang Luong, Graham Neubig, and Yusuke Oda. 2018. Findings

---

[4] The significance test was performed using the multeval tool (Clark et al., 2011) at a significance level of 5% ($p < 0.05$). `https://github.com/jhclark/multeval`

	Training		BLEU $\uparrow$ (Dev. $LR \simeq 0.988$)			BLEU $\uparrow$ (Dev. $LR \simeq 0.973$)		
	#Epoch	PPL $\downarrow$	2013	2014	2015	2013	2014	2015
Original Parallel Corpus Only	49	4.37	26.03	26.81	29.35	25.77	26.95	29.67
One-best w/o Dynamic Generation	61	4.43	26.17	26.19 (-)	28.49 (-)	25.94	26.43 (-)	28.91 (-)
Self-Training $1/\tau = 1.0$	83	4.20	**26.84** (+)	**27.59** (+)	**30.19** (+)	26.65 (+)	27.92 (+)	30.65 (+)
Self-Training $1/\tau = 1.2$	112	4.21	27.01 (+)	27.70 (+)	29.80	26.67 (+)	27.92 (+)	30.00
Self-Training $1/\tau = 1.5$	98	4.25	26.75 (+)	27.74 (+)	30.17 (+)	26.51 (+)	28.04 (+)	30.27 (+)

Table 2: Results of Marian NMT (Transformer Model)
The bold values denote the results of the submitted system. (+) and (-) symbols denote results that are significantly improved and degraded from the "original parallel corpus only," respectively.

	Training		BLEU $\uparrow$ (Dev. $LR \simeq 0.988$)			BLEU $\uparrow$ (Dev. $LR \simeq 0.973$)		
	#Epoch	PPL $\downarrow$	2013	2014	2015	2013	2014	2015
Original Parallel Corpus Only	20	5.58	23.45	22.69	25.70	23.23	22.94	25.96
One-best w/o Dynamic Generation	20	5.75	22.86 (-)	22.36	24.35 (-)	N/A (No Word Penalty)		
Self-Training $1/\tau = 1.0$	20	5.34	23.56	23.15 (+)	26.03	23.38	23.49 (+)	26.33
Self-Training $1/\tau = 1.2$	20	5.46	23.59	22.95	25.71	23.38	23.15	25.96
Self-Training $1/\tau = 1.5$	20	5.41	23.58	23.13 (+)	26.32 (+)	23.55	23.45 (+)	26.50 (+)

Table 3: Results of OpenNMT (Seq-to-Seq Model)
(+) and (-) symbols denote results that are significantly improved and degraded from the "original parallel corpus only," respectively.

of the second workshop on neural machine translation and gen eration. In *Proceedings of the Second Workshop on Neural Machine Translation and Generation (NMT-2018)*, Melbourne, Australia.

Jonathan H. Clark, Chris Dyer, Alon Lavie, and Noah A. Smith. 2011. Better hypothesis testing for statistical machine translation: Controlling for optimizer instability. In *Proceedings of the 49th Annual Meeting of the Association for Computational Linguistics: Human Language Technologies*, pages 176–181, Portland, Oregon, USA.

Kenji Imamura, Atsushi Fujita, and Eiichiro Sumita. 2018. Enhancement of encoder and attention using target monolingual corpora in neural machine translation. In *Proceedings of the 2nd Workshop on Neural Machine Translation and Generation (NMT-2018)*, Melbourne, Australia.

Marcin Junczys-Dowmunt, Roman Grundkiewicz, Tomasz Dwojak, Hieu Hoang, Kenneth Heafield, Tom Neckermann, Frank Seide, Ulrich Germann, Alham Fikri Aji, Nikolay Bogoychev, André F. T. Martins, and Alexandra Birch. 2018. Marian: Fast neural machine translation in C++. *arXiv preprint arXiv:1804.00344*.

Guillaume Klein, Yoon Kim, Yuntian Deng, Jean Senellart, and Alexander M. Rush. 2017. OpenNMT: Open-source toolkit for neural machine translation. In *Proceedings of ACL 2017, System Demonstrations*, pages 67–72, Vancouver, Canada.

Taku Kudo. 2018. Subword regularization: Improving neural network translation models with multiple subword candidates. In *Proceedings of the 56th Annual Meeting of the Association for Computational Linguistics (ACL-2018)*, Melbourne, Australia.

Makoto Morishita, Jun Suzuki, and Masaaki Nagata. 2017. NTT neural machine translation systems at WAT 2017. In *Proceedings of the 4th Workshop on Asian Translation (WAT2017)*, pages 89–94, Taipei, Taiwan.

Yusuke Oda, Katsuhito Sudoh, Satoshi Nakamura, Masao Utiyama, and Eiichiro Sumita. 2017. A simple and strong baseline: NAIST-NICT neural machine translation system for WAT2017 English-Japanese translation task. In *Proceedings of the 4th Workshop on Asian Translation (WAT2017)*, pages 135–139, Taipei, Taiwan.

Rico Sennrich, Barry Haddow, and Alexandra Birch. 2016a. Improving neural machine translation models with monolingual data. In *Proceedings of the 54th Annual Meeting of the Association for Computational Linguistics (ACL-2016, Volume 1: Long Papers)*, pages 86–96, Berlin, Germany.

Rico Sennrich, Barry Haddow, and Alexandra Birch. 2016b. Neural machine translation of rare words with subword units. In *Proceedings of the 54th Annual Meeting of the Association for Computational Linguistics (Volume 1: Long Papers)*, pages 1715–1725, Berlin, Germany.

Ilya Sutskever, Oriol Vinyals, and Quoc V. Le. 2014. Sequence to sequence learning with neural networks. In *Proceedings of Advances in Neural Information Processing Systems 27 (NIPS 2014)*, pages 3104–3112.

Ashish Vaswani, Noam Shazeer, Niki Parmar, Jakob Uszkoreit, Llion Jones, Aidan N. Gomez, Lukasz Kaiser, and Illia Polosukhin. 2017. Attention is all you need. *CoRR*, abs/1706.03762.

Fast Neural Machine Translation Implementation

Hieu Hoang[†]   Tomasz Dwojak[*]   Rihards Krislauks[‡]
Daniel Torregrosa[¶]   Kenneth Heafield[†]

[†]University of Edinburgh   [*]Adam Mickiewicz University
[‡]Tilde   [¶]Universitat d'Alacant

Abstract

This paper describes the submissions to the efficiency track for GPUs at the Workshop for Neural Machine Translation and Generation by members of the University of Edinburgh, Adam Mickiewicz University, Tilde and University of Alicante. We focus on efficient implementation of the recurrent deep-learning model as implemented in Amun, the fast inference engine for neural machine translation. We improve the performance with an efficient mini-batching algorithm, and by fusing the softmax operation with the k-best extraction algorithm. Submissions using Amun were first, second and third fastest in the GPU efficiency track.

1   Introduction

As neural machine translation (NMT) models have become the new state-of-the-art, the challenge is to make their deployment efficient and economical. This is the challenge that this shared task (Birch et al., 2018) is shining a spotlight on.

One approach is to use an off-the-shelf deep-learning toolkit to complete the shared task where the novelty comes from selecting the appropriate models and tuning parameters within the toolkit for optimal performance.

We take an opposing approach by eschewing model selection and parameter tuning in favour of efficient implementation. We use and enhanced a custom inference engine, Amun (Junczys-Dowmunt et al., 2016), which we developed on the premise that fast deep-learning inference is an issue that deserves dedicated tools that are not compromised by competing objectives such as training or support for multiple models. As well as delivering on the practical goal of fast inference, it can serve as a test-bed for novel ideas on neural network inference, and it is useful as a means to explore the upper bound of the possible speed for a particular model and hardware. That is, Amun is an inference-only engine that supports a limited number of NMT models that put fast inference on modern GPU above all other considerations.

We submitted two systems to this year's shared task for the efficient translation on GPU. Our first submission was tailored to be as fast as possible while being above the baseline BLEU score. Our second submission trades some of the speed of the first submission to return better quality translations.

2   Improvements

We describe the main enhancements to Amun since the original 2016 publication that has improved translation speed.

2.1   Batching

The use of mini-batching is critical for fast model inference. The size of the batch is determined by the number of inputs sentences to the encoder in an encoder-decoder model. However, the number of batches during decoding can vary as some sentences have completed translating or the beam search add more hypotheses to the batch.

It is tempting to ignore these considerations, for example, by always decoding with a constant batch and beam size and ignoring hypotheses which are not needed. Figure 1 illustrates a naïve mini-batching with a constant size batch. The downside to this algorithm is lower translation speed due to wasteful processing.

Amun implements an efficient batching algorithm that takes into account the actual number of hypotheses that need to be decoded at each decoding step, Figure 2.

Proceedings of the 2nd Workshop on Neural Machine Translation and Generation, pages 116–121
Melbourne, Australia, July 20, 2018. ©2018 Association for Computational Linguistics

Algorithm 1 Naïve mini-batching

> **procedure** BATCHING(encoded sentences i)
>   Create batch b from i
>   **while** hypo $h \neq EOS, \forall h \in b$ **do**
>   Decode(b)
>   **end while**
> **end procedure**

Algorithm 2 Mini-batching

> **procedure** BATCHING(encoded sentences i)
>   Create batch b from i
>   **while** $b \neq \emptyset$ **do**
>   Decode(b)
>   **for all** hypo $h \in b$ **do**
>   **if** $h = EOS$ **then**
>   Remove h from b
>   **end if**
>   **end for**
>   **end while**
> **end procedure**

We will compare the effect of the two implementations in the Section 4.

2.2 Softmax and K-Best Fusion

Most NMT models predict a large number of classes in their output layer, corresponding to the number of words or subword units in their target language. For example, Sennrich et al. (2016) experimented with target vocabulary sizes of 60,000 and 90,000 sub-word units.

The output layer of most deep learning models consist of the following steps

1. multiplication of the weight matrix with the input vector $p = wx$

2. addition of a bias term to the resulting scores $p = p + b$

3. applying the activation function, most commonly softmax $p_i = \exp(p_i)/\sum \exp(p_i)$

4. a search for the best (or k-best) output classes $\text{argmax}_i\, p_i$

Figure 1 shows the amount of time spent in each step during translation. Clearly, the output layer of NMT models are very computationally expensive, accounting for over 60% of the translation time.

We focus on the last three steps; their outline is shown in Algorithm 3. For brevity, we show the algorithm for 1-best, a k-best search is a simple extension of this.

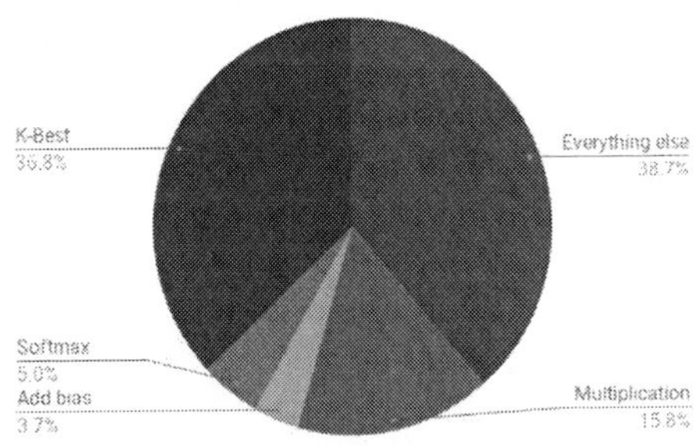

Figure 1: Proportion of time spent during translation

Algorithm 3 Original softmax and k-best algorithm

> **procedure** ADDBIAS(vector p, bias vector b)
>   **for all** p_i in p **do**
> $p_i \leftarrow p_i + b_i$
>   **end for**
> **end procedure**
>
> **procedure** SOFTMAX(vector p)
>   ▷ calculate max for softmax stability
> $max \leftarrow -\infty$
>   **for all** p_i in p **do**
>   **if** $p_i > max$ **then**
> $max \leftarrow p_i$
>   **end if**
>   **end for**
>   ▷ calculate denominator
> $sum \leftarrow 0$
>   **for all** p_i in p **do**
> $sum \leftarrow sum + \exp(p_i - max)$
>   **end for**
>   ▷ calculate softmax
>   **for all** p_i in p **do**
> $p_i \leftarrow \frac{\exp(p_i - max)}{sum}$
>   **end for**
> **end procedure**
>
> **procedure** FIND-BEST(vector p)
> $max \leftarrow -\infty$
>   **for all** p_i in p **do**
>   **if** $p_i > max$ **then**
> $max \leftarrow p_i$
> $best \leftarrow i$
>   **end if**
>   **end for**
>   **return** $max, best$
> **end procedure**

As can be seen, the vector p is iterated over five times - once to add the bias, three times to calculate the softmax, and once to search for the best classes. We propose fusing the three functions into one kernel, a popular optimization technique (Guevara et al., 2009), making use of the following observations.

Firstly, softmax and exp are monotonic functions, therefore, we can move the search for the best class from FIND-BEST to SOFTMAX, at the start of the kernel.

Secondly, we are only interested in the probabilities of the best classes during inference, not of all classes. Since they are now known at the start of the softmax kernel, we compute softmax only for those classes.

Algorithm 4 Fused softmax and k-best

> **procedure** FUSED-KERNEL(vector p, bias vector b)
>> $max \leftarrow -\infty$
>> $sum \leftarrow 0$
>> **for all** p_i in p **do**
>>> $p_i' \leftarrow p_i + b_i$
>>> **if** $p_i' > max$ **then**
>>>> $\Delta \leftarrow max - p_i'$
>>>> $sum \leftarrow \Delta \times sum + 1$
>>>> $max \leftarrow p_i'$
>>>> $best \leftarrow i$
>>> **else**
>>>> $sum \leftarrow sum + \exp(p_i' - max)$
>>> **end if**
>> **end for**
>> **return** $\frac{1}{sum}, best$
> **end procedure**

Thirdly, the calculation of max and sum can be accomplished in one loop by adjusting sum whenever a higher max is found during the looping:

$$
\begin{aligned}
sum &= e^{x_t - max_b} + \sum_{i=0...t-1} e^{x_i - max_b} \\
&= e^{x_t - max_b} + \sum_{i=0...t-1} e^{x_i - max_a + \Delta} \\
&= e^{x_t - max_b} + e^\Delta \times \sum_{i=0...t-1} e^{x_i - max_a}
\end{aligned}
$$

where max_a is the previous maximum value, max_b is the now higher maximum value, i.e., $max_b > max_a$, and $\Delta = max_a - max_b$. The outline of our function is shown in Algorithm 4.

In fact, a well known optimization is to skip softmax altogether and calculate the argmax over the input vector, Algorithm 5. This is only possible for beam size 1 and when we are not interested in returning the softmax probabilities.

Algorithm 5 Find 1-best only

> **procedure** FUSED-KERNEL-1-BEST(vector p, bias vector b)
>> $max \leftarrow -\infty$
>> **for all** p_i in p **do**
>>> **if** $p_i + b_i > max$ **then**
>>>> $max \leftarrow p_i + b_i$
>>>> $best \leftarrow i$
>>> **end if**
>> **end for**
>> **return** $best$
> **end procedure**

Since we are working on GPU optimization, it is essential to make full use of the many GPU cores available. This is accomplished by well-known parallelization methods which multi-thread the algorithms. For example, Algorithm 5 is parallelized by sharding the vector p and calculating $best$ and max on each shard in parallel. The ultimate $best$ is found in the following reduction step, Algorithm 6.

2.3 Half-Precision

Reducing the number of bits needed to store floating point values from 32-bits to 16-bits promises to increase translation speed through faster calculations and reduced bandwidth usage. 16-bit floating point operations are supported by the GPU hardware and software available in the shared task.

In practise, however, efficiently using half-precision value requires a comprehensive redevelopment of the GPU code. We therefore make do with using the GPU's Tensor Core[1] fast matrix multiplication routines which transparently converts 32-bit float point input matrices to 16-bit values and output a 32-bit float point product of the inputs.

3 Experimental Setup

Both of our submitted systems use a sequence-to-sequence model similar to that described in Bahdanau et al. (2014), containing a bidirectional

---

[1] https://devblogs.nvidia.com/programming-tensor-cores-cuda-9/

Algorithm 6 Parallel find 1-best only

> **procedure** FUSED-KERNEL-1-BEST(vector p, bias vector b)
>>   ▷ parallelize
>> Create shards $p^1...p^n$ from p
>> **parfor** $p^j \in p^1...p^n$ **do**
>>> $max^j \leftarrow -\infty$
>>> **for all** p_i^j in p^j **do**
>>>> **if** $p_i^j + b_i > max$ **then**
>>>>> $max^j \leftarrow p_i^j + b_i$
>>>>> $best^j \leftarrow i$
>>>> **end if**
>>> **end for**
>> **end parfor**
>>   ▷ reduce
>> $max \leftarrow -\infty$
>> **for all** $max^j \in max^1...max^n$ **do**
>>> **if** $max^j > max$ **then**
>>>> $max \leftarrow max^j$
>>>> $best \leftarrow best^j$
>>> **end if**
>> **end for**
>> **return** $best$
> **end procedure**

RNN in the encoder and a two-layer RNN in the decoder. We use byte pair encoding (Sennrich et al., 2016) to adjust the vocabulary size.

We used a variety of GPUs to train the models but all testing was done on an Nvidia V100. Translation quality was measured using BLEU, specifically multi-bleu as found in the Moses toolkit[2]. The validation and test sets provided by the shared task organisers were used to measure translation quality, but a 50,000 sentence subset of the training data was used to measure translation speed to obtain longer, more accurate measurements.

3.1 GRU-based system

Our first submitted system uses gated recurred units (GRU) throughout. It was trained using Marian (Junczys-Dowmunt et al., 2018), but Amun was chosen as inference engine.

We experimented with varying the vocabulary size and the RNN state size before settling for a vocabulary size of 30,000 (for both source and target language) and 256 for the state size, Table 1.

After further experimentation, we decided to use sentence length normalization and NVidia's

[2]https://github.com/moses-smt/mosesdecoder

	State dim		
Vocab size	256	512	1024
1.000	12.23		12.77
5,000	16.79		17.16
10,000	18.00		18.19
20,000	-		19.52
30,000	18.51	19.17	19.64

Table 1: Validation set BLEU (newstest2014) for GRU-based model

	Vocab size	
Beam size	40,000	50,000
1	23.45	23.32
2	24.15	24.04
3	24.48	
4	24.42	
5	24.48	

Table 2: Validation set BLEU for mLSTM-based model

Tensor Core matrix multiplication which increased translation quality as well as translation speed. The beam was kept at 1 throughout for the fastest possible inference.

3.2 mLSTM-based system

Our second system uses multiplicative-LSTM (Krause et al., 2017) in the encoder and the first layer of a decder, and a GRU in the second layer, trained with an extension of the Nematus (Sennrich et al., 2017) toolkit which supports such models; multiplicative-LSTM's suitability for use in NMT models has been previously demonstrated by Pinnis et al. (2017). As with our first submission, Amun is used as inference engine. We trained 2 systems with differing vocabulary sizes and varied the beam sizes, and chose the configuration that produced the best results for translation quality on the validation set, Table 2.

4 Result

4.1 Batching

The efficiency of Amun's batching algorithm can be seen by observing the time taken for each decoding step in a batch of sentences, Figure 2. Amun's decoding becomes faster as sentences are completely translated. This contrasts with the Marian inference engine, which uses a naïve

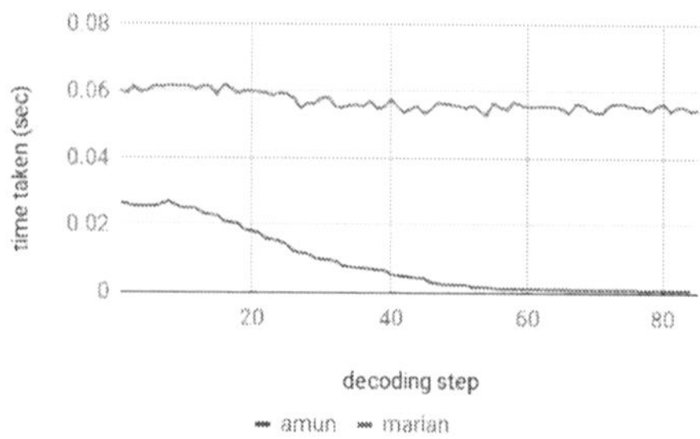

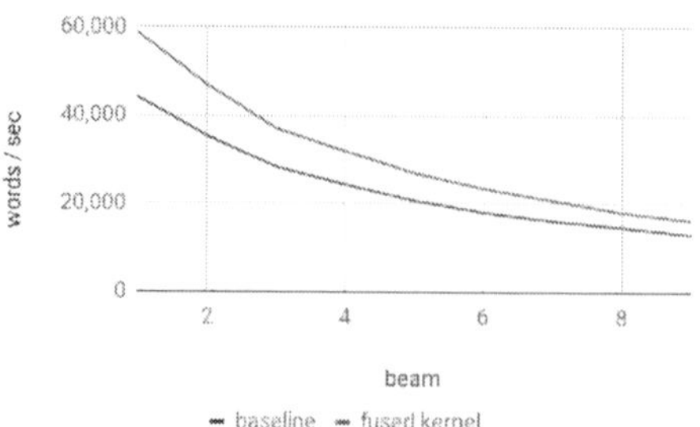

Figure 2: Time taken for each decoding step for a batch of 1280 sentences

Figure 4: Using fused operation

best list is begins to impact on speed.

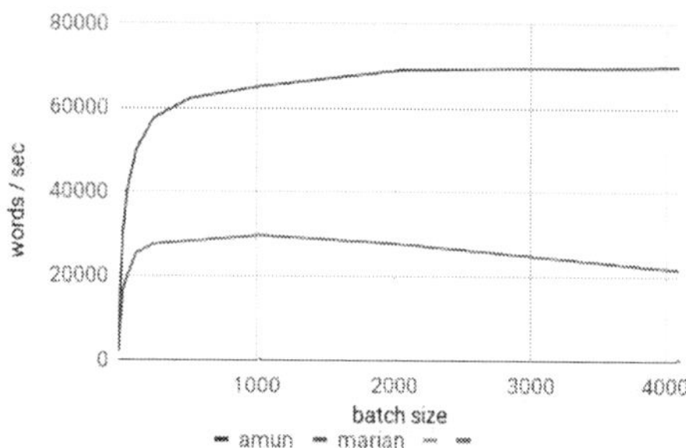

Figure 3: Speed v. batch size

	Baseline	Fused
Beam size 1		
Multiplication	5.39	5.38 (+0%)
Add bias	1.26	
Softmax	1.69	2.07 (-86.6%)
K-best extr.	12.53	
Beam size 3		
Multiplication	14.18	14.16 (+0%)
Add bias	3.76	
Softmax	4.75	3.43 (-87.1%)
K-best extr.	18.23	
Beam size 9		
Multiplication	38.35	38.42 (+0%)
Add bias	11.64	
Softmax	14.4	17.5 (-72.1%)
K-best extr.	36.7	

Table 3: Time taken (sec) breakdown

batching algorithm, where the speed stays relatively constant throughout the decoding of the batch.

Using batching can increase the translation speed by over 20 times in Amun, Figure 3. Just as important, it doesn't suffer degradation with large batch sizes, unlike the naïve algorithm which slows down when batch sizes over 1000 is used. This scalability issue is likely to become more relevant as newer GPUs with ever increasing core counts are released.

4.2 Softmax and K-Best Fusion

Fusing the bias and softmax operations in the output layer with the beam search results in a speed improvement by 25%, Figure 4. Its relative improvement decreases marginally as the beam size increases.

Further insight can be gained by examining the time taken for each step in the output layer and beam search, Table 3. The fused operation only has to loop through the large cost matrix once, therefore, for low beam sizes its is comparable in speed to the simple kernel to add the bias. For higher beam sizes, the cost of maintaining the n-

4.3 Tensor Cores

By taking advantage of the GPU's hardware accelerated matrix multiplication, we can gain up to 20% in speed, Table 4.

Beam size	Baseline	Tensor Cores
1	39.97	34.54 (-13.6%)
9	145.8	116.8 (-20.0%)

Table 4: Time taken (sec) using Tensor Cores

5 Conclusion and Future Work

We have presented some of the improvement to Amun which are focused on improving NMT inference.

We are also working to make deep-learning faster using more specialised hardware such as FP-GAs. It would be interesting as future work to bring our focused approach to fast deep-learning inference to a more general toolkit.

References

Bahdanau, D., Cho, K., and Bengio, Y. (2014). Neural machine translation by jointly learning to align and translate. *CoRR*, abs/1409.0473.

Birch, A., Finch, A., Luong, M.-T., Neubig, G., and Oda, Y. (2018). Findings of the second workshop on neural machine translation and generation. In *The Second Workshop on Neural Machine Translation and Generation*.

Guevara, M., Gregg, C., Hazelwood, K. M., and Skadron, K. (2009). Enabling task parallelism in the cuda scheduler.

Junczys-Dowmunt, M., Dwojak, T., and Hoang, H. (2016). Is neural machine translation ready for deployment? a case study on 30 translation directions. In *Proceedings of the 9th International Workshop on Spoken Language Translation (IWSLT)*, Seattle, WA.

Junczys-Dowmunt, M., Grundkiewicz, R., Dwojak, T., Hoang, H., Heafield, K., Neckermann, T., Seide, F., Germann, U., Aji, A. F., Bogoychev, N., Martins, A. F. T., and Birch, A. (2018). Marian: Fast Neural Machine Translation in C++. *ArXiv e-prints*.

Krause, B., Murray, I., Renals, S., and Lu, L. (2017). Multiplicative LSTM for sequence modelling. *ICLR Workshop track*.

Pinnis, M., Krišlauks, R., Miks, T., Deksne, D., and Šics, V. (2017). Tilde's Machine Translation Systems for WMT 2017. In *Proceedings of the Second Conference on Machine Translation (WMT 2017), Volume 2: Shared Task Papers*, pages 374–381, Copenhagen, Denmark. Association for Computational Linguistics.

Sennrich, R., Firat, O., Cho, K., Birch, A., Haddow, B., Hitschler, J., Junczys-Dowmunt, M., Läubli, S., Miceli Barone, A. V., Mokry, J., and Nadejde, M. (2017). Nematus: a toolkit for neural machine translation. In *Proceedings of the Software Demonstrations of the 15th Conference of the European Chapter of the Association for Computational Linguistics*, pages 65–68, Valencia, Spain. Association for Computational Linguistics.

Sennrich, R., Haddow, B., and Birch, A. (2016). Neural Machine Translation of Rare Words with Subword Units. In *Proceedings of the 54th Annual Meeting of the Association for Computational Linguistics (Volume 1: Long Papers)*, pages 1715–1725, Berlin, Germany. Association for Computational Linguistics.

OpenNMT System Description for WNMT 2018:
800 words/sec on a single-core CPU

**Jean Senellart, Dakun Zhang,
Bo Wang, Guillaume Klein,
J.P. Ramatchandirin, Josep Crego**
SYSTRAN Research, Paris
`first.last@systrangroup.com`

Alexander M. Rush
School of Engineering
and Applied Sciences
Harvard University
`srush@seas.harvard.edu`

Abstract

We present a system description of the
OpenNMT Neural Machine Translation
entry for the WNMT 2018 evaluation. In
this work, we developed a heavily optimized NMT inference model targeting a
high-performance CPU system. The final
system uses a combination of four techniques, all of them leading to significant
speed-ups in combination: (a) sequence
distillation, (b) architecture modifications,
(c) pre-computation, particularly of vocabulary, and (d) CPU targeted quantization. This work achieves the fastest performance of the shared task, and led to the development of new features that have been
integrated to OpenNMT and made available to the community.

1 Introduction

As neural machine translation becomes more
widely deployed in production environments, it
becomes also increasingly important to serve
translations models in a way as fast and as
memory-efficient as possible, both on dedicated
GPU and on standard CPU hardwares. The WN-
MT 2018 shared task[1] focused on comparing different systems on both accuracy and computational efficiency (Birch et al., 2018).

This paper describes the entry for the OpenN-
MT system to this competition. Our specific interest was to explore the different techniques for
training and optimizing CPU models for very high
throughput while preserving highest possible accuracy compared to state-of-the-art. While we did
not put real focus on memory and docker size foot-

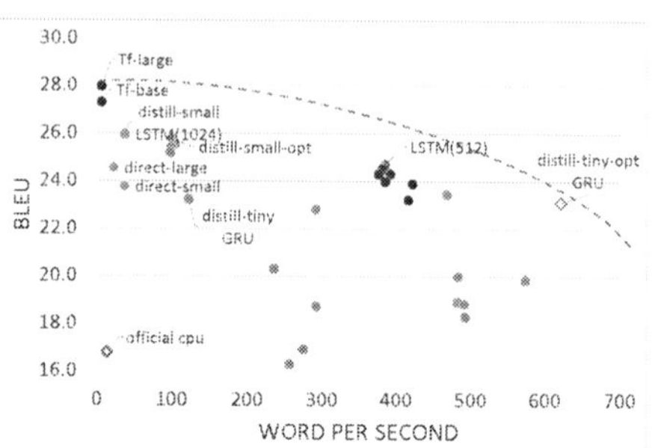

Figure 1: Pareto on accuracy and throughput. The different
models on the plot are described in the paper, the corresponding BLEU score calculated on *newstest2014*, and throughput
in word per second measured on <u>non dedicated</u> M5 instances.

print, we applied basic optimization techniques to
reduce the final size of our models.

Our strategy for the shared task was to
take advantage of four main optimization techniques: (a) sequence-level *distillation*, in particular cross-class distillation from a transformer model (Vaswani et al., 2017) to an RNN, (b) *architecture search*, changing the structure of the network
by increasing the size of the most efficient modules, reducing the size of the most costly modules and replacing default gated units, (c) specialized *precomputation* such as reducing dynamically the runtime target vocabulary (Shi and Knight,
2017), and (d) *quantization* and faster matrix operations, based on the work of Devlin (2017) and
`gemmlowp`[2]. All of these methods are employed
in a special-purpose C++-based decoder *CTranslate*[3]. The complete training workflow including
data preparation and distillation is described in
Section 2. Inference techniques and quantization
are described in Section 3.

Our experiments compare the different approaches in terms of speed and accuracy. A meta

---

[1] `https://sites.google.com/site/wnmt18/
shared-task`

[2] `https://github.com/google/gemmlowp`
[3] `https://github.com/OpenNMT/CTranslate`

Proceedings of the 2nd Workshop on Neural Machine Translation and Generation, pages 122–128
Melbourne, Australia, July 20, 2018. ©2018 Association for Computational Linguistics

question of this work is to decide which models represent interesting and useful points on the Pareto curve. The main results are described in Figure 1. From these results we highlight two models which were submitted to the shared task: Our first system `distill-small-opt` is a 2-layer LSTM network that is only -2.19 BLEU points behind the reference transformer model, but with a speed-up of x18. Our second system achieves 23.11 on WNMT 2018 English-German *newstest2014* (-4.85 behind the reference model) but with an additional decoding speed-up of x8. The final model reaches 800 words/sec on the dedicated evaluation CPU hardware and is the fastest CPU model submitted[4].

We additionally report several new results about recent work in NMT and model efficiency: (a) we show that distillation of transformer model to a simple RNN outperforms direct training of a strong RNN model - extending findings of Crego and Senellart (2016) who reported that student models could outperform their teacher for reference RNN-based model. (b) We compare quantitatively different quantizations, and (c) we give an improved algorithm to dynamically select target vocabulary for a given batch. Finally, we also report several complementary experiments that resulted in systems inside of the pareto convex border. For instance, we compare using 8-bit quantization to 16-bit quantization.

2 Training and Distillation

Following the shared task setup, we use the data set provided by WNMT 2018, which is a pre-processed and tokenized version of WMT 2014 on English-German translation[5]. The training data contains about 4.5M sentence pairs. We use *newstest2013* as the validation set and *newstest2014* and *newstest2015* as the testing sets. Before training, we trained a 32K joint byte-pair encoding (BPE) to preprocess the data (Sennrich et al., 2015) (actual vocabulary size of 34K). We limit the sentence length to 100 based on BPE preprocessing in both source and target side (excluding only 0.31% of the training corpus). After decoding, we remove the BPE joiners and evaluate the tokenized output with multi-bleu.perl (Koehn et al., 2007).

2.1 Teacher Model: Transformer

Transformer networks (Vaswani et al., 2017) are the current state-of-the art in many machine translation tasks (Shaw et al., 2018). The network directly models the representations of each sentence with a self-attention mechanism. Hence much longer term dependencies than with standard sequence-to-sequence models can be learned, which is especially important for language pairs like English-German. In addition, transformer allows to easily parallelise the MLE training process across multiple GPUs. However, a large number of parameters are needed by the network to obtain its best performance. In order to reduce the model size, we applied knowledge distillation, a technique that has proven successful for reducing the size of neural models. We considered the transformer network as our teacher network.

We used *OpenNMT-tf*[6] to train two transformer based systems: base and large described in Table 2 with their evaluation in Table 3. For both, the learning rate is set to 2.0 and warmup steps 8000, we average the last 8 checkpoints to get the final model. Our baseline system outperforms the provided baseline Sockeye model by +0.37 BLEU on *newstest2014*.

2.2 Distillation to RNN

To train our smaller student system, we follow the sequence-level knowledge distillation approach described by Kim and Rush (2016). First, we build the full transformer as above. Next, we use the teacher system to retranslate all the training source sentences to generate a set of simplified target sentences. Then, we use this simplified corpus (original source and newly generated target) to train a student system. The student system can be assigned with smaller network size, in our case a RNN-based sequence-to-sequence model similar to Bahdanau et al. (2014)

Results from Crego and Senellart (2016) show that the distillation process not only improves the throughput of the student models and reduce their size, but can also improve the translation quality. Also, these distilled systems have the interesting feature that they performed almost identically when reducing beam search size K from $K = 5$ to $K = 2$. Seemingly the smaller model learns from more consistent translations and can produce effective results with simpler syntactic structure and

---

[4]On non dedicated hardware, our best benchmark shows 621 words/sec, see section 4.3 for analysis of the difference.

[5]`https://nlp.stanford.edu/projects/nmt/`

[6]`https://github.com/OpenNMT/OpenNMT-tf`

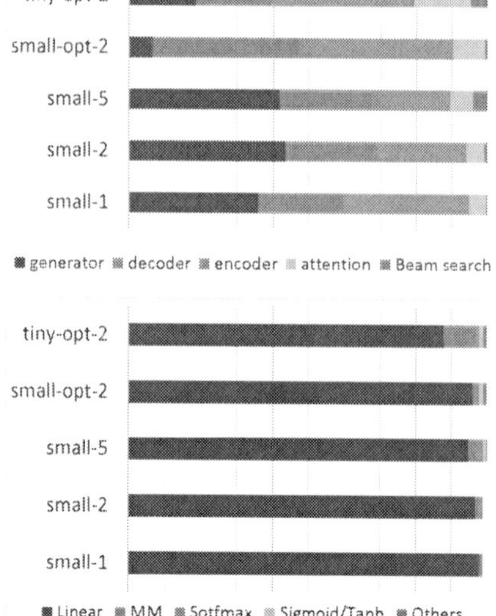

Figure 2: Profiling of the throughput during inference on *newstest2014*. Each line is a different system. The `small-1,2,5` are distilled systems with respective beam size of 1, 2, 5. `distill-tiny-opt` and `distill-small-opt` are the final systems. The decoding time for each of these systems range from 90 to 1800 seconds. The top table shows the distribution of time per component of the network, while the bottom table shows the distribution of time for network operators.

even word choices. One major question here was to find out whether cross-class distillation works as well, here from a transformer model to student RNN model. Remarkably, Figure 3 shows that a distilled simple RNN system outperforms the direct strong RNN model[7] by a significant +1.4 BLEU score.

2.3 Model Analysis

Profiling of the throughput of our student system, before and after further optimizations, is presented in Figure 2. Here we compare along two splits, the components of the system: encoder, decoder, attention, word generation, and beam search; and model components: linear, MM (matrix multiply, primarily in attention), softmax, activations, and others. From this analysis we gather the following facts:

- The most costly part of the inference is the generator, that is the final Linear layer feeding Softmax with weights corresponding to each single vocab of the target language. This is by far the largest matrix multiplication of the system: $(B, W) * (W, V)$ (with B being the batch*beam size, W the width of the network, and V the size of the vocabulary).

- Although the cost of the encoder for beam size 1 is higher than the decoder, the decoder cost - including generator and attention model - grows linearly with the beam size.

- The most costly operations are the multiplication of the Linear matrix-vector in the RNNs and generator, contributing for more than 95% of the complete processing time.

From these facts, it is obvious that we need to optimize the efficiency of linear matrix-vector operation, to reduce the amount of such required operations, and have a special focus on the generation layer.

These observations led us to several further model experiments. First we tried different model combination based on a "fat encoder, thin decoder" spirit: ie. increasing if necessary the number of operations in the encoder part if we can in parallel reduce the number of operations in the decoder. Second, we experimented with replacing LSTM cells with GRU cells (Cho et al., 2014). Indeed LSTM cells have 4 gates while GRU cells only 3, so a potential 25% improvement in speed with similar performance can be reached. Note though, that we found that GRU requires more care in optimization while a naive SGD optimization is generally sufficient for LSTM-RNN training.

3 Inference Optimizations

3.1 Implementation: CTranslate

CTranslate is the open-source inference engine for OpenNMT models (initially designed for Lua Torch). The code is implemented in raw C++ with minimal dependencies using the popular Eigen linear algebra library. CTranslate's goal is to offer a lightweight and embeddable solution for executing models. It benefits from Eigen efficiency and is about 20% faster than a Torch application using Intel MKL. Additionally, the use of C++ over a garbage-collected language ensures a predictable and reduced memory usage. All additional optimizations are built on top of this library.

---

[7] Both NMT systems follow the standard architecture of Luong et al. (2015). It is implemented as an encoder-decoder network with multiple layers of a RNN with Long Short-Term Memory (Hochreiter and Schmidhuber, 1997) hidden units and attentional architecture. Full details of the *OpenNMT* system are given in Klein et al. (2017).

3.2 Generator Vocabulary Reduction

As seen in the last section, the word generation matrix operations and softmax require significant time. This time is scaling linearly with the effective target language vocabulary, which starts at 34K.

There has been significant work in reducing this cost. We start with the word alignment method, presented in Shi and Knight (2017), which uses alignments computed on the training corpus and for each sentence, selects target words aligned to each source word, that way building a reduced vocabulary of target words to be used when translating a source sentence.

To increase the coverage of the selected meanings without increasing the size of the mapping model, we first extract words in the target language that are unaligned - e.g. determiners when translating from English to French. We kept the 100 most frequent such words and call them 0-gram meanings. Then we go through 1-gram, 2-gram, ..., n-gram sequences of words in the source sentence. For each source sequence, we consider its N-best translation hypotheses. All target words present in such N-best hypotheses are kept in the target vocabulary. To account for translation hypotheses we use a phrase table extracted from word alignments.

The method extends single word vocabulary mappings to multi-word expressions[8]. We have multiple criterion to extract a vocabulary map: the maximal sequence size n, the maximum number N of translation hypotheses, the minimum frequency of a phrase pair. The efficiency of a vocabulary map can be evaluated through the coverage of the predicted meanings for a reference test set, the final translation quality, the average number of meaning per vocab and the actual time spent in generator layer (Linear and Softmax).

Table 1 compares several vocabulary maps with these different metrics. Compared to Shi and Knight (2017), our approach with multiple n-gram length phrase enables better match-rate than the 1-gram approach (saturating the Test Coverage (TC) at 80%).

---

[8]For instance `speed test` translated by `test de vitesse` in French is covered by 0-grams $\varnothing \rightarrow$`de`, and 1-grams `speed`→`vitesse`, `test`→`test`. However, `once more` translated by `à nouveau` will need the 2 additional meanings `à` and `nouveau` that are only covered when using 2-gram meanings.

3.3 Quantization

Another important area of optimization is the cost of linear matrix-operations. To speed these up, we use 16-bit signed integer quantization method proposed in Devlin (2017). To further optimize on the AWS M5 instance used in the competition and powered with INTEL Skylake processors, we extend the approach to AVX2 and AVX512 SIMD instruction sets. Switching from SSE4 to AVX2, then from AVX2 to AVX512 instructions set gave additional speed boost of respectively +12% and +6%.

3.4 Other Experiments

We explored several other methods which largely resulted in negative results but could be interesting for other contexts.

Decrease the sentence length: For BPE preprocessing, we try using 64K merges which can generate shorter sentences. The average sentence length for 32K BPE is about 29.1 and for 64K BPE, it is about 27.7 tokens. Assuming the same efficiency in the vocabulary mapping, increasing the size of the vocabulary could therefore have a gain of about 5% additional speed-up just by the reduction of the sentence length. However, the tradeoff here was not clearly a win.

8-bit quantization: To reduce further the system size, we also considered use of `gemmlowp`[9]. `gemmlowp` is a library allowing quantization to unsigned 8 bits integer through dynamic offset/multiplier/shift parameters. Like our implementation of 16-bit quantization, the low precision is only for storing the parameters, the dot product is using larger register for accumulating intermediate result of the operation. `gemmlowp` usage is for embedded application where speed but also power usage is critical. The idea was tempting, but it was not clear if such quantization schema could actually outperform quantization using SIMD extended instruction set on modern processors. We ran comparative tests using AVX2 instructions set and found out that for multiplications of large matrixes $(20, 1024) * (1024, 512)$ - optimized INT16 implementation was about 3 times faster than `gemmlowp` UINT8 implementation[10]. Main reason being that AVX2 (and AVX512 twice faster)

[9]`https://github.com/google/gemmlowp`
[10]On Intel(R) Core(TM) i7-6850K CPU @ 3.60GHz

Max Sequence	Min Freq	# Meaning	vocab per token	Test Coverage	Linear Time [s]	SoftMax Time [s]	File Size	BLEU
					143.86	4.97	239M	23.24
1	1	50	2	30%	3.78	0.11	295M	21.98
2	1	100	24	86%	5.97	0.16	902M	23.13
2	1	150	25	86%	6.63	0.18	918M	23.16
2	1	50	22	85%	5.34	0.14	846M	23.09
2	2	100	22	85%	4.08	0.11	324M	23.02
2	2	150	22	85%	3.95	0.11	324M	23.02
2	2	50	20	84%	3.95	0.11	322M	23.03
3	1	50	30	90%	5.23	0.15	1127M	23.16

Table 1: Evaluations of n-gram vocabulary mappings on newstest2014.

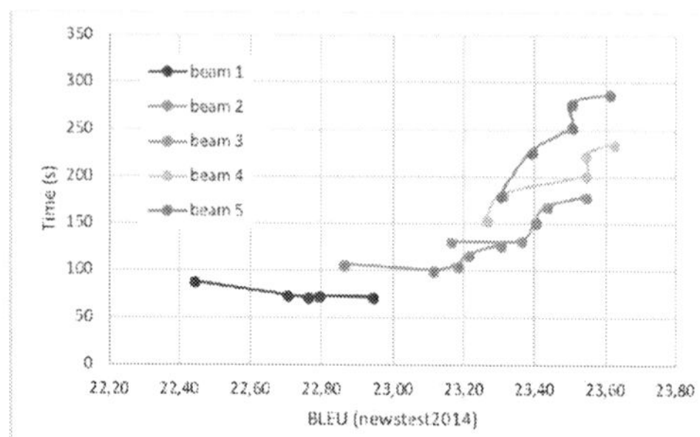

Figure 3: Evaluations on different beam size and batch size

have very powerful multiply and add instructions[11] allowing to perform in one single cycle the dot product of vectors 32*INT16 and at the same time, the pair accumulation in a vector 16*INT32.

4 Results

After tuning, we settled on two optimal NMT systems based on the distilled training data. Table 2 lists the different configurations for these two systems:

- `distill-small`, uses a bidirectional RNN with 2 LSTM layers with each hidden layer having 1024 nodes. We use a word embedding size of 512 and set the dropout to 0.3. The batch size is set to 64 and the default learning rate is 1.0 with sgd optimization.

- `distill-tiny`, uses a smaller network, with GRU layers, 512 hidden size. On the encoder side, we have 2 layers, while on the decoder side, only 1 layer is set. We use Adam optimization with the starting learning rate 0.0002.

Both systems are trained up to 10 epochs.

[11] _mm256_madd_epi16 and _mm512_madd_epi16

Table 3 shows our internal evaluations. For system `distill-small-opt`, the CPU time during decoding improves from 1694.16 seconds to 621.17 seconds (saving 63.3%), with a loss of only 0.19 BLEU score, on *newstest2014*. For system `distill-tiny-opt`, the trends are similar. 80.3% cpu time is saved, while only 0.13 BLEU score is lost.

We also compare the influence of quantization hyperparameters, e.g. vmap and quantize model, on tiny distilled RNN (`distill-tiny`). Quantize runtime and vmap both can save about 50% of the decoding time. The quantized model also halves the model size.

4.1 Beam size and Batch size

We further test the impact on the decoding performance (BLEU) and CPU time of different beam size and batch size on system `distill-tiny-opt`. Figure 3 shows that for a fixed batch size, when we increase the beam size from 1 to 3, the accuracy increases as well. While for beam size 3, 4 and 5, there is no significant difference in accuracy which is consistent with previous findings on distilled system. Interestingly, for a fixed beam size, we notice also a slight improvement of accuracy when increasing the batch size. This is a side-effect of the dynamic vocabulary mapping per batch.

These experiments also show that the decoding cost increases with larger beam and batch size. For beam size $K = 1$ (in blue), we process more sentences inside each batch and the CPU cost reduces along the increasing of batch size. While for the others, larger beam size and larger batch size both cost more computational effort.

As a result, we choose beam $K = 2$ and batch 2, balancing the performance and computation cost.

126

Transformer	Large	N=6, d=512, d_{ff}=4096, h=8
	Base	N=6, d=512, d_{ff}=2048, h=8
direct RNN	Large	b-LSTM, 4 layers*1024, embed=512, optim=sgd
	Small	b-LSTM, 2 layers*1024, embed=512, optim=sgd
distilled RNN	Small	b-LSTM, 2 layers*1024, embed=512, optim=sgd
	Tiny	GRU, enc:2, dec:1 *512, embed=256, optim=adam

Table 2: Configurations for the different systems presented in the paper

		quantize runtime	vmap	quantize model	newstest2014		newstest2015		model size
					cpu time [s]	BLEU	cpu time [s]	BLEU	
Transformer	Large	-	-	-	11279.97	27.96	8339.10	29.95	1.4G
	Base	-	-	-	10795.16	27.30	7511.08	29.36	1.2G
direct RNN	Large	-	-	-	2859.57	24.56	2073.90	27.24	618M
	Small	-	-	-	1713.54	23.78	1313.39	26.37	416M
distilled RNN	Small	-	-	-	1694.16	25.96	1300.24	28.62	416M
	Small-opt	Y	Y	Y	621.17	25.77	478.08	28.60	207M
	Tiny	-	-	-	506.67	23.24	384.76	26.09	141M
	Tiny	Y	-	-	286.89	23.24	219.85	26.03	141M
	Tiny	Y	Y	-	105.80	23.18	77.10	25.95	141M
	Tiny-opt	Y	Y	Y	99.81	23.11	77.76	25.75	72M

Table 3: Evaluations on NMT systems (the suffix "-opt" means it is the final submission)

4.2 Docker Image Size

We did not invest effort into reduce image size during the preparation of the submission. Our fastest system has a docker image of 200M for an effective 72Mb size for the model and less than 15Mb for additional code and resources. Post-submission, we looked at reducing this 110Mb overhead coming from operating system and misc tools. Without huge effort - we managed to reduced this overhead to 70Mb, and docker engineering could probably reduce it even further.

4.3 Other Engineering Considerations

We note that at this level of optimization, especially the use of quantization, the speed measurement is very dependent on low level memory management mechanisms[12], and therefore on other processes running on the same instance, especially due to the critical importance of the L3 cache shared between the different cores. In particular, we observed that 4 parallel processes using fastest model were only reaching a x3 speed boost. To go further on parallel decoding, one would need to implement different ad-hoc mechanisms such as:

- synchronization points between the parallel decoders to avoid waste of memory cache transfer

- grouping of the sentences by sentence-length to optimize CPU usage on the different cores

All the optimizations performed for that submission were focussed on the Linear layers - on the final fastest submitted system, and the profiling in Figure 2 shows emerging opportunities for optimization: even though the Linear share remains preponderant, some potential additional gain (between 5 and 10%) could be achieved by focusing on other operators (MM and non-linear).

5 Conclusion

This work presents the OpenNMT submission to the 2018 Shared Task of WNMT. We show that training with distillation using an optimized RNN sequence-to-sequence system we can produce a very competitive model for CPU demonstrating again the powerful effect of the distillation process and for the first time its application cross-class (Transformer→RNN). This positive result implies that text simplification through distillation could be applied to more contexts.

Even though our submission was dedicated to a specific RNN-based network, most of the presented optimizations, aiming by different means to reduce and optimize the matrix multiplication operations can apply for other types of architectures.

Our final system does show an impressive increase in speed of 110x compared to the baseline system and achieves a throughput of 800 word/sec on a single core which is the fastest reported so far.

---

[12] This effect was actually observed during the preparation of the system: a same test could benchmark with a fluctuation of up to 25% depending on the time of the day, and probable load of the shared server hosting the virtual instance.

References

Dzmitry Bahdanau, Kyunghyun Cho, and Yoshua Bengio. 2014. Neural machine translation by jointly learning to align and translate. *arXiv preprint arXiv:1409.0473*.

Alexandra Birch, Andrew Finch, Minh-Thang Luong, Graham Neubig, and Yusuke Oda. 2018. Findings of the second workshop on neural machine translation and generation. In *The Second Workshop on Neural Machine Translation and Generation*.

Kyunghyun Cho, Bart van Merrienboer, Çaglar Gülçehre, Fethi Bougares, Holger Schwenk, and Yoshua Bengio. 2014. Learning phrase representations using RNN encoder-decoder for statistical machine translation. *CoRR*, abs/1406.1078.

Josep Maria Crego and Jean Senellart. 2016. Neural machine translation from simplified translations. *CoRR*, abs/1612.06139.

Jacob Devlin. 2017. Sharp models on dull hardware: Fast and accurate neural machine translation decoding on the CPU. *CoRR*, abs/1705.01991.

Sepp Hochreiter and Jürgen Schmidhuber. 1997. Long short-term memory. *Neural Comput.*, 9(8):1735–1780.

Y Kim and Alexander M. Rush. 2016. Sequence-level knowledge distillation. *CoRR*, abs/1606.07947.

Guillaume Klein, Yoon Kim, Yuntian Deng, Jean Senellart, and Alexander M. Rush. 2017. Opennmt: Open-source toolkit for neural machine translation. In *Accepted to ACL 2017 Conference Demo Papers*, Vancouver, Canada. Association for Computational Linguistics.

Philipp Koehn, Hieu Hoang, Alexandra Birch, Chris Callison-Burch, Marcello Federico, Nicola Bertoldi, Brooke Cowan, Wade Shen, Christine Moran, Richard Zens, et al. 2007. Moses: Open source toolkit for statistical machine translation. In *Proceedings of the 45th annual meeting of the ACL on interactive poster and demonstration sessions*, pages 177–180. Association for Computational Linguistics.

Thang Luong, Hieu Pham, and Christopher D. Manning. 2015. Effective approaches to attention-based neural machine translation. In *Proceedings of the 2015 Conference on Empirical Methods in Natural Language Processing*, pages 1412–1421, Lisbon, Portugal. Association for Computational Linguistics.

Rico Sennrich, Barry Haddow, and Alexandra Birch. 2015. Neural machine translation of rare words with subword units. *arXiv preprint arXiv:1508.07909*.

Peter Shaw, Jakob Uszkoreit, and Ashish Vaswani. 2018. Self-attention with relative position representations. *CoRR*, abs/1803.02155.

Xing Shi and Kevin Knight. 2017. Speeding up neural machine translation decoding by shrinking runtime vocabulary. In *Proceedings of the 55th Annual Meeting of the Association for Computational Linguistics (Volume 2: Short Papers)*, volume 2, pages 574–579.

Ashish Vaswani, Noam Shazeer, Niki Parmar, Jakob Uszkoreit, Llion Jones, Aidan N Gomez, Łukasz Kaiser, and Illia Polosukhin. 2017. Attention is all you need. In *Advances in Neural Information Processing Systems*, pages 6000–6010.

Marian: Cost-effective High-Quality Neural Machine Translation in C++

Marcin Junczys-Dowmunt[†]   **Kenneth Heafield**[‡]
Hieu Hoang[‡]   **Roman Grundkiewicz**[‡]   **Anthony Aue**[†]

[†]Microsoft Translator
1 Microsoft Way
Redmond, WA 98121, USA

[‡]University of Edinburgh
10 Crichton Street
Edinburgh, Scotland, EU

Abstract

This paper describes the submissions of the "Marian" team to the WNMT 2018 shared task. We investigate combinations of teacher-student training, low-precision matrix products, auto-tuning and other methods to optimize the Transformer model on GPU and CPU. By further integrating these methods with the new averaging attention networks, a recently introduced faster Transformer variant, we create a number of high-quality, high-performance models on the GPU and CPU, dominating the Pareto frontier for this shared task.

1 Introduction

This paper describes the submissions of the "Marian" team to the Workshop on Neural Machine Translation and Generation (WNMT 2018) shared task (Birch et al., 2018). The goal of the task is to build NMT systems on GPUs and CPUs placed on the Pareto Frontier of efficiency in accuracy.[1]

Marian (Junczys-Dowmunt et al., 2018) is an efficient neural machine translation (NMT) toolkit written in pure C++ based on dynamic computation graphs.[2] One of the goals of the toolkit is to provide a research tool which can be used to define state-of-the-art systems that at the same time can produce truly deployment-ready models across different devices. Ideally this should be accomplished within a single execution engine that does not require specialized, inference-only decoders.

The CPU back-end in Marian is a very recent addition and we use the shared-task as a testing ground for various improvements. The GPU-bound computations in Marian are already highly optimized and we mostly concentrate on modeling aspects and beam-search hyper-parameters.

The weak baselines (at 16.9 BLEU on newstest2014 at least 12 BLEU points below the state-of-the-art) could promote approaches that happily sacrifice quality for speed. We choose a quality cut-off of around 26 BLEU for the first test set (newstest2014) and do not spend much time on systems below that threshold.[3] This threshold was chosen based on the semi-official Sockeye (Hieber et al., 2017) baseline (27.6 BLEU on newstest2014) referenced on the shared task page.[4]

We believe our CPU implementation of the Transformer model (Vaswani et al., 2017) and attention averaging networks (Zhang et al., 2018) to be the fastest reported so far. This is achieved by integer matrix multiplication with auto-tuning. We also show that these models respond very well to sequence-level knowledge-distillation methods (Kim and Rush, 2016).

2 Teacher-student training

2.1 State-of-the-art teacher

Based on Kim and Rush (2016), we first build four strong teacher models following the procedure for the Transformer-big model (model size 1024, filter size 4096, file size 813 MiB) from Vaswani et al. (2017) for ensembling. We use 36,000 BPE joint subwords (Sennrich et al., 2016) and a joint vocabulary with tied source, target, and output embeddings. One model is trained until convergence for eight days on four P40 GPUs. See tables 3 and 4 for BLEU scores of an overview of BLEU scores for models trained in this work.

---

[1]See the shared task description: `https://sites.google.com/site/wnmt18/shared-task`
[2]`https://marian-nmt.github.io`

[3]We added smaller post-submission systems to demonstrate that our approach outperforms systems by other participants when we take part in the race to the quality bottom.
[4]`https://github.com/awslabs/sockeye/tree/wnmt18/wnmt18`

Proceedings of the 2nd Workshop on Neural Machine Translation and Generation, pages 129–135
Melbourne, Australia, July 20, 2018. ©2018 Association for Computational Linguistics

Model	Emb.	FFN	MiB
Transformer-big	1024	4096	813
Transformer-base	512	2048	238
Transformer-small	256	2048	101
Transformer-tiny-256*	256	1536	84
Transformer-tiny-192*	192	1536	60

Table 1: Transformer students dimensions. Post-submission models marked with *.

2.2 Interpolated sequence-level knowledge-distillation

As described by Kim and Rush (2016), we re-translate the full training corpus source data with the teacher ensemble as an 8-best list. Among the eight hypotheses per sentence we choose the translation with the highest sentence-level BLEU score with regard to the original target corpus. Kim and Rush (2016) refer to this method as interpolated sequence-level knowledge-distillation. Next, we train our student models exclusively on the newly generated and selected output.

2.3 Decoding with small beams

Whenever we use beam size 1, we skip softmax evaluation and simply select the output word with highest activation. The input sentences are sorted by source length, then decoded in batches of approximately equal length. We batch based on number of words. For CPU decoding we use a batch size of at least 384 words (ca. 15 sentences), for the GPU at least 8192 words (ca. 300 sentences).

3 Student architectures

3.1 Transformer students

For our Transformer student models we follow the Transformer-big and Transformer-base configurations from Vaswani et al. (2017). Additionally we investigate a Transformer-small and post-submission two Transformer-tiny variants on the CPU. We also use six blocks of self-attention, source-attention, and FFN layers with varying embedding (model) and FNN sizes, see Table 1.

Transformer-big is initialized with one of the original teachers and fine-tuned on the teacher-generated data until development set BLEU stops improving for beam-size 1. The remaining student models are trained from scratch on teacher-generated data until development set BLEU stalls for 20 validation steps when using beam-size 1.

3.2 Averaging attention networks

Very recently, Zhang et al. (2018) suggested averaging attention networks (AAN), a modification of the original Transformer model that addresses a decode-time inefficiency, apparently without loss of quality. During translation, the self-attention layers in the Transformer decoder look back at their entire history, introducing quadratic complexity with respect to output length. Zhang et al. (2018) replace the decoder self-attention layer with a cumulative uniform averaging operation across the previous layer. During decoding, this operation can be computed based on the single last step. Decoding is then linear with respect to output length. Zhang et al. (2018) also add a feed-forward network and a gate to the block. We choose a smaller FFN size than Zhang et al. (2018) (corresponding to embeddings size instead of FFN size in table 1) and experiment with removing the FFN and gate.

3.3 RNN-based students

Our focus lies on efficient CPU-bound Transformer implementations. However, Marian and its predecessor Amun (Junczys-Dowmunt et al., 2016) were first implemented as fast GPU-bound implementations of Nematus-style (Sennrich et al., 2017b) RNN-based translation models. We use these models to cover the lower end of the quality spectrum in the task. We train a standard shallow GRU model (RNN-Nematus, embedding size 512, state size 1024), a small version (RNN-small, embedding size 256, state size 512) and a deep version with 4 stacked GRU blocks in the encoder and 8 stacked GRU blocks in the decoder (RNN-deep, embedding size 512, states size 1024). This model corresponds to the University of Edinburgh submission to WMT 2017 (Sennrich et al., 2017a).

4 Optimizing for the CPU

Most of our effort was concentrated on improving CPU computation in Marian. Apart from improvements from code profiling and bottleneck identification, we worked towards integrating integer-based matrix products into Marian's computation graphs.

4.1 Shortlist

A simple way to improve CPU-bound NMT efficiency is to restrict the final output matrix multiplication to a small subset of translation candidates. We use a shortlist created with fastalign (Dyer et al., 2013). For every mini-batch we restrict the output vocabulary to the union of the 100 most frequent target words and the 100 most probable translations for every source word in a batch. All CPU results are computed with a shortlist.

4.2 Quantization and integer products

Previously, Marian tensors would only work with 32-bit floating point numbers. We now support tensors with underlying types corresponding to the standard numerical types in C++. We focus on integer tensors.

Some of our submissions replaced 32-bit floating-point matrix multiplication with 16-bit or 8-bit signed integers. For 16-bit integers, we follow Devlin (2017) in simply multiplying parameters and inputs by 2^{10} before rounding to signed integers. This does not use the full range of values of a 16-bit integer so as to prevent overflow when accumulating 32-bit sums; there is no AVX512F instruction for 32-bit add with saturation.

For 8-bit integers, we swept quantization multipliers and found that 29 was optimal, but quality was still poor. Instead, we retrained the model with matrix product inputs (activations and parameters but not outputs) clipped to a range. We tried $[-3, 3]$, $[-2, 2]$, and $[-1, 1]$ then settled on $[-2, 2]$ because it had slightly better BLEU.[5] Values were then scaled linearly to $[-127, 127]$ and rounded to integers. We accumulated in 16-bit integers with saturation because this was faster, observing a 0.05% BLEU drop relative to 32-bit accumulation.

The test CPU is a Xeon Platinum 8175M with support for AVX512. We used these instructions to implement matrix multiplication over 32 16-bit integers or 64 8-bit integers at a time.[6]

4.3 Memoization

To ensure contiguous memory access, the integer matrix product $\mathrm{dot}'_{\mathrm{int}}(A, B)$ calculates AB^{T} instead of AB. It also expects its inputs A and B to be correctly quantized integer tensors. Therefore, we have to compute $\mathrm{dot}'_{\mathrm{int}}(\mathrm{quant}_{\mathrm{int}}(A), \mathrm{quant}_{\mathrm{int}}(B^{\mathrm{T}}))$ to use the quantized integer product as a replacement for the floating point matrix product.

In most cases, B is a parameter, while A contains activations. Repeating the quantization and trans-

Model	1s	384w	BLEU
Transf.-base-AAN	1018.8	397.5	27.5
+shortlist	758.1	293.7	27.5
+int16	2703.2	491.4	27.5
+memoization	572.9	294.3	27.5
+auto-tuning	574.8	273.2	27.5
Transformer-big	4797.0	1537.8	28.1
+clip=2 (+mem.)	5006.9	1737.1	27.7
+int8 (+mem.)	1772.6	1169.9	27.5

Table 2: Time to translate newstest2014 with batch-size equal to 1 sentence (1s) and around 384 words (384w) using integer multiplication variants vs 32-bit float matrix multiplication.

position operations for every decoder parameter at every step would incur a significant performance penalty. To counter this, we introduce memoization into Marian's computation graphs. Memoization caches the values of constant nodes that will not change during the lifetime of the graph.

During inference, parameter nodes are constant. Apart from that any node with only constant children is constant and can be memoized. In our example, B is constant as a parameter, B^{T} is constant because its only child is constant, so is $\mathrm{quant}_{\mathrm{int}}(B^{\mathrm{T}})$. $\mathrm{dot}'_{\mathrm{int}}(\mathrm{quant}_{\mathrm{int}}(A), \mathrm{quant}_{\mathrm{int}}(B^{\mathrm{T}}))$ itself is not constant, as the activations A can change. Values for constant nodes are calculated only once during the first forward step in which they appear; subsequent calls will use cached versions.

4.4 Auto-tuning

At this point, the float32 (Intel's MKL) product and our int16 matrix product can be used interchangeably for small and mid-sized models (we see overflow for the large Transformer model). While trying to choose one implementation, we noticed that both algorithms will outperform the respective other in different contexts. In the face of many different matrix sizes and access patterns it is difficult to determine reliable performance profiles. Instead, we implemented an auto-tuner.

We hash tensor shapes and algorithm IDs and annotate each node in an alternative subgraph with a timer. We collect the total execution time across 100 traversals of each alternate subgraph. Once this limit has been reached, usually within a few sentences, the auto-tuner stops measurements and selects the fastest alternative for all subsequent calls.

---

[5]This might however have been an artifact of the posterior clipping process rather than an effect of quantization.

[6]The only packed 8-bit multiplication instruction is `vpmaddubsw`, which requires AVX512BW. Interestingly, Amazon's hypervisor hides support for AVX512BW from CPUID but the instruction works as expected so we used it.

4.5 Optimization results

Table 2 illustrates the effects of the optimizations introduced in this section for sentence-by-sentence and batched translation. Adding a shortlist improves translation speed significantly. Enabling int16 multiplication without memoization hurts performance; with memoization we see improvements for single-sentence translation and similar performance to MKL for batched translation. With auto-tuning, single-sentence translation achieves the same performance as before and batched translation improves. In both cases the auto-tuning algorithm was able to choose a good solution. In the single-sentence case we would always use the int16 product. In the batched case a mix performs better than a hard choice.

We also see respectable improvements for the Transformer-big model with int8 multiplication. Most of the loss in BLEU is due to the fine-tuning process with clipping during training.

5 Results and cost-effective decoding

In tables 3 and 4, we summarize our experiments with GPU and CPU models. Bold rows contain results for our task submissions. We report model sizes in MiB, translation time without initialization and BLEU scores for newstest2014. Time has been measured on AWS p3.x2large instances (NVidia V100) and AWS m5.large instances, the official evaluation platforms of the shared task.

All our student models outperform the baselines in terms of translation speed and quality, but as stated before, we are mostly interested in models above a 26 BLEU threshold. It seems that the new AAN architecture is a promising modification of the Transformer with minimal or no quality loss in comparison to its standard equivalent. We also see that teacher-student methods can be successfully used to create high-performance and high-quality Transformer systems with greedy decoding.

We compare our systems on a common cost-effectiveness scale expressed as the number of source tokens translated per US Dollar $\left[\frac{w}{USD}\right]$. Given the hourly price for a dedicated AWS GPU (p3.x2large, 3.259 USD/h) or CPU (m5.large, 0.102 USD/h) instance[7] and the time to translate newstest2014 consisting of 62,954 source tokens with a chosen model and instance, we calculate:

$$\frac{62,954\ [\text{w}]}{\text{Translation time [s]}} \cdot \frac{3,600\ [\text{s/h}]}{\text{Instance price [\$/h]}}.$$

---

[7]The same instance types were used for the shared task.

This representation has multiple advantages:

- Systems deployed on different hardware can be compared directly;
- The linear mappings into the common space are scale-preserving and correctly represent relative speed differences between systems on the same hardware;
- We can relate three important categories — speed, quality, and cost — to each other in a single visualization.

Figures 1 and 2 illustrate cost-effectiveness of our models, the baselines and submissions by other participants versus translation quality on newstest2014. Figure 1 contains all models with a cost-effectiveness log-scale. This reflects a trend that speed gains are exponential in quality loss. Based on Figure 1, it seems that our models dominate the Pareto-frontier for high-quality models for CPU and GPU models compared to the baselines and other participants.

We added post-submission systems (23i) and (24i) on the CPU to demonstrate that we can outperform the results of other participants for speed and quality when lowering our quality threshold.

In Figure 2 with a linear cost-effectiveness scale, we emphasize models around and above the quality threshold of 26 BLEU which were our main focus in this work. It is interesting to see that similar Marian models have surprisingly similar cost-effectiveness across different hardware types.

6 Conclusions

We demonstrated that Marian can serve as an integrated research and deployment platform with highly efficient decoding algorithms on the GPU and CPU. Transformer architectures can be efficiently trained in teacher-student settings and then used with small beams or with greedy decoding. To our knowledge, this is also the first work to integrate Transformer architectures with low-precision matrix multiplication. By combining these methods with the new averaging attention networks, we created a number of high-quality, high-performance models on the GPU and CPU, dominating the Pareto frontier for this shared task.

Acknowledgments

We thank Jon Clark who suggested the graphing in USD. Partly supported by a Mozilla Research Grant.

No	Model	MiB	Time	BLEU
(1)	Baseline GPU	–	51.6	16.8
(2)	Sockeye GPU (Transformer-base b=5)	–	231.9	27.6
(3)	Teacher - Transformer-big b=8	813	109.7	28.1
(4)	Teacher - Transformer-big×4 b=8	3252	410.8	29.0
(5)	Transformer-big b=4	813	52.0	28.4
(6)	**Transformer-big b=2**	**813**	**31.9**	**28.4**
(7)	Transformer-big	813	19.9	28.2
(8)	Transformer-base b=4	238	40.5	27.8
(9)	Transformer-base b=2	238	22.9	27.8
(10)	Transformer-base	238	12.8	27.6
(11)	Transformer-base-AAN b=4	220	15.9	27.7
(12)	**Transformer-base-AAN b=2**	**220**	**8.9**	**27.7**
(13)	Transformer-base-AAN	220	7.2	27.6
(14)	Transformer-small	101	10.8	26.4
(15)	Transformer-small-AAN	100	5.9	25.8
(16)	**Transformer-small-AAN -ffn**	**98**	**5.7**	**26.2**
(17)	Transformer-small-AAN -ffn -gate	95	5.6	25.8
(18)	**RNN-small-Amun**	**88**	**1.6**	**24.1**
(19)	RNN-Nematus-Amun	199	2.2	24.8
(20)	RNN-small	88	1.8	24.1
(21)	RNN-Nematus	199	2.5	24.8
(22)	RNN-Deep	323	2.9	25.7

Table 3: Results on newstest2014 - GPU systems. Submitted systems in bold. All student systems have been used with beam-size 1 unless stated differently (b=n).

No	Model	MiB	Time	BLEU
(1)	Baseline CPU	–	4492.2	16.8
(2)	Sockeye CPU (Transformer-base b=5)	–	1168.6	27.4
(7)	**Transformer-big**	**813**	**1537.8**	**28.1**
(7i)	**Transformer-big-int8**	**813**	**1169.9**	**27.5**
(10)	Transformer-base	238	393.1	27.4
(10i)	Transformer-base-int16	238	400.2	27.4
(13)	Transformer-base-AAN	220	288.7	27.5
(13i)	**Transformer-base-AAN-int16**	**220**	**273.2**	**27.5**
(14)	Transformer-small	101	134.1	26.5
(14i)	Transformer-small-int16	101	133.2	26.5
(15i)	Transformer-small-AAN-int16	100	108.8	25.8
(16i)	Transformer-small-AAN-int16 -ffn	98	108.3	26.2
(17)	Transformer-small-AAN -ffn -gate	95	100.6	26.0
(17i)	**Transformer-small-AAN-int16 -ffn -gate**	**95**	**94.1**	**26.0**
(23i)	Transformer-tiny-256-AAN-int16 -ffn -gate*	84	79.7	25.3
(24i)	Transformer-tiny-192-AAN-int16 -ffn -gate*	60	61.1	24.4

Table 4: Results on newstest2014 - CPU systems. Submitted systems in bold. Post-submission systems marked with *. All student systems have been used with beam-size 1 unless stated differently (b=n).

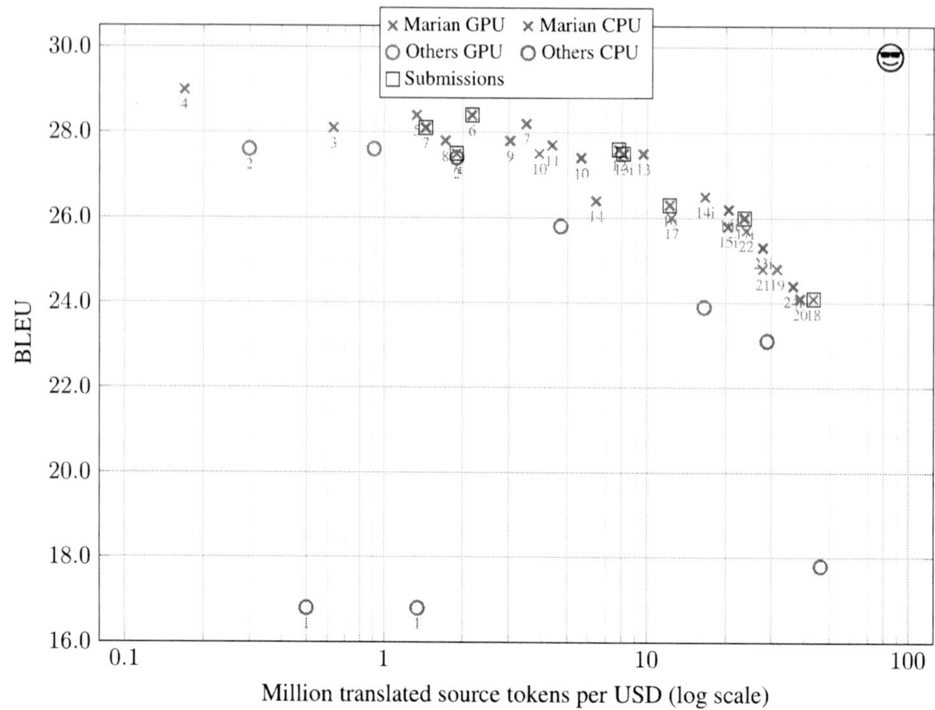

Figure 1: Cost-effectiveness (logarithmic scale) vs BLEU for all systems and baselines.

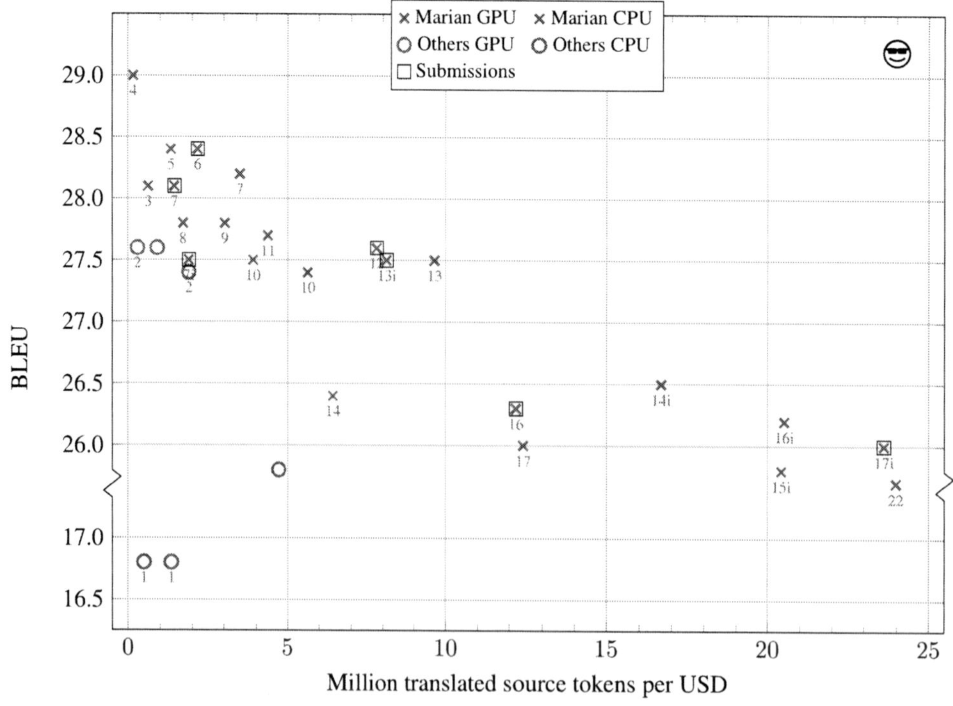

Figure 2: Cost-effectiveness (linear scale) vs BLEU for systems around and above 26 BLEU and baselines.

References

Alexandra Birch, Andrew Finch, Minh-Thang Luong, Graham Neubig, and Yusuke Oda. 2018. Findings of the Second Workshop on Neural Machine Translation and Generation. In The Second Workshop on Neural Machine Translation and Generation.

Jacob Devlin. 2017. Sharp models on dull hardware: Fast and accurate neural machine translation decoding on the CPU. In Proceedings of the 2017 Conference on Empirical Methods in Natural Language Processing, pages 2820–2825.

Chris Dyer, Victor Chahuneau, and Noah A. Smith. 2013. A simple, fast, and effective reparameterization of IBM model 2. In HLT-NAACL, pages 644–648. The Association for Computational Linguistics.

Felix Hieber, Tobias Domhan, Michael Denkowski, David Vilar, Artem Sokolov, Ann Clifton, and Matt Post. 2017. Sockeye: A toolkit for neural machine translation. CoRR, abs/1712.05690.

Marcin Junczys-Dowmunt, Tomasz Dwojak, and Hieu Hoang. 2016. Is neural machine translation ready for deployment? A case study on 30 translation directions. In Program of the 13th International Workshop on Spoken Language Translation (IWSLT 2016).

Marcin Junczys-Dowmunt, Roman Grundkiewicz, Tomasz Dwojak, Hieu Hoang, Kenneth Heafield, Tom Neckermann, Frank Seide, Ulrich Germann, Alham Fikri Aji, Nikolay Bogoychev, André F. T. Martins, and Alexandra Birch. 2018. Marian: Fast neural machine translation in C++. In Proceedings of the 56th Annual Meeting of the Association for Computational Linguistics, Melbourne, Australia.

Yoon Kim and Alexander M. Rush. 2016. Sequence-level knowledge distillation. In Proceedings of the 2016 Conference on Empirical Methods in Natural Language Processing, EMNLP 2016, Austin, Texas, USA, November 1-4, 2016, pages 1317–1327.

Rico Sennrich, Alexandra Birch, Anna Currey, Ulrich Germann, Barry Haddow, Kenneth Heafield, Antonio Valerio Miceli Barone, and Philip Williams. 2017a. The University of Edinburgh's neural MT systems for WMT17. In Proceedings of the Second Conference on Machine Translation, Volume 2: Shared Task Papers, pages 389–399, Copenhagen, Denmark. Association for Computational Linguistics.

Rico Sennrich, Orhan Firat, Kyunghyun Cho, Alexandra Birch, Barry Haddow, Julian Hitschler, Marcin Junczys-Dowmunt, Samuel Läubli, Antonio Valerio Miceli Barone, Jozef Mokry, and Maria Nadejde. 2017b. Nematus: a toolkit for neural machine translation. In Proceedings of the Software Demonstrations of the 15th Conference of the European Chapter of the Association for Computational Linguistics, pages 65–68, Valencia, Spain. Association for Computational Linguistics.

Rico Sennrich, Barry Haddow, and Alexandra Birch. 2016. Neural machine translation of rare words with subword units. In Proceedings of the 54th Annual Meeting of the Association for Computational Linguistics (Volume 1: Long Papers), pages 1715–1725, Berlin, Germany. Association for Computational Linguistics.

Ashish Vaswani, Noam Shazeer, Niki Parmar, Jakob Uszkoreit, Llion Jones, Aidan N Gomez, Łukasz Kaiser, and Illia Polosukhin. 2017. Attention is all you need. In I. Guyon, U. V. Luxburg, S. Bengio, H. Wallach, R. Fergus, S. Vishwanathan, and R. Garnett, editors, Advances in Neural Information Processing Systems 30, pages 5998–6008. Curran Associates, Inc.

Biao Zhang, Deyi Xiong, and Jinsong Su. 2018. Accelerating neural transformer via an average attention network. In Proceedings of the 56th Annual Meeting of the Association for Computational Linguistics (Volume 1: Long Papers), Berlin, Germany. Association for Computational Linguistics.

Author Index